The
Black
Manager

THE BLACK MANAGER

Making It in the Corporate World

FLOYD DICKENS, JR.
JACQUELINE B. DICKENS

Generously Donated to
The Frederick Douglass Institute
By Professor Jesse Moore
Fall 2000

American Management Association

Library of Congress Cataloging in Publication Data

Dickens, Floyd.
  The black manager.

  Bibliography: p.
  Includes index.
    1. Afro-American executives.   2. Success.   I. Dickens,
Jacqueline B.   II. Title.
HF5500.3.U54D5   658.4′09′08996073   81-69377
ISBN 0-8144-5678-2   AACR2
ISBN 0-8144-7564-7 Pbk.

Third Printing

To our three little ones, Daphne, Floyd III, and Karen: We have opened the door to success; may you enter with dignity, pride, and joy.

To Dr. Price M. Cobbs and Dr. Ronald B. Brown for their inspiration, encouragement, assistance, time, and energy: Be assured that you have wrought change in the lives of two black Americans and we thank you.

Foreword

For the past 20 years, black managers have been engaged in a vigorous drive to learn and assume positions of power in American corporations. The few who entered in the early 1960s have paved the way for the many who now seek to achieve and master the corporate world. There have been success stories along the way and sadly some failures within this pioneering group. We know very little about the how-to's of the success of this first generation of black managers. In particular, the tools and skills used have been hidden and obscured by the sheer energy and efforts expended by those managers who have been successfully scaling the heights of the corporate pyramid.

As management consultants working with many different companies and organizations, we have had the opportunity to meet and work with many of these black managers. They occupy the full spectrum of management positions from management trainees to vice presidents of major Fortune 500 companies, financial institutions, and public organizations. One consistent and widespread request from these managers is for information, tools, and skills that relate to the different experiences of black managers. We refer to the differences implied when blacks manage whites, when women manage men, when whites manage blacks, or when someone comes from a different cultural background than that of the majority group. There is little, if any, written documentation on how successful black managers become successful and function in this different experience. There is a burning need to document such how-to information that can be used by blacks and other minorities in their quest to become successful.

The challenge for black managers in the 1980s is to capitalize on the learnings and experiences of the first generation of black managers. The themes for black managers are excelling and excellence. The spirit of these themes is captured by Floyd and Jacqueline Dickens in this book.

Floyd and Jacqueline, as a living part of the first generation of black managers, have over a period of years documented many of the how-to's for success; they have presented them in a most interesting way. To meet the challenge of the 1980s, their efforts have been focused to translate and transfer this information to the growing corps of black managers, especially those in the second generation. It is our belief that this information will be helpful to blacks and other minorities in becoming successful in American institutions. We have witnessed the successful use of many of the techniques talked about in this book. This text is beneficial to both minority and majority managers.

Dr. Price M. Cobbs
Dr. Ronald B. Brown

Preface

For many years we wondered why some blacks were successful and moved up in white institutions (corporations, school systems, armed services, and so on) while others of equal intelligence struggled, floundered, gave up, and were set aside. Our wonderment and deep curiosity took a positive turn in early 1970. We started to document our personal observations of blacks and whites as they interacted. During 1972–1974 we attended night school to take courses in psychology and social psychology. This helped tremendously as we sought to explain what made some blacks successful and what caused failure in others. We subsequently participated in and led racial awareness and personal development groups consisting of both blacks and whites in community, service, and profit-making organizations. We also attended numerous seminars on personal development and management techniques. Throughout this time period, we counseled and coached both blacks and whites on how to become more effective in an integrated work environment. There was a personal payout for both of us: Floyd became successful in a major white profit-making institution, and Jackie became successful in working with community and profit-making institutions. As a result we discovered a behavioral process blacks undergo while working in white institutions. We then developed a four-phase structured black developmental model.

Jackie returned to school in 1976 and obtained a master's degree in social work from Ohio State University in 1978. She fulfilled her thesis requirements by conducting exploratory research on some factors that were utilized by a group of black managers who became successful in major white corporations.

These events, coupled with our burning desire to share information that might be helpful to others, caused us to feel we should publicly document our learnings; therefore, in 1978 we decided to write a book.

There are four primary reasons why we wrote this book. The first and foremost reason was because no book existed in the marketplace that gave practical day-to-day how-to solutions to the management problems faced by black men and women managers. The second reason was because there is a need for blacks to have basic information on how their blackness and culture impact their daily work interactions. The third reason was a need to collect, organize, and share data and techniques on how both blacks and whites become successful in a multicultural environment. The fourth reason was to share new, creative, and different ways of managing in the multicultural environment that resulted from blacks and other minorities entering the professional ranks of all-white institutions.

This book is based on research data collected from a number of black managers who shared their experiences to help Jackie realize a thesis requirement. The overwhelming response to the thesis findings by all who have read them led to the expansion of the data and the development of this book. Hopefully this will be the first comprehensive book on multicultural management—an emerging theme in organizations of today and tomorrow.

The research study was conducted in an attempt to pinpoint some attitudes, emotions, behaviors, and job skills learned by a number of black male managers in adjusting and becoming successful in the white corporate world. In the study, success was identified as earning at least one promotion in the company.

Corporations and other institutions represent a microcosm of our larger society. Racism pervades every walk of our lives and presents barriers to success for the minority person in addition to whatever his or her individual shortcomings may be. For that reason, the minority managers must acquire additional coping behaviors other than those acquired by managers in general. Also, many black managers feel they bring some cultural differences to the white organization that may enhance or hamper their development and success attainment.

As a result of this study, we created a four-phase structured model of development for black managers in white corporations. The model identifies and organizes the experience of black managers and provides a means of understanding the personal dynamics that occur on the job.

The undertaking of producing a book can be quite a staggering experience, especially for those who have never tried it before. Often what sustained us most was our firm conviction of purpose. We feel there is an ever increasing and continuing need to share our experiences, as well as those of the people we interviewed, with blacks and whites—both males and females. We believe this is important because each year more and more minorities enter the professional ranks of white institutions. Because minorities have been in these institutions long enough to begin building a body of successful operational learnings, they should no longer need to operate solely by trial and error. Many of us are aware that minorities are being stymied at the entry levels, with little hope of advancement. There is little evidence of equitable dispersion throughout most white institutions.

Information about the psychological and behavioral processes of minorities in white settings and the movement or development that evolves as a result of struggling for success is missing from the existing literature. We will identify common experiences and patterns of behavior and fit them into a model of predictable behaviors and commonly held attitudes and emotions. We will also present some successful strategies used by successful black managers.

We want to help make individuals in business environments aware of some prevalent problems blacks face in succeeding in white corporations. Bosses and subordinates may be alerted to the everyday issues and problems blacks must overcome to succeed. Many white managers who feel a need or commitment to help minorities succeed have few places to go to find out how to proceed; they will find many of the answers here.

We feel a personal commitment to point out the positive aspects of black success models in white corporations. Some of these aspects may have previously been seen in a negative light. Blacks often experience confusion and self-doubt. These reactions may become understandable with clear explanations of what is happening to them. We also would like to assure blacks in white corporations that they are not alone in their experience.

By now you may have realized this book is for everyone who wants to be an effective manager. It is critical to the white manager who works with or for minorities. For the minority manager in a white corporation, being able to recognize issues and formulate solutions may make the difference between success and failure.

The structured model of development can assist minority readers in organizing their experiences into a usable framework in preparing for success. White readers can use the model to understand and facilitate the movement needs of the minority manager.

There are whites who feel a responsibility as a part of the dominant system to provide fair and equal treatment and offer opportunities to minorities. For those persons, the information presented in this book tells what can be expected in terms of growth and coping attitudes and behaviors of minorities in white organizations as minorities seek success. How whites prepare themselves to respond to the needs of minorities so that both white and minority managers can be successful in their interactions is also discussed.

The patterns of successful black managers are embodied in the model. It offers specific tools people can use to understand what is necessary to get ahead in a predominantly white working environment.

Our intent was to write a book that was theory based and practically oriented but written in a simplified format in everyday language for a wide general audience. This text, therefore, can be used by individuals who are already managers or by those starting new jobs. We not only describe what happens but also offer viable solutions that have been successfully used by others. We present good practical management strategies that emerged because of the existence of minorities in white institutions; however, the strategies can be used successfully by *all* managers.

Even though blacks are generally not found in policymaking positions in major white institutions in this country in the 1980s, blacks are learning and forming the precepts of multicultural management. Unfortunately, since blacks tend not to be at the top of various organizations, the multicultural management skills are being learned at the middle and bottom of hierarchies. Somehow, this learning must be moved to the top, because it will be crucial for the future. American productivity is on a downward slide; we, therefore, need to make better use of the existing resources. A lot of those resources happen to be blacks, women, and other minorities. If these resources are to be properly and efficiently utilized, then the managers in charge of the resources are going to have to learn multicultural management.

The number of black professionals entering the work force before the 1970s was only a trickle compared to the number of white professionals. Some of the black professionals became successful but at a great cost to their self-esteem, self-respect, and self-concept. These blacks paid a price that must no longer be extracted from them. Much black talent was lost as a result of both racism and sexism. In the 1980s America cannot afford to lose *any* creative talent in our professional work force.

Today black professionals are still faced with racism. Yes, blacks have made great strides, but given their potential, only the surface has been scratched and the valuable resources of this underutilized group of people have not been fully tapped. The future challenge for our country relative to black professionals is to remove those barriers that prevent blacks from fully utilizing their creativity and competencies.

This book represents a consolidation of our struggles, our pain, our joy, our excitement, and our learnings. To the best of our knowledge, this is the first text to discuss multicultural management; we hope that there will be others.

We thank our friends and readers, Lonnie and Janice Cochran and Charles and Carletta Johnston, for their valuable help. We thank our friends Dr. Duke Ellis and Dr. Beverly Toomy for their encouragement and faith in us. A very special thanks to Janice Cochran for her editing and typing skills and to Rob Kaplan of AMACOM for his faith in us, his encouragement, and his patience. Last, we thank all those black managers who participated in the research effort.

Floyd Dickens, Jr.
Jacqueline B. Dickens

Contents

Introduction

Minorities have been seen in research and the literature as constantly struggling to attain success in all areas of life. Many problems have been identified—most of these are true—but many of the data collected are seen as negative, and few solutions to these identified problems have been offered for consideration. This book will deal with the most recent phenomenon, the influx of minorities as managers into previously all-white corporations and institutions.

The book has been divided into four parts to facilitate its use as a reference. Part One explains the developmental model and how the reader can use it for personal survival and growth. The model may also be used to help the individuals gauge where they are in their personal development.

Part Two contains four chapters that show the reader how each phase of the model works, step by step, as a manager develops within the organization. The model provides an understanding of the phases that successful black managers traverse. Each chapter points out the general critical issues involved for managers as they negotiate that phase of their development. The critical issues are analyzed in terms of the process involved, and how-to solutions are developed. Lastly, the basic concepts involved in arriving at the solutions are explored. Understanding the concepts allows readers to develop and apply solutions to whatever unique situations they find in each phase of development.

1

Part Three contains three chapters, each focusing on critical guidelines for the manager. The guidelines are strategies involving the internal, external, and environmental systems in which the black manager must operate. This part of the book discusses in a step-by-step fashion what to do in order to implement effective behavior to overcome difficulties.

In Part Four, the reader will find two chapters that address long-range planning steps needed by the black manager. Careers need to be developed far in advance of their realization. Too often black managers fail to consider long-range plans. Part Four provides a framework in which the manager may plan for upward mobility in the corporation. This book speaks to a process and a plan for success.

SOME TRUTHS ABOUT BLACK PROFESSIONALS

In the 1960s America found itself in the midst of racial disorders. Although the specific grievances varied from area to area, certain basic issues were held in common. The National Advisory Commission on Civil Disorders appointed by President Lyndon B. Johnson in 1967 identified at least 12 grievances deeply held by the black population. The second greatest injustice felt by blacks was unemployment and underemployment; the fourth was inadequate education.

With the passage of the Civil Rights Act of 1964, educational and professional job opportunities were opened in fields previously closed to blacks. The private industrial sector established programs to encourage the hiring of blacks in more varied professional fields. For the first time in history, blacks in relatively large numbers were entering previously all-white universities. They were obtaining degrees and jobs previously available only to whites; however, gross inequalities still existed.

The 1970 census of the population showed that, of the 78.6 million people employed in the United States, 70.2 million, or 89.3 percent, were white and 8.4 million, or 10.7 percent, were nonwhite. (The specific number of blacks employed is not available.)* Significant gains in equality have been made in the job

*The statistics on population and labor force are found in *Statistical Abstract of the United States 1976*, 97th Annual Edition, U.S. Department of Commerce, Bureau of the Census.

market, but clearly not enough. The accompanying table shows the percentage of blacks among various groups of workers in 1975. As the statistics show, blacks are still heavily employed in the between the doors opened by equal employment opportunity legislation.

	Total Population	Percentage Black
White-collar workers	41,738,000	9
Blue-collar workers	29,776,000	12
Service workers	11,373,000	19
Farm workers	3,048,000	7
Total workers	85,935,000	11

Looking back at the 1960s, we can see the upheaval was an important ingredient to the knowledge we have gained about blacks. Racial violence is not new to America, but this time two important events resulted. The Civil Rights Bill was signed into law, and the National Advisory Commission on Civil Disorders was established. This commission identified central issues that the nation was ordered to rectify—discrimination in employment and in education were high on the list. If orders were not complied with, penalties were to be issued by the government. Some of the penalties would be in the form of loss of funds, loss of government contracts, and fines. Colleges, universities, and professional schools all over the country opened their doors to blacks. Then companies started to seek black professionals.

When companies first started hiring black professionals, they hired *qualifiable* people. These were blacks who supposedly were not qualified but could be trained. Many companies felt they were lowering their standards to admit blacks. Whether this was true or not, blacks managed to move into the higher levels of management in these companies. Generally speaking, industry has not found workable means of training and developing blacks for higher managerial positions; but neither have existing racial barriers stopped the trickle of upward movement of blacks.

In the late 1960s and early 1970s, many corporations established affirmative action programs to help identify qualified blacks and to continue to ensure equal employment opportunities. This includes identifying and developing blacks with high potential; seeking to help industry learn ways of evaluating black growth and development for upward mobility; and helping to ensure that discriminatory practices are not used in hiring and firing blacks. The expressed purpose of these plans was to increase the number of black professionals in a particular corporation. Corporations had not yet begun to deal with the internal problems that arose after the black professionals were hired.

If blacks have managed to slip between the doors opened by equal employment opportunity legislation and, in addition, have moved into higher levels with little help from the white industries, then what kind of factors were involved in surviving in these institutions? The historical data indicate the institutions were hostile to the survival of blacks. How is it some blacks have managed to be successful in spite of the barriers presented to them? What kinds of attitudes did they have? How did they behave? What was their emotional set? What kinds of job skills did they develop in order to survive and be successful?

When whites have been successful under adverse conditions, then the human behavior professionals want to know how they did it. Blacks have managed to survive and be successful for hundreds of years in a society that has been hostile to them. How then do we proceed to gain knowledge about what the avenues for survival and success have been for black people? One way we may be able to begin to understand what has happened is to look at the attitudes, emotions, behaviors, and job skills of blacks who have been successful under adverse conditions.

Many of the studies about blacks in the past have been completed by white researchers who did not attempt to understand or accept racial differences as positive factors. Many of these studies have been of blacks who have not been able to survive, not been able to cope with a hostile environment. These blacks have not presented us with characteristics of success or what it takes to be successful. It is certainly time to take a look at the positive side of survival and success for blacks in the white setting.

MULTICULTURAL MANAGEMENT

Multicultural management is defined as the act, art, and practice of leading and directing people other than white males in the attaining of organizational goals. With an increased number of minorities and women joining the work force, there is a need to manage different people differently and appropriately. Minorities and women cannot produce to their maximum potential as long as they are managed with the standard management techniques that were designed for white males. While most of us can understand that *all* peoples are biologically the same and emotionally capable of the same responses to external and internal stimuli, we must also remember that we *are* culturally different. Our society makes different demands on its various groups of people and specifies different roles. Therefore, we need additional management techniques to include those different needs and motivations to reach members of minority cultures and capitalize on their potential. We cannot afford to lose these valuable resources in today's organizations. Multicultural management can provide the body of knowledge that can be used to effectively manage blacks and other minorities. Below are some key aspects of this new management technology.

1. *Feedback or input on minorities must be probed.* Supervisors must probe both negative and positive feedback from others on minority subordinates more than they do for white subordinates. Testing the feedback for validity is a way of removing racism and sexism from the input. Blacks, women, and other minorities must insist that this be done.

2. *Minorities must be included in decision-making processes.* If not, the assumptions made by white managers will generally be wrong. It is essential that minorities be included very early in making decisions that will have a major impact on them. For example, women should have early input when organizational policy is set on maternity leaves. In this way, supervisors or organizations can ensure that the appropriate minority perspective is obtained and that trust barriers do not become operative as a result of the decision. Such action is not necessary in an organization where all the people are of one race and gender.

3. *Be sensitive to and include a minority's perceptions and assumptions about a situation.* Before transmitting organizational skill information to a minority, a white supervisor must explore the minority individual's perceptions and assumptions about the situation. Otherwise, it is difficult for a white supervisor to understand that use of the skill information may have negative consequences for the minority individual. White supervisors must

realize, when telling a minority to use an organizational resource, that some of the resources may be racist and sexist. The supervisor may need to include additional information that will help the minority obtain information effectively from the resource.

4. *Supervisors must interact in an open, up-front, and to-the-point manner with minorities.* Effective interactions occur between white supervisors and minorities when supervisors behave in this way. The white American corporate style of interaction is not as open and up-front as the cultural style of minorities, especially blacks. Because minorities continue to be victims of racism and sexism, they tend to be suspicious of white managers who are not open in interactions with minorities.

5. *Racism and black rage (anger and resentment) must be managed by both whites and minorities.* White supervisors must be sensitive to racism and manage it in the boss–subordinate relationship. This enables blacks to manage their rage. Black rage is a reaction to the racism of others.

6. *Entry-level jobs for minorities must be programmed.* Appropriate attention must be given to programming the proper jobs and preparing the work environment for minorities as they enter an organization. A hostile environment can program a minority for failure. It is of the utmost importance that a sensitive and skillful first boss be selected for a minority individual to *help* ensure success. The first job should be one in which the minority can realize early success while also being challenged.

7. *Supervisors should be aware of differential consequences.** A white supervisor must be attuned to the *differential consequences* that a given behavior can have for a minority versus a white individual operating in a similar manner. This means that when a white supervisor asks a black subordinate to perform a task, the supervisor should examine it to see if a negative situation could result. If so, corrective and/or supportive action must be taken. An example of differential consequences would be a manager addressing or referring to a subordinate as "boy." This word would be taken quite differently if it were spoken to or about a black subordinate than if it were spoken to or about a white subordinate.

Differential consequences is a term coined by Dr. Duke Ellis, Assistant Dean of Student Affairs, School of Professional Psychology, Wright State University, Dayton, Ohio

The above are but a few concepts of the new multicultural management technology. This field of study needs to be further expanded and developed. We have only begun the task of adding to the larger body of management knowledge.

CONCRETE COPING BEHAVIORS

This book provides a framework for understanding what happens to minorities psychologically and what learnings they gain pertaining to survival and success in the corporate setting. We will present a road map of what minorities might expect to encounter and offer strong suggestions about which roads to travel. If properly used, these data can steer minorities on a course of *positive* coping that will enable them to grow and develop. For whites, there is information that will help them understand how they might approach minorities in order to facilitate the development process.

An important aspect of our book is that it focuses on the strengths in minorities and the output of positive concrete coping behaviors. As stated earlier, much of the information gathered in the past about minorities, blacks in particular, has pointed up deficits or weaknesses in the minority's struggles. Most blacks, regardless of their position or status, tend to be lumped with the poor and defeated. As blacks and women have moved into white male institutions over the past 20 years, we have been presented with a wealth of positive coping behavior displayed by those individuals who have been continously successful.

Let us look at an example of such behavior. Our experience and the experience of many other minorities have shown that white managers tend to accept information more readily from minority managers if the information is first asked for. So it is to the minority's advantage to position the white manager to ask for the information before attempting to give it. Otherwise racism and negative thoughts about the minority may prevent the information from being heard, understood, or accepted.

One way to position a group of managers to listen and seek understanding of data given by a minority is to allow the group to become involved or to nearly reach a decision, then to ask a question that will make the group reexamine the direction in which it is headed. If the group cannot answer the question, then the white managers will turn to the minority person and ask for more information. This is one hell of a way to operate, but it works.

Successful blacks have developed a facility for focusing on behavior. They have learned the art and process of behavioral observation—that is, they have learned to recognize the conditions in which behavior should be closely observed. They know what to look for, especially in a conflictual situation. Successful black managers have learned how to extract key messages by observing behavior and then to design and implement a plan to get what they want from an interaction.

COMMONALITY OF EXPERIENCES SHARED BY MINORITIES

For blacks and other minorities in an organization, the information in this book can be supportive in helping them realize that what they are experiencing is not an individual but a group experience—that this experience results from a minority person entering a corporation staffed predominantly by another race whose norm is to be in a position superior to that of the minority. History tells us that difficulties will exist when these individuals must operate on a peer level or when the minority person holds the superior position.

This book moves us from the ostrich stance of "We do not have any problems," to a position of "We do have problems; so what can we do about them?" Many of the experiences, feelings, frustrations, and attitudes of minorities are shared by *all* managers seeking the few positions available at the top. Minorities, however, share the common additional experience of an environment that is hostile to their attainment of success because of their lesser status assignment in society.

Let us look for a moment at two examples that illustrate what we mean by the commonality of experiences of minorities. The first example relates to what we call the Entry Phase, or the early part of a minority's entry into a corporation or institution. On entering a corporation, most minorities seem to display a need to fit into the corporate community. While this may be a characteristic of people in general, minorities have a particular need not to feel different from their white peers.

At this juncture in their early careers, minorities tend to behave in one of two extremes. They exhibit either "fit-in" or "avoidance" behavior. Fit-in behavior is characterized by acting "nice" around white managers. "Nice," as used here, means that although many minorities do not see themselves as actively and freely associating with whites, they do see themselves as not doing anything that might cause trouble. They therefore behave in a "nice" manner around whites so they can be seen in a favorable light.

Some minorities will go out of their way to stay away from whites as much as possible. This is avoidance behavior. Given a choice of using a white or a minority individual as a resource, the minority will normally use another minority. If a minority resource does not exist in that person's environment, he or she may feel forced to consult someone outside of that environment, or worse, may not use resources at all. Some of this behavior results because the minority is not comfortable in the presence of whites and is either too angry or too hostile to relate to them. Some of this behavior also results from a lack of background and skill in relating to whites.

The second example relates to individuals who have been in a corporation or institution more than one year. Most minorities working in white corporations at some time have been told by a white manager that they cannot write. Of course, many whites have also been told that they cannot write. Because of differential consequences, however, a black person will tend to interpret the message in a more derogatory way. A black person is apt to personalize the message and think that the white manager has said that he or she has a lack of training and is therefore not capable of writing properly. We remind the reader that the tendency to personalize in this way is the result of the inferior status position that society assigns to blacks. Therefore, it is easy to see how this can become another way of saying to a black person, "Your education is inferior in some manner." White subordinates will tend to interpret the message as saying that they will have to acquire a writing style that is different from their present style in order to respond to organizational needs and to fit organizational norms.

We are sure most minorities reading this section will see themselves in one or both examples. White managers may have witnessed minority isolation behavior or wondered about a seeming overreaction displayed by a minority manager being given data about an organizational norm. Suffice it to say at this point, these behaviors and attitudes are reactions to society's prejudicial expectations of minorities.

LEARNINGS MUST BE SHARED

In order for managers to become most productive in their settings and companies to realize optimum productivity from workers, our learnings must be shared. Whites must understand the importance of sharing the dominant organizational norms and goals with minorities. Minorities must learn to appropriately share their attitudes and perceptions; our mutual success depends on each other.

A win–win boss–subordinate environment can be created by sharing the kinds of learnings that will be discussed in this book. In a win–win environment, minority and white bosses with minority and white subordinates can all win in their pursuits of organizational and personal goals. Wasted time and energy used in reactive behavior to racism and sexism will be greatly reduced. People tend not to misinterpret or fear things that they understand. Understanding can be fostered by the sharing of multicultural management knowledge.

Unfortunately, fear and mistrust still exist, particularly between whites and blacks. There are many causes for the fear and mistrust between groups; racism and sexism are two of these. A lack of contact and a lack of information sharing are products of racism and sexism. Many whites still fear violence and retribution from blacks for past injustices. There are still remnants of beliefs by some whites that blacks are inherently incapable of measuring up to white standards. There is a belief that the old tried-and-true methods of performance (that is, white male) are best. The list can go on and on.

Some blacks, on the other hand, perpetuate the above beliefs by deliberately withholding certain information from whites. Sometimes this is because blacks feel as though they have cultural secrets that would be sullied and spoiled if known by whites. Much of the reasoning behind withholding information from whites is the firm belief by many minorities that whites will in some way use the shared information to the detriment of the minority. This belief has historical foundation in truth for blacks and for this reason is fervently held by many black individuals.

We are at a point in this country, however, when the fears, mistrusts, and misunderstandings we cling to may well ruin the future for all. As our society learns more about itself through the comparative study of other cultures, whites may learn more about themselves through the study of blacks and other minorities. Insights into how and why others behave the way they do often lead to insights about ourselves. People do not live in isolation but are related one to another and in that relatedness lie solutions to many of our problems if we take the time to understand. This book is dedicated to helping achieve that end.

PART ONE
The Developmental Model

Chapter 1, "Emergence of a Developmental Model," deals heavily with the effects of racism on the black manager in his or her everyday work life. This is important for two basic reasons. Subsequent chapters will concentrate primarily on providing learnings on how black managers can effectively operate and succeed in a predominantly white setting without much explanation of how and why these learnings have come about. Second, this chapter offers the reader an understanding of why some behaviors and skills blacks learn are either different or different by degree from what whites learn.

Chapter 1 may shock, surprise, and anger some readers who are unaware of how institutional and personal prejudices can critically impact what appear to be insignificant behaviors and attitudes of black individuals. The "colored" and "white" signs of yesterday have been removed from public facilities, but unfortunately not from all people's minds. This chapter not only presents a working model of behaviors but also sets a foundation that helps the reader understand why certain behaviors need to be displayed by blacks, what attitudes will be displayed in the presence of certain stimuli, and the reasons behind the behaviors and attitudes of blacks doing their jobs.

If you are white, it is important to understand that the information presented is from a black perspective and some of it may be alien to you. It is important for you to understand rather than react. In learning about each other, we *all* must learn to look at some things through the eyes of the other person.

If you are black, it is important to understand that the elimination of the effects of prejudice must be a *shared* task. Responsibility for terminating injustices in the work place cannot rest on one group alone. Understanding personal motivations and controlling personal responses are critical to becoming an equal participant in the corporate world.

We have not attempted to dilute the information in this chapter. We are sharing the material because in the past many people have been less than candid in sharing this kind of information. If we are to truly understand ourselves, then we must at some point be honest with each other in facing some truths about how we see our world and how we feel about each other.

Within any culture, there are observable patterns of behavior, and in any situation, these cultural behavior patterns tend to be repeated. In any research endeavor, observation is the first step in forming a new theory about the behavior of people. Over a period of about ten years, we observed and recorded the attitudes, emotions, behaviors, and job skills displayed by a number of black managers from their entry into white organizations to at least their first promotion. We made our observations in corporations, educational institutions, and community groups, and while helping individuals with personal development. As a result of our observations, we determined that black managers who are successful in predominantly white organizations have similar patterns of behavior, and we were able to group these behavior patterns into a developmental model for the attainment of success for black managers.

An added benefit has accrued to the model. White managers have become successful because they were able to use the concepts in the model to learn how to successfully manage blacks.

This chapter will take a comprehensive look at how the model was developed, the contents of the model, how it can be used, and its transferability to other minorities in their attainment of success.

1

Emergence of a Developmental Model

In 1968, we became very sensitive to and interested in the behavior exhibited by blacks and whites as they interacted. Our interest was motivated by the racial conditions existing in the country at that time and our experiences as members of a new breed of black managers in white corporations. At this point, we were limited to observations. In 1970, we started to take notes on our personal interactions with whites and our observations of the interactions of others. The notes included data that led us to identify helpful and dysfunctional concepts.

Night school course work provided us with a framework in which to place the results of our observations. We now knew the "legitimate labels" that we could use to verbalize our experiences and observations.

Frustration and a strong desire to be successful motivated us to attend seminars on personal development and management. Often we had to experiment with what we learned to adapt it to our own experiences, because for the most part, these seminars were developed for white male managers. During this period, we worked as consultants in team building and racial awareness workshops, both inside and outside of corporations, and developed various affirmative action programs. With this experience as background, in 1975 we placed our observations and knowledge in a tentatively structured five-phase black developmental model.

The purpose of the exploratory research Jacqueline decided to conduct was to ascertain if the data we had collected and the tentative model we had formulated would stand up under the scrutiny of research.

A structured questionnaire was given to a group of black male managers. The questions were designed to identify attitudes, emotions, behaviors, and job skills held by the managers from work entry to their present status in the company. This questionnaire was followed by a taped, private interview during which each manager could talk freely about his experiences. This provided a broad overview of what happened to the black managers from their entry into the white corporation to the present. We then compared the research data to our model and to the data we had previously collected. The research data verified our developmental model as well as supplied additional refinements to it. One refinement occurred because we found two of the phases were closely related. Therefore, we moved to a more concise four-phase developmental model.

We did not initially consider writing a book. We undertook our research because we were striving to survive and control our destiny as we sought success in a white-oriented world of big business and large corporations. Often our major efforts were geared toward survival and circumventing painful experiences and costly mistakes.

EXPLANATION OF THE DEVELOPMENTAL MODEL

In compiling and analyzing the data in the research project, from the entry period through the success period, we recognized a growth pattern. From this pattern, we developed a model that can be used as a guide to the movements of a black individual in a large white corporate setting. These movements represent the learning process exhibited by black managers as they pass through the four phases of development: Entry Phase, Adjusting Phase, Planned Growth Phase, and Success Phase.

At the start of any new job, the employee enters the Entry Phase of the developmental model. This phase is characterized by:

- No movement in terms of job growth.
- Little or no direction from the boss.

- Little or no direction in terms of personal goals.
- A feeling of "I've got it made" (because of securing the desirable job position).
- Contained anger; interpersonal and job discomfort is ignored or not dealt with.
- Reserved behavior, "Don't make waves."

In time, the individual moves into the Adjusting Phase of the model. This phase is divided into two parts, a dissatisfaction stage and a frustration stage. The dissatisfaction stage is characterized by:

- A negative reaction to whites (regarding interactions with whites and a desire to mete out punishment).
- Rage that slips out periodically; minorities begin to display anger.
- Low self-confidence.
- Beginning to see inequalities but still hold anger inside most of the time; may complain a lot.
- Negative reaction at seeing white peers get better jobs and more responsibility and the company taking more chances on white potential.

The frustration stage is characterized by:

- Rage that cannot be contained or managed (may be seen by whites as a "bad attitude").
- A lot of verbal, interpersonal fights with whites (may be seen by whites as "militant" or "noncooperative").
- No movement in personal growth or job growth and production. (The degree of anger inhibits growth.)
- No increased job results. (Dysfunctional behavior can help produce job stagnation.)
- Becoming more vocal, tending to speak out about feelings, usually inappropriately.

At some point, managers will come to a crossroad in their development. It may be precipitated by a number of things. They may become weary and see their behavior become debilitating in the area of job growth. Managers may become fearful of losing their jobs or may realize they are getting less job responsibility and are being shoved aside. Whatever the reason, successful black managers move into a phase of planned growth. This is a time when managers make a conscious and concentrated effort to grow in their jobs and in personal development. The Planned Growth Phase is characterized by:

- Management of rage; controls indiscriminate outbursts; chooses things at which to become angry.
- Style changes; behavior becomes smoother; tends to initiate fights with whites less and less often.
- A start to move toward goals; career plan is established.
- Establishment of firm goals; begins to see what to reach for.
- Rough periods; may slip back to the frustration and dissatisfaction stages.

As the Success Phase is reached:

- Basic goals are met; progress can be seen.
- New and harder goals are set.
- Style is developed. (There is no longer a need to fight with or punish whites in interactions.)
- High confidence is developed (as a result of successes).
- High-quality results are produced; managers become aware of how the system works and acquire skill in using it.
- Strokes become less important. (Managers no longer depend on verbal OKs and praise from others, particularly from whites.)
- Results become more important. (Jobs well done speak for themselves.)
- A success affect is developed; self-confidence and importance are displayed.

Our research has shown that these phases are never skipped, nor do they occur out of sequence. The time spent in each phase varies, however, because of individual differences. Different levels of awareness of self and the environment can reduce the time spent in each phase. A person may also become stuck in one phase or even regress to an earlier phase. This regression can take place even from the Success Phase, since nothing remains static. Getting comfortable, dropping one's guard, and getting tired of the output of energy can be causes for regression. Failing to realize that growth must continue may be another cause.

The thesis research clearly showed that black managers felt they must develop a higher degree of job skills, especially in management, than their white peers. They felt that, in order to survive and be successful in a major white corporation, there were some skills blacks had to learn that were different from the skills learned by whites. Two of these, which will be discussed later, are the management of racism and the management of conflict.

To sum up, the two major issues of concern in our model are survival and success. The two main phases associated with survival are Entry and Adjusting. Planned Growth and Success are the main phases associated with success. Each phase is characterized by different attitudes, emotions, behaviors, and job skills. In separating these factors, we will look first at what they mean in terms of the black manager's survival—how they operate and why they exist. Then we will look at them in terms of attaining success.

Entry Phase
Entry Phase Attitudes. Most minority readers of this book can personally connect with the early feeling of doubt about making it in the white corporate world. Several factors can cause this doubt. As with all people, personal feelings about oneself can cause a black person to have doubts about making it. Blacks, however, are affected by additional doubts caused by other factors that do not plague whites. Racism in this country and the way our society perceives the competence of blacks can cause blacks to feel unsure of themselves. Blacks are affected by these perceptions even if they are not actively aware of this situation. These negative perceptions are usually internalized to some degree by all blacks. However, all blacks do not believe "all" the negative perceptions that society has about them and their competence.

Another factor contributing to the doubts of blacks is the realization that they are sometimes hired "because" they are black. Many blacks still must face the fact that they are being hired for reasons other than being the best person available for the job. Since this possibility always exists for the black individual, this doubt can get translated into, "I wonder if I'm as prepared for my job as my white peers." This perception can be further compounded if the black manager has graduated from a black university. Even though this does not make the training inferior or the black person less qualified than white peers, prejudicial perceptions about the quality of education at black schools can cause further doubts.

We are all reminded today in various books and journals that education does not prepare the newly hired person for the realities of the everyday work environment. For blacks, this can be a particularly crushing blow. Naiveté often causes blacks to assume that racial attitudes within the company will be more positive than those of society outside the company. Blacks expect to be treated fairly and to be rewarded for their hard work. They may not expect to have to work in very close conjunction with whites as a team. In other words, blacks often expect the company and its members to disregard their blackness and judge them in the same manner their white peers are judged.

Lastly, the word *career* does not hold the same meaning for blacks as it does for whites. Gratitude for having acquired a "good job" with a "high salary" can cloud the black manager's vision beyond basic day-to-day responsibilities and task accomplishment. Also, the stereotypical white boss–black subordinate role status continues to make it difficult for many blacks to see themselves in the upper-level positions normally held by whites.

Entry Phase Emotions. At entry level, most blacks experience a moderate to high degree of stress. Many managers may see this stress as typical of any person in a new situation. However, the degree of stress depends on how black managers interpret their preparedness to work in a white corporation. Among the concerns that produce stress are (1) how they will fit into the normal corporate picture; (2) how they will fit in socially; (3) whether they will get the quality of help needed to do the job; (4) whether their education will compare favorably to that of their white peers.

Shortly after coming into the company and beginning the job, some blacks become angry and hostile without knowing why. Blacks are aware of racism in the larger community but are often not aware of the subtle ways it gets translated into behavior by whites in the corporation. Blacks may feel certain levels of visceral discomfort in some of their job interactions with whites but cannot pinpoint where and how that discomfort originated. A common emotion that blacks experience in their job interactions with whites is "feeling crazy."*

Entry Phase Behaviors. Entry-level behaviors were discussed in the Introduction to illustrate the commonality of experiences shared by minorities. To briefly recap, the two primary behaviors

*Edward W. Jones, Jr., "What It's Like to Be a Black Manager," *Harvard Business Review*, July–August 1973, pp. 108–116.

displayed are fit-in and avoidance behavior. The two extremes are indicative of the black manager's need either to "overcome" blackness and belong or to avoid the "unpleasant" task of any interaction with whites beyond getting the job done. Both extremes can be dysfunctional for the black individual.

Entry Phase Job Skills. Most blacks, like their white peers, feel technically competent to do the job for which they were hired. A major difference, however, appears to be in the area of awareness of the need for managerial skills. Neither black nor white managers have overcome the "normal" American white boss–black subordinate relationship. Still too few companies have role models for changing this relationship. For this reason, many blacks at the entry level do not truly see themselves becoming managers of whites, and therefore it takes some time for blacks to recognize the need for managerial skills.

During the Entry Phase, companies often neglect to offer training or encourage black employees to seek it and develop managerial skills. Since blacks are not a normal part of the corporate "club," the informal opportunities for encouragement that whites are privy to are, for the most part, denied blacks. The corporate club that exists in most companies refers to the after-work socializing done by members of the various organizations who have common interests and enjoy activities together—for example, playing cards, golfing, and fishing. Minorities tend to be excluded from these activities.

We would like to remind the reader that the time spent in each phase of the model varies from person to person and depends on differences in the environmental situation. In reality, there is considerable blending or overlapping as the person moves from one phase to another. The speed at which the person develops is determined by individual learning rates. Keeping this in mind, we are now ready to move into the next phase of survival, the Adjusting Phase.

Adjusting Phase

Adjusting Phase Attitudes. Gradually the doubts experienced by black managers dissipate as the managers become more acclimated to the white corporate setting. Usually, the gradual gain in confidence results from experiencing successes on the job. Blacks who do not experience these successes, however, will become increasingly less confident and will continue to operate with entry-level attitudes for a long time. The more successes black managers have, the more confidence they gain. The obvious conclusion is that, since blacks who enter white corporations experience an initial drop in confidence, they need to be positioned in the kinds of jobs where they can see early successes and quick results.

Black managers usually change their attitudes about a company after they start work. One important attitude change is dropping the general belief that hard work alone will net a reward. Blacks tend to come into companies believing in the Protestant work ethic—work hard, keep your nose clean, and you will be rewarded accordingly. Highly successful people, however, are successful because they do more than adhere to the work ethic. Because there are limited positions at the top, other considerations come into play in competing for those places. For blacks, the barrier of racism prevents them from receiving their appropriate reward. Black managers cannot *just* follow the work ethic and automatically get fair treatment from a company or realize a lot of positive results from their efforts. Black managers must use strategy to make others see what they have produced and to push an organization in some way to obtain an appropriate reward. The large number of black managers who believe the work ethic applies to them is surprising. They do not realize corporations are large entities with very few managerial slots relative to the number of employees. Therefore, opportunities for a reward in the form of a promotion are limited.

The naiveté of black managers about the norms and values of the white corporation creates a painful adjustment period for most blacks. Since the Protestant work ethic alone does not determine who gets ahead, then the question becomes, what does? Corporations have developed a method by which certain people are moved ahead. This is accomplished by people higher up in the hierarchy sponsoring other people for managerial slots. The sponsor may coach and guide the individual who is being sponsored. The sponsor may also push the organization to gain a promotion for that person. Many blacks are still not aware of this, and many whites do not know how to sponsor blacks. Whites' sponsorship of whites is a normal corporate process for pushing bright young whites up the corporate ladder. This process breaks down with blacks because companies do not initially possess the criteria for selecting blacks with potential nor do blacks know how to give whites this information. Blacks tend not to know how to develop or affect a relationship with a potential white sponsor. The reverse also tends to be true; whites do not know how to develop or affect a relationship with a potential black sponsoree.

A factor that inhibits blacks from getting sponsors is the black manager's need to feel emotionally attached to the sponsor. Whites tend not to have this need. Anger and hostility as a result of the racism felt by the black manager can also inhibit the black person from seeking a sponsor. Many blacks stubbornly refuse to affect any kind of relationship with whites in the hierarchy and instead focus on their anger. Many blacks ask themselves, "Why do I have to take the initiative? I didn't create this situation; why do I have to be responsible for changing it?" This can prolong the period of adjustment.

Understanding the company's norms and values is an important factor for black managers in adjusting their attitudes to the corporate milieu. Most companies, regardless of the product they produce, have established a norm that states "technical competence is more valued than managerial competence."

When black professionals enter white corporations, they tend not to possess the managerial experience to manage the black–white interactions necessary to do their jobs. This happens because they have not had preparation or work experience in the area of multicultural management. This is true of most white managers, also. In most instances, however, whites are not required to use good black–white management skills. But a black manager's survival depends on it. On entering the company, blacks appropriately sense that technical competence is more important than managerial competence for the company. They, however, have to deal with racial barriers and issues using managerial skills and interventions. White managers are only required to manage with the same managerial skills they have always used.

Black managers have to accomplish their jobs by using managerial competence, which is less highly valued than technical competence by the manager's company. In essence, white managers will tend to judge the technical competence of blacks by the way they display managerial competence.

Lastly in the area of adjusting attitudes, a gradual realization occurs with black managers that racism directly affects them. In the entry period, most black managers can identify an uncomfortable feeling in their interactions with whites. In the adjusting period, they come to understand that race is a real issue and that it does affect their work output. They also realize that racial issues have to be dealt with and cannot be avoided. It is in this phase that blacks begin to be aware of some specific kinds of barriers that affect their progress.

Adjusting Phase Emotions. In the Adjusting Phase, a very important psychological event takes place with black managers. As we said earlier, blacks come into corporations with some degree of stress, as all new employees do. Blacks, however, are hit head on with institutional racism and neoracism* in terms of their work task accomplishments. Neoracism refers to the more sophisticated, subtle, and indirect forms of racism that are evidenced by individual white attitudes and behaviors.

Today, neoracism is the danger in the integrated community and its assault is most commonly aimed at undermining the black's self-confidence, self-esteem, and self-worth.

At this point, most blacks will be stunned and will consequently experience a lack of technical and managerial growth. However, all is not lost; most blacks will start to grow again when they discover what is occurring. Two things that will allow them to grow and develop are the acquisition of cultural paranoia† and the use of protective hesitation.‡ Cultural paranoia as used in the context of this book is a sociological and anthropological concept referring to a person's expectations of mistreatment. It is a cultural phenomenon that has evolved as a group coping mechanism to deal with the real consequences of racism. It does *not* refer to the psychological concept that implies individual mental disorders. Protective hesitation is the behavior associated with cultural paranoia in which a black individual hesitates in order to protect

---

*The term *neoracism* was suggested by Robert Blaunder and discussed in John P. Fernandez, *Black Managers in White Corporations*. (New York: John Wiley & Sons, 1975), pp. 196–197.

†William H. Grier and Price M. Cobbs, *Black Rage* (New York: Basic Books, 1968), p. 149.

‡*Protective hesitation* is a phrase coined by Dr. Duke Ellis, Assistant Dean of Student Affairs, School of Professional Psychology, Wright State University, Dayton, Ohio.

himself or herself from possible psychological assault before interacting or preparing to interact with a white individual. Cultural paranoia and protective hesitation are healthy coping reactions of a black individual to the very real dangers of racism.

Another emotional reaction of blacks in the Adjusting Phase is the very strong negative feelings that result from prejudicial interactions with whites in the corporation. Blacks are culturally sensitive enough to pick up prejudicial behavior in whites, and this in turn affects a black person's work output.

As a result of their sensitivity to whites' negative behavior, black managers tend to seek closer contact with other blacks in a company. This is done for psychic support and to determine whether other blacks are experiencing the same kinds of situations. The need of blacks to seek close contact with other blacks points out why companies should, when possible, hire blacks and other minorities in groups rather than one at a time when they initially hire minorities into a previously all-white environment.

Adjusting Phase Behaviors. In the Adjusting Phase, the behavior exhibited by black managers usually results from trial and error in interactions, using resources, and linking with the informal communications network. An informal communications network exists in most companies; however, blacks are normally excluded from this network. To become a part of the network, blacks have to be friendly with whites. They do this by either seeking an authentic friendship or, as a minimum, affecting a relationship with whites in order to get them to share company information. Blacks must behave in what appears to be a friendly manner with whites to be able to function more effectively in the corporation.

There are some other prominent behaviors that black managers exhibit in the Adjusting Phase. Confrontive behavior is more important to the survival and success of black managers than it is to their white peers. White managers can afford the luxury of avoiding confrontation as much as possible, but for blacks, confrontation is seen as necessary in many situations to avoid constantly running the risk of having their input dismissed. Unfortunately, in this period of development, confrontation can often be dysfunctional for blacks. It is in a later period that the black manager learns to become smooth with confrontational interactions with whites.

Blacks tend to take greater risks in the Adjusting Phase than in the Entry Phase. They are literally forced to do this because of a high level of frustration. The frustration results from an inability to effectively manage various black–white interactions. Whereas in the Entry Phase, behavior is restrained because of perceptions of punishment resulting from aggressive actions or because of a high need to fit in and be accepted, the Adjusting Phase is a time to cast off restraints and aggressively pursue one's goals at all costs. Generally speaking, the higher the level of risk taken, the higher the potential rewards granted.

In the Adjusting Phase, blacks exhibit a great deal of sensitivity to people. Since blacks have historically been disadvantaged, it is fairly easy for them to understand the needs and desires of others. One reason this occurs is probably because blacks have always had to be sensitive to some degree to survive from slavery time to the present. Even in the cotton fields, blacks had to be sensitive to the overseers to survive from day to day under the tremendous demands placed on them. Therefore, we see this sensitivity as a cultural trait handed down from generation to generation.

Another important behavior that can be seen in blacks at this point is resistance to organizational power. Blacks in this phase are able to resist power more than they could in the Entry Phase. This resistance is important because, when blacks enter previously all-white institutions, some whites may position blacks to fulfill their negative and prejudicial stereotypes. To prevent this, blacks begin to learn how to resist that power.

An overall conclusion we reached is that blacks enter a corporation armed with their own cultural behavioral patterns, which they soon find cannot be *fully* used in the corporation to accomplish results. It becomes obvious during the Adjusting Phase that blacks have to develop additional behavioral styles and skills. This does not mean blacks should discard their cultural styles. It does, however, mean blacks should acquire an additional behavioral repertoire to accomplish results.

Adjusting Phase Job Skills. This phase is the beginning of a more active period of learning for blacks. It is when they learn the more subtle aspects of getting the job done. The desire to learn behaviors and skills that will help them advance in the organization is in contrast to the *self-induced* satisfaction that many blacks feel in the Entry Phase. We say this because we think some of the

difficulty experienced by blacks is self-induced for various legitimate reasons, as discussed in the Entry Phase.

In the Adjusting Phase, black managers start to test the environment in ways unlike those used in the Entry Phase. A new struggle
is begun, using trial-and-error behavior. To ascertain what can
and cannot be done, a person often acts inappropriately and may
get into difficulty with the organization in some way. At other
times, he or she will do things correctly and get appropriately
rewarded. The person will make a conscious or unconscious note
of the specific behavior and the reward that resulted from it.
Therefore, the job skills that the manager starts to acquire result
from the testing and probing of the environment.

Since black managers have not yet gained the self-confidence
they will hopefully gain later and do not have a lot of positive
experiences at this point, they do not have a good feel for what
they are doing. They seldom exhibit behavior in a planned manner. Instead, they act upon and react to various stimuli—the people, the values of the organization, and the norms—without
understanding them. Blacks do not have a clear understanding of
the organizational norms because they are just starting to learn
how to tap into and use resources.

Blacks can be seen adjusting their behavior in the areas of
managing rage and other emotions, managing interfaces with
other people in the organization, managing conflict, and reading
corporate cues. Let us look more closely at one of these areas.

White managers of blacks often complain that blacks are too
emotional. Blacks and women in general tend to display and use
emotions very openly. This behavior in a corporation can cause
problems for them. White male managers tend not to behave as
emotionally as blacks and women do. Therefore, most corporate
norms present a rule that states, "Keep emotions down to the bare
minimum to get the job done." Blacks will restrain themselves
emotionally in the Entry Phase. In the Adjusting Phase, however,
they cast aside restraint and vigorously display rage and other
emotions. Blacks respond emotionally at this point because of a
high level of frustration. They become frustrated because they
have high job interest and energy but cannot seem to produce the
correct job outputs. Emotions tend to be close to the surface; rage
cannot be constrained or managed.

Extreme emotions can cause a person to become almost irrational. We are not suggesting, however, that the display of emotions is wrong or bad. There are many occasions when the display of strong emotions is both right and very functional if they are used as a part of a person's strategy.

Another Adjusting Phase struggle for black managers is connected to the corporate messages they receive. Most organizations emphasize the technical aspects of the job more than the managerial aspects. Rewards seem to be given for results produced and not how well the people doing the job were organized, directed, and developed. Therefore, during this phase, black managers seldom get rewarded for displaying managerial competence; however, they will get punished for displaying a lack of it. The ambiguity of the situation adds to the frustration of black managers in the Adjusting Phase. They must work to find some balance of job performance between what is seen by the organization as technical competence and what is seen as managerial ability. Black managers in this phase struggle to be seen as technically sound while attempting to handle personal and group interfaces in a functional manner.

In essence, in the Adjusting Phase, black managers are dissatisfied and frustrated. The resultant behavior is often volatile and emotionally charged. This action can be frightening for whites and dysfunctional for blacks.

Planned Growth Phase

Planned Growth Phase Attitudes. The Planned Growth Phase is a period of consciously structured activity for black managers. The attitudes of planned growth center around personal improvements that facilitate growth and development. Since the organization may not become less racist, black managers begin to accept the responsibility for changing their own styles and methods of operating.

Black managers will work hard to improve their personal style of interacting with whites in an effort to be more productive and get needs met. They will consciously look for successes and for strokes from others to help build self-confidence. Black managers will start not only to recognize others' prejudicial attitudes toward them but to learn how to keep those attitudes from being obstacles to their progress. This action causes some whites to become less prejudiced.

Black managers in the Planned Growth Phase will work to make better use of resources. Many black managers discover the importance of sponsors and will actively seek out one or more and cultivate relationships with them. In this phase of development, black managers give up much of their reactiveness to the environment and learn how to become proactive on the job. Here, they become involved in success issues rather than survival issues. In this manner, barriers are overcome, prejudice is managed, and rewards are obtained.

This period represents a major milestone for black managers because it is a turning point in their development. Bitterness and anger in the extreme inhibit growth when an individual decides the system owns all the problems. Managers moving toward success will separate the system's problems from their own. In this development phase, black managers make a conscious effort to change those attitudes and behaviors that prevent them from being effective.

Planned Growth Phase Emotions. In the Planned Growth Phase, black managers begin to control their angry outbursts and to understand how anger can work for them if it is used strategically. As confidence grows, presentation of personal style becomes smoother. The need to fight with whites diminishes because now black managers can channel their frustrations into consciously planned goal-seeking activities directed at their own personal growth.

Planned Growth Behaviors. Overcoming mistrust of input from whites is a lingering issue for most black managers. Trust may be established in a one-to-one relationship between a black and white manager, but it is seldom a generalized attitude held by blacks. However, in the Planned Growth Phase, black managers will elect to keep their misgivings to themselves, choosing instead to behave in a manner of trust. Sponsors must be identified, sought out, and accessed. Resources must be used, racist or not. A commitment to succeed becomes the paramount goal.

By now, black managers know that waiting to be adopted by a white sponsor in the hierarchy is chancy. Instead, they must take the initiative to access potential individuals in the hierarchy and select a sponsor. Then it becomes a matter of establishing a relationship and contacting the sponsor when there are certain needs. Black managers must make sure their sponsors have an understanding of their value and potential in the company. A reciprocal relationship may be encouraged by the black manager so the white sponsor can learn more about blacks and thereby put the black person in a giving and sharing position.

In most corporations, people have to interact with other people to accomplish work tasks. Because many technologies and work processes are very complex, it is difficult to do most jobs without seeking the expertise of others. In the Planned Growth Phase, black managers will more readily use white resources than in earlier phases. However, they may still be hesitant to do so and may distinguish between the kinds of information sought from whites and from blacks. Black managers will more readily seek whites as resources for technical job issues but may hesitate on questions of strategy, particularly pertaining to interpersonal relations. Blacks continue to seek out other blacks for help in interpersonal strategic planning. There are reasons other than trust for this; these include common experiences, the perception by blacks of more honest feedback from each other, and the tendency to be straightforward with each other.

Black managers in the Planned Growth Phase often find that their organization has allowed them to fall behind their white peers in job growth and development. Their first concern then becomes having to expend extra energy to catch up to where they should have been all along. Other black managers fortunate enough to have stayed afloat with their white peers will begin to use resources to help them chart career paths—that is, to plan their advancement in some structured manner. Many blacks will in various ways exert pressure on their organization in order to advance. For instance, a black manager may be able to point out the company's inequities toward its black managers or may confront the organization directly about his or her current status in relation to white peers. Whatever the initial activity, black managers in the Planned Growth Phase begin to take conscious charge of their destiny.

Planned Growth Job Skills. Two of the most important job skills acquired by black managers in the Planned Growth Phase are what we call conflict management and the management of racism. These skills are seen as necessary if blacks are to continue to advance in white corporations. Many behaviors and strategies make up these management skills. Conflict management is seen by blacks as a skill that must be more highly developed by blacks than by whites. The management of racism is seen as a uniquely black management skill.

Conflict management is just as it sounds—that is, managing conflicts between people, groups, and situations. Most blacks have learned that whites have options to confronting conflicts. They may deal with conflicts or, as is usually done in organizations, avoid them. Black managers must learn how to deal with conflict productively, or they are apt to be scapegoated as a cause of the conflict. Culturally, confronting conflicts has been a simpler process for blacks than it has been for whites. As we stated previously, blacks tend as a group to be more open and straightforward in their interactions than whites. (In recent years, we have seen some white managers learn from black managers how to confront conflict directly and gain rapid results to problem solving—a heady experience for white managers in conflict-avoiding companies.)

A big difference in the way blacks and whites handle conflict is in the approach. When faced with the conflictual situation, a black manager will more likely confront the person immediately. If that is inappropriate, a black manager will do it later in private. Whites, on the other hand, will tend to discuss the conflictual situation with the person's boss.* The white manager may also talk about the situation indirectly with the person or with peers, usually to get the unpleasant feelings off his or her chest, or the white manager may opt to do nothing. The success of a black manager often depends on how well conflict is handled on the job because, as we said earlier, invariably some part of the conflict will be attributed to the black individual.

Management of racism involves a group of behaviors uniquely developed by blacks to counteract and neutralize demeaning, prejudicial behavior directed toward them by persons of another race or ethnic group. The management of racism is connected with both the survival and success of the black manager. A large amount of energy goes into the development of this uniquely black management skill. Whites do not need to develop this as a job skill because they are not targets of racial discrimination.

---

*For a personal account of such an experience, see Edward W. Jones, Jr., "What It's Like to Be a Black Manager," *Harvard Business Review*, July–August 1973.

Black managers need this skill above all others in the Planned Growth Phase. They can survive without managing conflict, although it may limit their success, but black managers will not survive for long without managing the racism of others.

Some management of racism is learned by all blacks by virtue of their survival in the society at large. It is like being a member of a big family and having the skill passed down from parent to child. How much the black manager learns in the corporate setting and how difficult it is to acquire additional skills in this area often depends on accessibility to other "family members." Blacks provide each other with coaching, guidance, feedback, and so forth just as whites provide other whites with an understanding of corporate norms and expectations. Unfortunately, there are no formal training sessions dedicated to teaching the management of racism. Black managers learn it from other blacks through shared experiences and shared knowledge on a one-to-one or a group basis.

From a shared perspective, black managers learn how to manage racism through planning and implementing strategy. They learn by controlling the behavior of others and by self-control. Racism is managed by using the company's norms, values, and communications network effectively. The individual behaviors used in the acquisition of these skills will be discussed in later chapters.

Success Phase

Success Phase Attitudes. In the Success Phase, black managers combine all they have learned and felt and understood as they struggled to reach this phase. The degree of success is directly linked to their degree of sensitivity to themselves as well as to the environment. Black managers are successful when they have learned the appropriate skills that apply to their unique position in the white corporation.

One of the key learnings in the Success Phase is that making mistakes or failing is not an option for black managers. When a white person fails, the failure is on that person. When a black person fails, that person fails for the group. Every failure blacks have reinforces the expectations of the white system.*

Black managers who have become successful have accepted

*This message is clearly communicated by John H. Johnson in "Failure Is a Word I Don't Accept, Harvard Business Review, March–April 1976.

protective hesitation as a way of life in the corporation. They are very careful about identifying and using resources, remaining cautious in their interactions with whites. (Complete openness is a luxury afforded to whites by whites.) Preplanning becomes a necessary part of the protective hesitation process. Careful thought is taken before a move is made.

Black managers in the Success Phase are aware of their blackness at all times and how this impacts the white corporation. Blacks must keep in mind that if they want to be successful, they must constantly remember who they are and how they are seen. Black managers must understand how that blackness impacts the people they work with and how it impacts relationships with others in the corporation.

Black managers have learned to be aware of the racism around them. To forget the impact of racism is tantamount to losing or giving up one's survival instincts. They have learned how to have peripheral vision in interactions with others. They must listen with "two sets of ears" and "three eyes." In other words, black managers must be sensitive to the many cues, especially the racist cues, around them—not to respond to them all but to be able to respond to those that threaten them or that offer them opportunities.

To briefly chart the attitudes of black managers from entry to success—they come to the corporation with a positive but naive attitude. They encounter personal as well as corporate racism and become angry, hostile, and culturally paranoid. Hopefully, they will make the decision to adjust and plan their growth rather than allow anger and resentment to stifle it. As black managers plan their growth, hard work must be applied to earlier attitudes to make them positive again. Once done, negative attitudes cease to be a barrier to learning. Therefore, successful black managers will retain a positive attitude even in the midst of racist behaviors.

Success Phase Emotions. In the Success Phase, black managers know they must sublimate emotions. They learn to use anger and rage as a part of their strategy to enhance job productivity. Through trial and error, they have taken the rage and channeled it into something that could produce better results. They no longer allow emotions to be a barrier to progress. Experience shows whites will not tolerate uncontrolled emotions from blacks. Whites will negatively evaluate the black manager who displays uncontrolled emotions and will make sure that manager does not succeed.

Success Phase Behaviors. Black managers in the Success Phase behave in a manner that conveys confidence, knowledge, and the appearance of being in charge. They now better understand how to negotiate the system. They have high control of self and others.

Successful black managers possess the unique ability to turn racism around and make it work *for* them, not against them. They know whites will allow other whites but not blacks to be dysfunctional. Therefore, successful black managers no longer allow the system to trap them into dysfunctional behavior.

A smoother interpersonal style emerges for the successful black manager, who develops a high ability to influence others. Black managers have to use more influential behavior than white peers do and charismatic power rather than real position power in order to get whites to work for them.

Black managers can now use resources that are obviously discriminatory. They learn they must confront whites in a way that leaves whites their dignity. If not, racism will dominate the white person's behavior and will cause him or her to become illogical. This prevents the reaching of closure on any issue. As previously stated, being sensitive to the environment is more important to blacks than to whites because blacks have had to protect themselves from hostile surroundings to survive.

Under certain circumstances, black managers have to resist the power of whites in order to prevent the master–slave relationship from occurring. Blacks perceive they must use more physical and psychic energy to get tasks done than whites do. In addition, successful black managers discover ways to tap into informal communications networks to seek out the norms, values, and other information that is otherwise a normal part of their white peers' job system.

By the time black managers reach the Success Phase, they have forged a track record. They have produced outstanding results and gained respect from others. However, this merely means they have won the opportunity to work to keep the record, the opportunity to prove competence to the company again and again. This is a failure on the part of the system. The noticeable difference for white managers is that they normally move through the organization on the basis of perceived potential. Black managers can continue to cement their own confidence in their competence relative to white peers. They can look outward at the events that happen to them and place blame appropriately, instead of always turning inward and perceiving failure in themselves. At this point in time, black managers can make the system own more of the failures, and they can own fewer.

Success Phase Job Skills. One thing that stands out in execution of the job is the need for black managers to use strategy more than their white peers do. This is particularly true for the management of conflict and the management of racism. It is necessary because external forces work on blacks to reduce their impact on the system. It is difficult for minorities in general to get their input heard. Black managers must develop a strategy against racist resistance in order to impact the system. Preplanning must be done in order to affect the outcome of any given situation. Everything becomes important—dress, style, and timing.

To implement the strategy, successful black managers develop high levels of interpersonal–behavioral skills. Blacks in the Success Phase understand that their interpersonal style is quickly evaluated in an all-white organization. Black managers also learn that getting the title and position at the next level is often anticlimactic. This occurs because, in reality, a black manager has usually been carrying the responsibility and doing the job at the next level for some time prior to the actual promotion. One plausible explanation for this action is that it eliminates the fear among white managers of setting back affirmative action goals by promoting a black who then fails. The system continues to test the black manager to make sure the job can be handled. Successful black managers must continue to reestablish their credibility with each new job, as if their track records will not hold.

HOW THE MODEL CAN BE USED

For Black Managers. In general, the developmental model can be used to explain what happens, why it happens, and how individuals can change to become successful or more successful. Specifically, the model relates the black experience in the white corporation to the experience of other blacks in the same circumstances. It helps explain, in part, what happens to blacks psychologically as they face the difficulties of prejudice and discrimination. The model can be used to help black managers ascertain where they are in relation to their organizational growth. It can also help in ascertaining where the black individual is in relation to his or her organizational skills.

The model can give personal insight into oneself and the reasons for certain behaviors. Black managers can become more aware of how racism impacts their daily life so that they may gain more control over themselves and their responses to the environment.

The essence of the model for the black manager is that it offers an explanation of what is real, insight into how to go about changing things, and a personal hope for one's future.

For White Managers. For the white manager, the model also offers an explanation of what happens to blacks in predominantly white corporations. White managers can be very anxious about a situation involving blacks if they do not have a clear picture of what is occurring. Knowledge of the model can help a white manager speed up the joining-up process for blacks. The white manager will have a clearer picture of what to expect from a black in the Entry Phase. Proactive steps can be formulated by the white manager to help speed up the development process for blacks. The model suggests that whites can help eliminate institutional racism. Since white managers will know what behaviors to expect as well as the reasons why blacks behave the way they do, whites will have a responsibility to remove the institutional barriers that cause dysfunctional behavior. The model will make both blacks and whites aware of some of those barriers. It is of the utmost importance for managers to understand that much of the behavior they see in a black subordinate is a minority group experience as opposed to an individual experience. Taken as a whole, the model gives white managers hope that the interface between a white manager and a black subordinate can change to a more effective one.

TRANSFERABILITY OF THE MODEL AND DATA TO OTHER MINORITIES

Because of the response to our model by members of other minority groups, it is our firm conviction that the developmental model and data are transferable to other minorities. Historically,

Hispanics and blacks have been, and are, members of an oppressed class of people; to some extent this is also true of white women. Hispanics and blacks are not an equally accepted part of American society. Discrimination separates them from the mainstream of life. Oppression creates issues within and between groups of people.

Minority psychology is a field of study that applies to all minority groups. Some commonalities among minorities are:

- Oppression
- Exclusion from mainstream activities of society
- Feelings of being different (in a negative way) from those in a dominant position
- Low self-concept, self-esteem, and self-confidence
- Being positioned in a one-down status
- Being prohibited from and not encouraged to seek a better position and status in the society—or in life
- Lack of equal opportunities

The subordinate position of various minority groups to a dominant group makes the model transferable because similar attitudes and behaviors are displayed in reaction to being in that subordinate position.

PART TWO
The Way to Success

America's racial attitudes are a subtle part of the everyday functioning of the black individual. In defense of their status, blacks have developed a unique way of operating in an interracial setting and as a result have learned a group of interpersonal skills that can be helpful for *all* interactions by *all* minorities.

Part Two will illustrate the dynamic functioning of the developmental model as it intimately affects the black manager. Each chapter will begin with a chart listing the critical issues that black managers deal with on the job. An in-depth discussion of these issues will follow.

In Part Two, you will meet Jack, a black manager. Jack will talk to you about his development as he moves through each phase of the model. Jack is a composite of the experiences, feelings, perceptions, and realities of most minorities who work in a white setting. He could just as easily be Evelyn, Ruby, Maria, Huiling, or Carlos. The ethnic background may vary, but the experiences remain essentially the same. His story offers white readers an opportunity to look into and feel the world of a black individual. It offers minority readers insight into the confusion and questions they may now be experiencing.

Following the story of Jack in each chapter is an analysis of the issues involved in that particular phase. Solutions to how to deal effectively with the critical issues of the particular phase will then be presented. Each chapter will end with the basic concepts that are used in these solutions so that the reader will be able to apply the general concepts to many situations that are individually different.

2

Entry Phase

CRITICAL ISSUES

Attitudes

1. Lack of self-confidence (especially in a racial context)
2. Attributing job situation to luck
3. Inadequate preparation for the realities of what is involved in the work world (especially interpersonal interactions)
4. Naiveté (particularly about racial attitudes in the work place)
5. Belief in the Protestant work ethic
6. Overly satisfied with job
7. Feelings of gratitude
8. Lack of clear job goals and/or understanding of career objectives and advancement opportunities
9. Unawareness of racial issues in day-to-day operations or interfaces

Emotions

10. High stress level (particularly in interactions with whites)
11. Confusion in interactions; willingness to accept responsibility for poor interactions with others
12. Inability to identify sources of visceral discomfort in interactions with whites
13. Feeling crazy

Behaviors

14. High need to fit in with whites or, at the opposite extreme, avoidance of whites
15. Being "nice" no matter what the situation; smiling, agreeing, laughing at jokes, etc.
16. Seeking support for psychic well-being
17. Problematic behavior style
18. Interpersonal style overshadows work or job competence
19. Concern mostly for job tasks with little concern for managerial interactions

Job Skills

20. Lack of managerial skills
21. Lack of understanding of how organizations function; concerned only with tasks
22. Lack of opportunity to obtain training and development in job
23. Inability to translate white-oriented training material to effective use by the black person
24. Unrealistic expectations of job and people (or lack of expectations)
25. Not future oriented in job
26. Inability to — and lack of understanding of how to — effectively use the communications network

ANALYZING THE CRITICAL ISSUES

Attitudes

That first significant job as an adult is important to most of us— whites and blacks alike. All of us have critical issues to deal with on any new job, and these include promotions into new positions as well as new assignments. Minorities must face and resolve these issues as well as the additional issues that are a product of living as the victims of racism and sexism.

The lack of self-confidence can admittedly be a product of personal background and upbringing. For the black person, however, society is also responsible to a certain degree for this feeling. Individual and family experiences with discrimination determine how a black person will feel about him- or herself in relation to functioning in the larger society.

"I felt I was capable of doing a good job, but I feared asking questions of whites. They would think I was dumb. I felt whites had better training and experience than I."

"I felt college had prepared me to do the job, but I never had whites as peers before and I felt they had to test me first."

"I felt whites had a lot of negative ideas about blacks. I felt evaluated when I asked questions. Asking questions became painful for me."

"I didn't go to whites because I felt they would think I was dumb, I should already know it all. So I tried to know it all alone as fast as I could so I wouldn't be seen as dumb."

"I thought I'd do well, but my performance review made me wonder how I was being seen by whites."

"I felt like the dumbest nigger in town, and whites treated me like I should have automatically known everything even though they had shared nothing about the job with me."

The above comments are but a small sample of the feelings and experiences expressed by blacks about their self-confidence in a predominantly white setting. Many also attributed the acquisition of their jobs, not to hard work and tenacity, but to luck, government pressure, or "they just needed another black."

One of the biggest complaints about education today is that it does not prepare people to deal with the day-to-day realities of the work environment. Often young *white employees* are jolted into the realities of the work world that they are not academically prepared to handle. For blacks, this experience is doubly or triply jolting, as evidenced by some of these comments.

"I expected to do my job with minimal help from whites."

"I expected to come in, do the job laid out for me, do nothing extra. I wasn't thinking of moving ahead, and that's how the company treated me."

"I expected hard work to get me recognition and reward. But it didn't, not by itself. There was no support for blacks, and I got evaluated on white standards and norms."

"I expected to struggle day by day to make the grade. I

*worked hard to be accepted by whites, but I got little infor-
mation or help."*

*"I thought I just needed technical things and that I wasn't
sure of myself. I expected to get help but instead got pro-
tected, sheltered, and killed with kindness."*

Naiveté in the Entry Phase, particularly about racial attitudes in
the work force, is a common characteristic of the black manager.
No matter how well versed blacks are about society's discriminatory practices, there seems to be a belief that it is not present on
the job. Blacks have generally bought into the Protestant work
ethic, and somehow racism has no place in this concept.

*"I was not prepared for interactions with whites. I didn't
understand racism behaviorally."*

*"I had no concept of what an organization was. I was just
doing a job without having to interact much with whites."*

*"I wasn't aware of racist issues or other goings on. I thought
people in a corporation would be more professional."*

*"I was very naive about subtle racism. I wanted to trust
whites and believe in goodness, fairness—to do the job and
get rewarded, not have to worry about interactions."*

*"I thought I would be evaluated on competence, nothing
else."*

*"I expected the company to give me what I wanted without
forcing it. I wasn't prepared for resistance. I had a basic lack
of understanding."*

*"I was naive, expecting to be seen and treated the same as
whites."*

*"I was arrogant and thought I would be rewarded because I
was so competent in my job."*

These statements and informal discussions between blacks often reveal how unaware they are of racial issues, except when
these issues result in negative evaluations and prevent their advancement in the work place. Whites and blacks often assume
most blacks know all there is to know about discrimination and its

effects. Much discrimination, especially today, is subtle. For this reason, blacks often miss much of the discriminatory behavior until it results in some harmful overt action.

Many black families, with the endorsement of the general dominant society, inadvertently teach their children that they must be grateful for the chances they get in life to better their status. This means being grateful to whites for that "good" job. With this in mind, is it any wonder that many black managers may be or may appear to be perfectly satisfied with their jobs? Although in reality black managers are often dissatisfied, they tend to inhibit their own feelings of dissatisfaction or be unable to see themselves in progressively higher positions of responsibility. With few role models and little or no support and encouragement from the whites in the organization, many blacks feel fortunate "just to have a good job."

"I didn't expect to be rewarded. I was concerned about keeping my job."

"I wasn't looking ahead to reward, just doing a job and getting paid."

"I wasn't looking for reward. I was just lucky to have a job with a great company."

"I had no goals for myself other than learning, alone, how to be good in my job."

"I wasn't thinking ahead to being rewarded for superior competence. I was too busy surviving day to day."

Emotions

The emotions experienced by blacks in the dominant white setting at the entry level can be confusing, debilitating, and often dysfunctional for the black manager. The dysfunctional aspect of the Entry Phase emotions is the willingness of blacks to accept responsibility for poor interactions with whites. In this phase black managers are unable to divorce themselves from the process of the interaction to ascertain what part they own, what the other person owns, and what the situation is contributing to the interaction. Often there is only visceral discomfort to cue the person that something is amiss. Black managers often experience a high level of stress because they cannot identify the source of the discomfort. All this confusion of emotion, self-debasement, and conflicting desire to acknowledge one's own competence leaves many black managers with the feeling of "going crazy."

> "I had not thought about how racism would affect me. I was not prepared for corporate life. I soon became bitter, and my self-confidence dropped."

> "I wasn't prepared to work with whites and was soon caught up in proving myself."

> "Sometimes I would go home after being in meetings half the day and ask myself if I was losing my mind."

> "I didn't know what was going on, but I began to be upset and became full of stress as I realized I was being stereotyped. I had been satisfied with wooing whites to be accepted and not be mistreated."

> "I was not prepared to deal with whites or know how to get what I wanted; I was generally satisfied; I believed the propaganda; I had some fear and a feeling of helplessness."

> "I was in no way prepared for anything I got on my job and was in and out of emotional upsets most of the time."

The most amazing finding among black managers in the Entry Phase is a lack of anger and hostility. This is probably due to an inability to identify the sources of their discomfort and a desire to see their organization as fair and paternal.

> "I had no anger or hostility. Intellectually I knew racism existed, could recognize it in the outside world, but I did not see the subtleties in the company. I just wanted to get along in the work setting."

> "I wasn't angry or hostile. I was unaware of how racism got played out. I wanted to fit in but couldn't seem to."

> "There was no anger or hostility in me. I ignored racism and acted white."

> "I felt no anger or hostility. I ignored racism. I wanted to fit in in the worst way, to be accepted. I wanted to be liked by whites, be on the bandwagon."

"I didn't feel any anger or hostility. I isolated myself. I was not involved with the racial issues around me. I didn't respond much to it."

Behaviors

One of the most obvious behaviors observed in blacks in the Entry Phase is the striving to belong to the group, to feel a part of the organization as they perceive whites would. Feeling accepted and being comfortable is of paramount importance. However, avoidance behavior can also be easily seen. It is almost as common as seeking to belong. These extremes in behavior are indicative of the alienation blacks feel from the mainstream of society. It boils down to trying too hard or not trying at all; it is all unnatural. Being "nice" and not making waves become critical to day-to-day well-being and to just being able to get the job done. Like it or not, everyone's behavior affects the cooperation of others, which is needed to do a job. This is especially true when blacks need the cooperation of whites; a black person's behavior affects how much others will cooperate.

"I didn't seek out my boss very often, nor did I speak up."

"I was quiet, didn't speak out. I didn't interact with anyone much."

"I didn't clique with the other workers. I had a fear of being seen as lazy, so I didn't do much socializing."

"I smiled a lot and made friends with whites. I ignored racial digs to be accepted."

"I laughed at the whites' jokes, even when they weren't funny. I wanted to make them think I was their friend. I worked to make them feel comfortable around me."

"I didn't interact much with whites. I am quiet, but whites saw that as a weakness in my style. I was told I'm too low key."

Intellectually, everyone can accept that there are individual differences in *all* people's personalities. However, for blacks, these differences often get exaggerated and usually are evaluated negatively by whites. For these reasons, interpersonal style becomes problematic for the black manager. More often than anyone imagines, interpersonal style overshadows work or job competence.

"I knew I was technically sound, so I thought I could run. But I got poor performance appraisals and suffered a lack of confidence for a long time. Now, I realize how much of that appraisal focused on personality differences and conflicts."

"I was told I was doing a good job, and I felt very arrogant about it. But I was not rewarded for it because of my interpersonal style, I was told."

"I expected to be evaluated on what I could do, nothing else. I stayed to myself. I thought I was doing well from the results. Later, when I was evaluated, I realized more went into the job than completing the tasks."

In the Entry Phase, blacks focus on the tasks, mostly because further advancement is seldom seen as a possibility. Whites enter corporations with careers on their minds. Until very recently, blacks felt fortunate merely to have been allowed to hold jobs once exclusively reserved for white males. Today, most blacks still hold limited visions of their chances to rise to the very tops of large corporations. Looking at the statistics of how many blacks hold such positions, these black managers have rather realistic expectations for advancement in most corporations.

Whether the black manager seeks to belong or to avoid social interaction with whites, the need for psychic support often overrides these considerations. The black manager will usually seek someone in the organization to talk to, gripe with, or glean information from. If there are no other blacks available, then often a sympathetic white will be sought. However, some blacks seek support outside the company from mates, family, or friends.

"I got support from blacks. I turned the place upside down to find other blacks."

"There were no other blacks around. I traveled a lot, so all my support had to come from my superior."

"I was isolated my first year, so I got most of my support from a black friend."

"I sought support and sharing with a black friend from another company."

"I really suffered. I had to listen to my boss, who told me

what to do. The only other black around wasn't at all sup-
portive."

Job Skills

The most damaging shortcoming for the black manager is the
lack of managerial skills. This becomes a critical issue for blacks,
because organizations will evaluate blacks, but not their white
peers, negatively if they do not very early display an ability to
manage others. This translates into showing such behaviors as
being able to (1) run meetings smoothly and handle the conflict
that arises; (2) use and manage resources; (3) manage one's frustrations and angers; and (4) manage the racism of others.

In the Entry Phase, newly hired black managers are destined to
failure in these areas for all the reasons discussed so far in this
chapter. In addition, most black managers do not initially have a
good working understanding of how organizations function.
Where would blacks as a group acquire this information? There
has been little or no historical basis or cultural opportunity for
blacks to learn. Few companies offer specific opportunity for
black managers to obtain the necessary training and development
in the areas of managerial and organizational skills.

Such training is not always necessary for white managers, because they can acquire most of the managerial and organizational
skills by generalizing their own cultural experience to the organization. That is, the primary style of interacting within an organization is a reflection of the behavioral styles of white America.
Therefore, white managers are normally accustomed to a style of
interaction that allows them to use resources and obtain new
skills in this environment. The style of white managers is generally consistent with the style of those who are evaluating them. In
this sense, whites can be said to inherit skills that are directly
related to their survival within the organization.

On the other hand, most blacks have a different cultural experience and, consequently, a different style from that of whites. This
is a handicap in the white organization, and blacks are consequently penalized for not having had the experiences of the dominant group. In this phase of development, black managers are
further handicapped by having to translate much of the training
material and data into a minority framework. Often black managers cannot use the training material as it is presented because
they would meet resistance or receive a negative evaluation.

"I couldn't use the mangerial training I got. It was all slanted to whites' needs. I didn't know how to translate it for my use."

"My company didn't deal with issues blacks would face. All the managerial stuff was white middle class."

"The managerial training was geared to white boys. I didn't get anything out of it."

"I was never encouraged to get any kind of training."

"I found out from a friend about management seminars. I went outside my company on my own to improve my interpersonal skills. My black friends helped me to strategize to go."

"My managerial training didn't give me an appreciation for what I was running into. When I used the training, it didn't work."

An additional handicap for most blacks in the Entry Phase is that they do not understand how they can effectively use the existing communications network. Whites can readily identify effective behavior and relate to successful managers through the formal and informal systems of sharing information. In this way they use the energy, skills, and knowledge of others who share a common cultural experience. Therefore, whites have a built-in support system. Circumstances allow white managers to have a forward-looking orientation. That is, whites generally have an image of the future that holds that growth in the organization is quite possible. On the other hand, black managers have trouble maintaining such a positive image of the future because of the absence of sufficient role models to support that belief. Black managers expend more energy in the Entry Phase on activities for the purpose of survival.

"I knew I wanted to do the best job they'd seen. That was all I was concerned about—not about becoming a manager or being successful."

Black managers in the Entry Phase tend to be unrealistic in their expectations of the quality of their jobs and about the people who share their work world. Their expectations are a product of wishful thinking. Continuous doses of the reality of their unique situation will sooner or later propel black managers either out the door or into the next stage of development.

JACK, A STORY OF BLUNDERS

My name is Jack, and I'm 32 years old. I've been asked to speak openly and frankly about the Entry Phase in my first job in a predominantly white organization. I don't profess to speak for all blacks, only about my experience and what I know and have seen. We all have different backgrounds, personalities, and have been in a myriad of different situations. Even I can't go into them all here. But one thing I do know—blacks in white institutions have faced the same problems, the same emotional responses and personal trials. I've found, though, that not all of us reach the same level of consciousness about it; nor are we all willing to face the brutal truth about ourselves or the discriminatory systems we work in. Still fewer of us are ready to speak out to others and tell it like it is.

Perhaps you'd like to know something about my personal background. OK, that might help you understand why I'm the kind of person I am. Let me get it straight with you, now. Just because I haven't reacted to my environment the same way you did or the way you've seen others do, don't think the same feelings weren't there. It was just a difference in training, friend.

I was born and reared in the South during the time before black was beautiful. It was an average-size town. It was just big enough for all the blacks *not* to know each other.

I was a good above-average student in my all-black, then-segregated, high school. When I graduated, I decided to go into the Army. My older brother, Fred, had not gone to college but had decided instead, two years before my graduation, to go into the small construction business our father owned.

My parents, like nearly all the black parents I knew, were working people. Both my parents had only a high school education. Now my brother also had stopped there. Fred and my father were pretty close. Fred hung around Daddy all the time, helping in the business, so no one was surprised when Fred started working full time with Daddy after high school. I never saw much of my father. He was always gone working on a job, sometimes until late at night. For blacks at that time, he made a good living for us.

My sister, who was a year behind me, wanted desperately to go to a teacher's college in another state. We had talked a lot about it, knew it was going to cost a lot of money, so I made things easy by joining the service. I'd thought about college for myself, but it didn't seem as important as having my sister go.

Not too long after going into the Army, I was sent to Germany. I worked as a personnel specialist, responsible for keeping track of people, making assignment changes, and keeping personnel records. Since I'd been a pretty good student in high school, I decided to fill some of my time by going to night school.

Now, you should understand where I was coming from, so you'll understand the why of some of the choices I made. Growing up in the South (I've since learned this happens all over the U.S. of A.), I was inadvertently taught that blacks are not as smart as whites.

Man! Now, there I was in night school with white guys. So what do I do? I start taking, not college courses, but high school courses. My first course was a ninth-grade English course. Of course, that was no challenge, so I took a twelfth-grade course next—then a twelfth-grade algebra course. Those weren't any challenge either.

But what surprised the hell out of me was the whites in the classes wanted to know how much college I had taken. I was impressed. I started to feel so good that I thought I'd move on and take some University of Maryland courses. So I took two years of college courses.

I had planned to make the Army my career, but a white sergeant encouraged me to leave and go to college. I enrolled in a black southern college and left the service, worked hard, and again was a very good student.

A large nationally known company hired me off my campus immediately after graduation. I was the first black person in my field of study to be hired at my school by this firm.

By then I had married and had an infant child. We moved North. Neither of us had lived in this area of the country before. The company provided no means to help us get settled. Theoretically, we could live anywhere (especially up North, we thought), but practically we had trouble finding housing. Many empty apartments were mysteriously filled when we showed up.

I started my job in an office with all whites around me.

I had replaced a black manager, James Peoples, who had been moved to another office. At first, everybody was really nice, you know—the people I talked to on my interview, the recruiting people. And, man, everybody was calling me "Mr."! I really felt like I had it made.

But everything got off on the wrong foot for me right away—the first day! My immediate boss was away from the office for two weeks. He left notes on my desk telling what he expected me to have done when he returned.

I looked through the papers; my anxiety shot straight up. How was I going to do this stuff? I didn't even understand it. There was nobody around to explain it to me. He'd just left me out there—on my own.

I thought about it for awhile. Frankly, there was reluctance on my part to go ask the whites around, so I went and found James and asked him about the work. I felt more comfortable doing that.

See, I felt I'd had an inferior education. That's what I had been taught, what I grew up with: that blacks who go to black southern schools have an inferior education.

You want to know why I felt that way? OK! I knew white companies had almost never recruited on black southern campuses before the civil rights laws. You learn this from other places, too. For instance, at school, our black teachers would say, "You've got to study and work hard because you know those whites are over there, too, and they've got better facilities and teachers and so on."

Another thing, you look around, and there are no black role models for us anywhere. At one time, teachin' and preachin' were high-status jobs in the black community. Even today, what few of us are out there making our mark seem to be invisible. Our black kids still don't see they can be somebody important.

Man, oh man! I'm getting on my soapbox! Where was I? So! I was reluctant to ask whites questions because I didn't want them to think I was dumb and didn't understand what I was doing.

I felt uncomfortable; I could look around and see there weren't any other blacks in my field except James. That told me something.

Two weeks later my boss returned. I hadn't finished the work because I didn't understand it. I had started and had tried to gather some material on it.

At this point I didn't know what my job was—didn't know how to go about accomplishing my job—and hadn't met very many people.

During this time, I felt lost. I had no direction. There was one white individual down the hall, a quiet, sympathetic-looking guy. I did go ask him questions. I depended on him a lot for help, and he gave me what he could.

Yeah! There was something else, too, that first year. I could sense the other people around me—as though they were smirking. It was like . . . a lack of respect. It's a strange feeling and difficult to explain. For instance, I had been on the job about two weeks when one of the whites in the office with a two-year degree . . . well, uh, I had asked him earlier in the day what I thought was a legitimate, intelligent question. In less than an hour, he had gone down the hall and told everybody how dumb I was because I had asked him a question. After finding that out, I was really afraid to ask whites any questions.

Of course, years later I realized that was the wrong thing to do because it hurt me in terms of my development and learning progress.

If I couldn't find a black person to ask a question of, I wouldn't ask questions. Oh! And there was another one. A young white peer of mine from the office across from me—a smart ass. He would come ask me basic kinds of questions. If I gave what he thought was the wrong answer, he'd look at me, smile, and then proceed to explain the correct answer to me. So I figured he was trying to find out if I really knew anything. I knew he had never interacted with blacks before because he would come in and try to get very intellectual with me.

Oh yeah! We had a white supervisor, too. He would come around and tell what amounted to "colored folks jokes." At first I used to laugh because . . . well, I guess, uhm . . . like a victim or a slave—if I didn't laugh and be nice, I'd be in some kind of trouble. Or maybe people wouldn't be nice back to me.

You know, I stayed to myself. I interacted with whites as little as possible, only when necessary. Now I know I hurt myself with this behavior. I'm sure I was negatively evaluated for this. I didn't socialize with whites; I didn't want to be around them after work; I didn't want to go to their parties—although I'd force myself to go in some instances.

Let me tell you what bugged and confused the hell out of me. I noticed white managers coming into the company the same time I did and after me, getting bigger jobs, larger projects to work on than I did. I know because I ate lunch with them every day.

I was damned uncomfortable most of the time. I really wanted to go eat with some black folks. I had met some other blacks, but they worked in other areas of the company. I didn't eat with the blacks, though, because I felt pressure to eat with my group. Because the whole group always ate together.

Occasionally, James and I would go out to eat—just to get away from everybody else. We wouldn't talk about the job. Instead, we talked about baseball, our families . . . to relax, laugh, talk, and enjoy each other's company.

Like with most companies, I had training and orientation sessions to attend during that first year. Needless to say, I was the only black manager at these sessions. We had to stand, give our name, and tell something about our background, including our school. When I mentioned my school, everybody wanted to know where that was—never heard of it before. The other people were mentioning Harvard, Yale, Princeton, Columbia, Stanford, schools like that. That was very intimidating to me. I dreaded having to go to these sessions. But, somehow, I hung in there.

Once, a vice president came to visit our sessions. At the time, the company was pushing equal opportunity, and they sent a photographer to take a picture of James and me to put in a brochure the company was putting together. A couple of the newer whites wanted to know why they weren't included, why only our pictures were being taken. The VP looked at me, and again I felt embarrassed, uncomfortable, and put on the spot. Somebody had to go explain to the whites what was going on.

But, you know, meetings in general were a hassle until I learned how to handle myself. I wouldn't speak up. And when I did, I'd always sense something wasn't right. It's like people would talk right over me. They wouldn't listen to me. For instance, in one of my meetings, we were dealing with a problem that was definitely in my area of expertise. My boss was in the meeting, too. So instead of asking me questions directly, whites asked questions of me through my boss by directing their questions to him. After about the third time this happened, I asked myself, "Didn't I make myself clear, or don't they know I speak English?" My white peers were there with their bosses. This didn't happen to them. They were talked to directly.

Oh, and another thing! Speaking of bosses, I didn't have regularly scheduled meetings with my boss. He told me I could come in if I had a problem. Now, think about that. The implication was, "Don't bother me unless you have a problem!" Now you *know* I certainly wasn't going to admit I had a problem I couldn't handle. Soooo, I had little interaction with my boss. Again, this hurt me.

You know what? During that first year especially, I really experienced periods of high stress. There were plenty of blacks around, but not in my area. I saw whites get better jobs than I had, and I didn't like that. James was from a northern city, and he didn't understand some of the things about southern blacks or what differences we had in some of our attitudes. He was just insensitive to what I might be going through.

James didn't understand, for instance, why I wasn't as aggressive as he was. Hell, I was from the South. I know I was pretty damn unaggressive. I always knew what the situation was. I've always been a fast learner.

I knew about racism, but I never thought it would exist in a large corporation like this. I thought they were in business to make money and wouldn't tolerate crap like that. Of course, that was an inappropriate assumption for me to make, because companies are just people from the larger society. I guess I just didn't think.

Being in a new city, having to make new friends added to my stress. I was used to a black society—now it was integrated.

Stress came from old learnings from my growing up in an environment—all of society—telling me, "Whites are smart; blacks are dumb and lazy." I guess, like a lot of blacks, I had unknowingly bought into a little piece of that.

Yeah! Sure it made me angry when I thought about it. I felt *if* whites were smarter, it was because they had better opportunities. And besides they made all the rules determining what was and was not considered smart.

Looking back, I see now that in order to escape some of the pressure I allowed myself to be maneuvered into becoming "the expert" in my work area. I've found out since, that's death for a minority. You get steered and directed so that you end up specializing in one piece of something because whites can feel that they know you can do that piece well. You're also comfortable being an "expert." But you don't get the broad-based training and development you need when that happens.

See, let me tell you. I had this one little piece that was mine. Later on, when they tried to broaden me, I fought it. They had channeled me into a narrow path to make sure I didn't fail. I knew this because I was only given this kind of work to do. They didn't introduce me to anyone else, either, to help me get my work done so I could move on to something else. So when they tried to broaden my area of responsibility, it was too late; I resisted. I had gotten their message. They wanted me to work in this narrow channel, and that was nice and safe. When they finally offered me others to help me on the project, I didn't want it! I didn't trust those other people. I felt they'd screw up what was mine.

I guess you know, I was really confused now. I said, "Wait a minute!

You wanted me to stay in this area, now you want me to get out." I couldn't read the messages. I didn't understand. And *nobody* took the time to explain it to me.

You better believe I felt anger from time to time—but I didn't express it at work. I knew if I did, I'd be looked down on and ostracized.

One day at work, my boss came in and asked me, "Why is it taking you so long to do this job?" I exploded! I told him I was upset—he was pressing me—I needed more time! I was new with the company! I hadn't been there ten years and didn't automatically know how to do that stuff. "I've got to learn how to do it like everybody else," I told him.

He thought I was taking too long. Looking back, I probably did take too long. But what he didn't understand was, being black and not having access to resources the way whites do, I would take damn near twice as long to make damn sure that everything was in order; I checked and rechecked.

The same thing in meetings—you have to get up in front of a bunch of white people and explain things. You're under a lot of stress when that happens. You're fearful that if you make a mistake that'll just confirm what you know whites are thinking in the first place.

At the time, I didn't know there were people someplace around there whose job it was to do some of the tasks on my projects. Hell, how was I supposed to know? I didn't even understand the organization or how things worked. No one ever explained it to me.

Sometimes my boss would stand over me and watch me work on my project and make comments about it. We argued all day one day over a simple decision I had made.

Now I'm feeling crazy! Why would a person do that? You know, if you asked me right now to explain it to you, I'd have to say I didn't think about trying to explain it to myself. I couldn't explain it! I just didn't think about it. I guess I didn't think about any of it much. I wasn't angry . . . and if anger threatened to surface over some incident, I'd usually swallow it. Sounds strange, doesn't it?

Thinking back, I guess I was thankful I had this job. In fact, when I joined this company I figured I might not last the year. Somewhere inside me, I felt that I might leave or they would fire me because they would discover some deficiency in me. I know that's not logical—but then neither is racism logical nor the effects it has on all of us.

I ran into a lot of things that worked to undermine my confidence. I saw younger whites come into the organization and other whites take them aside and tell them things, share information. I saw the new whites interacting with other people I didn't even know. That wasn't done with me or for me.

Now I'm feeling real strange.

At first—not for a long time, really—I didn't attribute my weird feelings to racism. I thought it was me! I thought I was doing something wrong.

James didn't even realize I was feeling this way. He'd been there longer and, being from the North, seemed to get along better than I did. James and I didn't discuss discrimination or many of the incidents at work or our real feelings about things.

Of course, there did come a time when everybody had just about had enough! Whew! Did we talk to each other then. Like when James got put on a really big project and ran headlong into several people who wouldn't work with him. But that's another story.

In retrospect, it took too long for me to get angry. I'm surprised I don't have an ulcer. I guess it had to come to the point where the damn job was less important than my dignity and self-respect.

There were even problems when I had to go out of town to one of the branch offices. Surprise showed on people's faces when they discovered that the troubleshooter sent out to them was black.

Once—get this—it got so bad that every time I made a suggestion this one big, red guy would stand up and ask insane questions, pick at my answers, and just agitate. It got so obvious, this guy's boss told him to get a cup of coffee. "Just leave!" he shouted.

At this point, I guess, it finally hit me—"This is happening because I'm black." No whites had complained about stuff like this. And the thoughtless racial remarks—but I was still "nice." Like Jackie Robinson—you can't fight back.

On another occasion, at 4 A.M., a white female passenger on an airliner made a big deal over not sitting in the seat next to me. She complained to the stewardess—"I'm not sitting *there!*" she said. Another passenger exchanged seats with her. I was so *damned mad!* The whole trip! But I didn't say anything.

Another time, returning to the northern city where I'd been transplanted, I had trouble getting a cab home, which was in the black part of town. I complained and learned other blacks had this problem, too.

Change came gradually. I found myself talking more to other blacks about survival issues. We were no longer merely seeking each other out for relaxation. Now we were also sharing experiences, asking questions of each other, and working strategies.

We discovered that we were all trying to survive . . . having the same kinds of problems and dealing with the same kinds of issues.

I know, I've often wondered myself why it took so long. I guess we all felt this couldn't possibly be happening to anyone else, so why even discuss it? Perhaps, too, in a way, we were covering up something we probably took more ownership of than we should have.

What precipitated my opening up? Yeah, I remember what happened. I had made friends with a black manager who had joined the company after I did. This was a few years later; I had gotten pretty fed up with a lot of things, and I told my friend, Harold, I was going to look for another job. I was going to leave the company.

Hal got alarmed and asked me why. I told him I didn't think I was getting anyplace here. That's when Hal looked at me and said, "I'd like to do the same thing."

Glory! Man, I felt . . . *good!* I was relieved. It wasn't just me! Yeah.

That's when we started to level with each other. In fact, all the black managers started leveling with each other after that.

Do you know what? I told my boss the same thing—that I was fed up and going to leave. I found out later that turkey didn't tell anyone about our conversation. That's also when I realized that, if I was going to get out of the survival state, I'd have to preplan my every move—to outwit and outfox some of those racist SOBs! Obviously, my boss didn't care if I quit or not.

At parties, over lunch, whenever we black managers were together, we talked more about what was happening to us. I could see the sad looks in my friends' faces as we talked about the crazy things we were putting up with.

Some of us were being checked upon to see if we were going where we said we were. Can you believe that?

Frank Smith told us he'd always ignored racism. It didn't touch his life much growing up sheltered in an all-black community. "I didn't perceive any problems," he said. "I thought things would be like they always were. But I got poor performance appraisals, even though no one offered to help me. I'd always succeeded before when I tried something. I asked myself, 'What's happening to me?' I've gotten bitter. They assigned me to a boss who's a company reject. I'd been thinking there was something wrong with me. My self-confidence has dropped to zero." Now where had I heard that before?

John Neil spoke up, "I was really impressed with this company coming in. But like a lot of you I've got small jobs, small projects. I didn't think anything of it at first, but I've noticed the new whites coming in getting big jobs and projects right off the bat."

We got the message—the company was going to test the blacks first to see what they could do before risking more.

John continued, "My jobs have been too easy. But I've been satisfied. Sure I've been mad, but I wouldn't dream of being aggressive. I know if I go to meetings and get aggressive, the whites would accuse me of being pushy."

You know, I'm glad there's a lot of us that don't care about those kinds of tags. Oh, no. Don't for a minute think that alone will get you over. You just get a different set of the same kind of problems. "Militant" is a tag that will get all kinds of doors shut for you. Knowingly or unknowingly, the black who's aggressive will get himself punished. The punishment most likely will come in the form of the type of jobs he'll get. He'll be passed over for promotion. His white peers will say he's "got a chip on his shoulder." He'll get cut out of what information flow whites might share—and so on.

The message to all of us is: Don't upset anyone. And for the love of God, don't act emotionally! One of the first things I noticed was that whites tended to be very unemotional. Show a white manager you're upset, or show you're angry, and watch his face and behavior. What'll happen? Chances are he'll try to shut you down by cutting you off—he'll just interrupt, that's what. He'll imply you don't know what you're talking about—say that you cause problems.

Evaluations were a revelation to all of us. I'd been on the job for nearly a year when I was called into my boss's office—my boss two levels up—and told that my immediate boss had given me the best performance evaluation he had ever seen. And that's essentially all he said. *Ten years later,* I got to see the performance evaluation, and it was damn near perfect.

But hell! I didn't need to see it ten years later. I needed to see it then—when I was feeling a gross lack of confidence. When I'd go to branch offices, people would write my bosses and tell them what a good job I'd done—but it was ten years later when I saw that information. So, they really withheld positive information from me.

Look, I'm going to tell you one more war story, and then I'm going to take a break. The more I talk, the more I remember, the madder I get! Man, this stuff is painful for me. I had to go out to one of the branch offices to help straighten out some foul-up in the books. We worked overtime until we got it all straightened out. Then I went back to the motel. Next morning, the books didn't check out. The branch supervisor got on me—asked, "What the hell is going on?"

What had happened was that one of the white clerks had tampered with the books—and he did it because he and some friends wanted to play a trick on the "nigger." That's what I heard later.

But you know what's interesting? I was walking around there, and it's like I wasn't really angry. I guess—out of frustration—I said, "What the hell! Why even get angry when somebody would do a stupid thing like that?"

OK, now I let you see a little piece of my world and get a feel of my gut. You said it would make a difference if I were honest about it. Sure, white America has run a number on me, but I let it happen. Hell, I'm no victim. Once I realized that, I started to do something about all this stuff. Yeah, yeah, whites helped, too, once I stopped hiding everything. Let me rest now; I'll tell you more later!

ANALYSIS OF CRITICAL ISSUES

Jack's story is a story of blunders—Jack's, his co-workers', and the company's. They are all casualties of ignorance and a racial system that discriminates against people like Jack. At this point, let us take a look at Jack's blunders and why the above statement is true.

When Jack came on board at his company, his boss was absent, and Jack did not understand what his job was or how the work he was given was to be accomplished. Jack made no attempt to seek out anyone who could provide him with the information he needed. Nor did he complain to his hierarchy about having to begin his job without proper assistance. Also, Jack's boss was not astute enough to understand that because his new employee was black he had to do something different to help Jack join up.

Jack refused to ask questions about his work, even to relieve his own stress. He laughed at jokes that were offensive to him without telling his co-workers he thought they were insensitive. By laughing at the jokes, Jack encouraged his co-workers' thoughtless and sometimes cruel behavior toward him.

In meetings, Jack allowed people to talk to his boss instead of to him. He never confronted that issue. This is an example of the subtle form discrimination can take. Often blacks will find their presence ignored. This lack of respect toward them is usually *felt* in the Entry Phase of development instead of *consciously acknowledged*. The person will feel uncomfortable without being able to pinpoint the source. Jack, typical of most minorities at this phase, disowned his negative feelings.

When Jack did make contact with another black in the company, James, he further hampered his progress by remaining closed to sharing his problems and seeking information from his black co-worker. If he had, he could have gleaned valuable information, since James had been in the organization longer and had a perspective and outlook similar to his own. In other words, at first Jack did not know how to effectively use his psychic support system.

Another blunder Jack made was not speaking up when it became obvious to him that his white peers were getting bigger jobs than he was. Again, Jack in his naiveté did not realize this was subtle discrimination against him. The company was sending Jack a message about its faith in his competence. Unconsciously, Jack picked this up. Since this message was not in conflict with all the other messages blacks get from the society as a whole, Jack accepted it and continued to doubt his own competence.

To relieve the resulting tension Jack felt between the messages he received from his environment about his lack of competence and his own desire to recognize and realize his competence, Jack allowed his company to position him as a specialist. This further prevented his growth and development. Jack's major blunder here was making *comfort* his prime objective.

Carl Sandburg said, "First, there must be a dream." Some years before, Jack had a dream that he worked to fulfill. He had left the Army, which held no real future for him, finished college, and entered a field that few blacks had dared to enter because there were so few jobs for them. Jack had gotten that job; his blunder was to stop his dream there. Without a dream, we become complacent. Without a dream, we do not push forward to obtain better things for ourselves. The first big barrier becomes a permanent block. Jack needed to set higher goals and career objectives for himself shortly after entering his job—or at the least, he needed to develop survival objectives.

Jack was too trusting of a system he knew, if only intellectually, was discriminatory against blacks. He blundered when he did not insist on *seeing* his boss's evaluation of him as opposed to just being told it was good. Jack inappropriately assumed everyone had his best interest at heart. His friends also made similar blunders when they did not insist on having their evaluations explained to them.

Jack should have demanded regular meetings with his boss for reasons other than discussing problems. Instead, he sat back and waited for people to come to him. Jack should have insisted that someone introduce him to all the people he would be working with in his area of responsibility. In addition, Jack should have let his boss know the kind of treatment, good or bad, that he was receiving at the branch offices.

In light of the information we have discussed, Jack's lack of self-confidence is understandable. Jack grew up in America and was taught as a child, in various ways, that whites are smarter than blacks and that whites are better educated. Therefore, any lack of self-confidence gets compounded for Jack because of the reinforcing messages he receives from the society at large.

Whites in America are also programmed to believe that blacks are mentally and educationally inferior to whites and many whites do believe this. Their beliefs are often sustained because they have no real interaction with blacks. Many whites still know very little about blacks except what they see and hear in the media. Because of these prejudices, blacks are constantly put in the position of having to prove themselves over and over. Jack's inexperience with subtle racism prevented him from realizing this. Since Jack did not understand, he was trapped. He had to work twice as hard to get the same evaluation as his white peers.

Many blacks get angry about this situation. Often a black individual will be angry and not realize it. This explains, in part, the feeling of "going crazy." This anger can affect a person's performance and output. It can manifest itself in a lack of confidence and cause withdrawal. In this case, the person will not seek external information that would be helpful to growth and development or in accomplishing the job tasks. Therefore, energy output, of necessity, will be twice as much as that of white peers.

The anger in the Entry Phase is different from the anger shown in the Adjusting Phase, when blacks seem to be angry at the whole world. In that phase, the anger and self-doubt is expressed by lashing out at everything and everybody and/or becoming bitter. People who react in this way are usually seen as having a chip on their shoulder. It is also understandable that their interactions with whites will be minimized.

Jack did not specifically point out his feelings of gratitude or good fortune at having gotten the job. However, that feeling is implicit throughout the narrative. Jack stated that he felt he had it made and never mentioned any other black who had attained a position similar to his. This strongly implies that Jack felt he had attained great heights not open to other blacks. He showed his gratitude to the company by not speaking up and by not making waves. Jack was careful not to cause problems. For example, he would not ask questions or complain about the lack of help in doing his job, even though he hurt himself by not doing so.

Because Jack felt lucky to have the job, he thought he must be careful or he might lose it or at least be somehow proven incompetent. Jack, during this phase, could not see that he had worked hard for his position in the company and that he had earned it. In the conversations Jack reported having with his friends, again the implication is one of gratitude, because they were for the most part satisfied with their jobs—and this was in the face of seeing their white peers get better jobs and more responsibility. A white manager can easily interpret this attitude as complacency and a lack of inner motivation, or the attitude can feed into a stereotype that says blacks do not want much out of life anyway. Neither of these conclusions could be further from the truth.

To sum up the situation in very general and rather simplified terms, blacks are subjected to the racial inferiority propaganda all Americans are subjected to. If blacks believe any part of that propaganda, then they are automatically grateful when given jobs. A person's attitude might sound something like this, "Even though whites don't think I'm worthy, at least they thought enough of me to give me this job, so I'm going to behave in a manner that will show them I'm grateful. I won't make waves, and I won't cause problems."

Jack was not prepared for the realities of his job. He was not prepared to be thrown out on the job to sink or swim. He lacked information about how his organization worked. For reasons already discussed, he was not about to ask. He expected to be given some tasks, laid out for him in very clear terms by someone, and then be left alone to do his job. He did not anticipate needing a lot of help. Jack certainly was not prepared for interactions with all kinds of people. As with most blacks, nothing in his background prepared him to be able to deal with corporate functioning, power, and politics. We would hazard to say that most blacks have adjustment problems in these areas, because these are the areas in which blacks have historically been the most powerless.

A lot of Americans, both black and white, believe in the Protestant work ethic. Very successful whites learn early that it often takes more than that belief to get what they want. For blacks, it becomes a painful lesson to learn that the system will not reward them in proportion to the results they obtain. One reason they are not sufficiently rewarded may be that some people are honestly not aware that blacks face greater obstacles in obtaining results than whites do. On the other hand, some people are aware but do not intend to give the extra credit deserved. In Jack's case, the Protestant ethic also worked against him because he did not realize he was putting forth extra effort to get the same results as whites.

Many people may find the degree of racial naiveté among blacks difficult to believe. The obvious discriminatory behavior is easy to see, but few blacks are aware and sensitive enough to see all the subtle ways they are excluded from mainstream participation. Jack and his friends are very typical in this respect.

Jack had enlisted in the Army, where he interacted in an interracial environment, yet he still made a basic assumption that a white profit-motivated corporation would not allow racial matters to become a hindrance to making a profit. These kinds of assumptions are common among blacks. Therefore, blacks are seldom prepared to deal with racial resistance. They tend not to be consciously sensitive to the subtleties of corporate interracial interfaces. Since most black adults today have essentially grown up in segregated surroundings and have also been somewhat restricted in their day-to-day interactions with whites, they are inexperienced in understanding the various cues of racial prejudice and the barriers they present to the black person.

It would seem that people in general are not aware of the effects that racial prejudices can have on a profit-making operation. That tells us a lot about the nature of racism. It can affect the bottom-line results. For an example, Jack could have produced more results per unit time from the beginning of his new job. In other words, Jack was paid for working 30 days, and he was unable to do what his boss had asked him to do. If Jack and the corporation had known what Jack was going to face, they both could have been positioned to work through some of the problems early. Then Jack could have finished his work and made a much smoother transition into the corporate milieu. So racial naiveté on the part of both blacks and whites can certainly affect bottom-line results.

Because of his inappropriate assumptions that race was not an issue in the corporation, Jack lowered the sensitivity he had acquired from previous experiences in interacting with whites, such as in the service. Jack, like most people without help, generally lacked sufficient insight into his own feelings and motivations. Without this, he could not see much of what was occurring to him.

A missing factor for Jack, as with many blacks, was the concept of career. Whites, on the other hand, are often brought up and educated with the idea of building a career in life. Blacks are generally brought up differently because in the past this country did not offer blacks opportunities to build careers. Jack did not go into the company thinking in terms of a career. He went in thinking in terms of a job. He was struggling wth such basic issues as keeping the job and doing well. He had not expanded his mind to the point of assuming he could have a career. Also, there were no black role models—no blacks he could look up to and say to himself that there is a possibility of having a career here. As Jack pointed out in his narrative, not much hope is offered young blacks in terms of what they can expect for themselves in the job world. They can verify the validity of that attitude when they look around and try to count how many blacks are on corporate boards.

At school no one taught Jack that you must set career goals when you go into an organization and that these should be well planned and laid out. This idea was alien to Jack. However, this is a responsibility Jack's boss should have assumed upon his return to the office. He should have helped Jack develop some goals. Companies need to let minorities know what they can ultimately offer them in terms of career opportunities. It is unfortunate that many companies are unclear themselves about their policies concerning career advancement for minorities.

For this reason, there is usually a lack of appropriate training opportunities for both minorities and whites to learn the kinds of managerial skills needed to effectively work together. Any kind of managerial training that the minority individual is exposed to is geared for the most part to meeting the needs of white male management. Black managers must translate the training material into something that they can use, because of their unique relationship to the dominant culture. Initially, few blacks are able to do the necessary translating; therefore, much of the training material is lost to them.

As we can now readily see, Jack's career opportunities were realistic from his viewpoint. He saw a lack of commitment from white institutions toward his equal participation and advancement, and there were no black role models to assure him that the opportunities were there. He was constantly reminded that his interpersonal style was problematic to whites, and he saw that his style often overshadowed others' evaluations of his job competence. Paradoxically, this usually drives black managers to become even more concerned about their work tasks rather than the interpersonal interactions that are in reality the crux of the issue.

In face of seemingly overwhelming odds, Jack, like many black managers, was able to overcome the various barriers and succeed. Now that we have some insight into many of the problems confronting the black manager, we will discuss how these problems may be solved.

DEVELOPMENT OF HOW-TO SOLUTIONS

Many critical issues and situations leap out from the story about Jack's Entry Phase. There are too many to deal with adequately in this volume. Therefore, we will present, in a general form, what we consider to be some of the key problems that hinder the progress of many blacks in the Entry Phase. Following each problem, we will present some solutions. These are certainly not the only solutions possible, but hopefully, they will trigger additional thoughts and approaches. In each case, the problem is clearly stated. Under each problem is a listing of the related critical issues; the numbers refer to the numbers in the list of critical issues that appears at the beginning of this chapter.

Problem I: How to overcome reluctance and hesitancy in asking work-related questions of whites. Problem relates to critical issues 1, 3, 9, 10, 20, 22

Solution 1: The first solution deals with yourself. Have a conversation with yourself and ask, "What is the worst thing that can happen to me if I ask questions of one or more white people?" The worst possible thing that can happen is you will get fired. That becomes the highest possible risk you have to be concerned about. Asking a question about your job is certainly not grounds for dismissal. Therefore, being fired is highly unlikely, and the risk becomes negligible.

Now ask yourself, "What is the best thing that can happen?" The answer to that is, " I will get an answer to my questions that will allow me to produce results."

Your next question may be, "But what if they think I'm dumb?" Then you will have to face your feelings about what is more important at this moment—the other person's perceptions of you or the fact that you now have information that will help produce results. In this case, the results are the important factor. This is a solution for individuals who are less concerned about the perceptions of others.

Solution 2: For individuals who are more concerned about their image with whites, the "power model" is useful. The power model is used in this fashion. When preparing to ask a question, preface the question with a statement like this: "Mr. Jones (or Ms. Jones), my boss told me that you would be a good resource for me on this kind of question and that if you can't help me I should come back and let him (or her) know." Then ask the question.

What that does is to position the resistant individual to give you an answer to prevent you from going back and reporting to the boss. It also implies you have the support of the boss. This can be done because you will have already had meetings with your boss. (See Problems II and III.)

Solution 3: A third way to approach this problem is to preposition the white individual to receive your question. You can say, for example, "I want to ask you a question. Now, the question may seem elementary to you, but I'm not really concerned about how you view it." Then ask your question.

This positions the person to focus on the question instead of evaluating the person who asked it. People don't like to be told beforehand how they are going to react to something, so they will work hard to do the opposite of what you suggested. It is simple reverse psychology.

Problem II: How to find out what your job is. Problem relates to critical issues 3, 8, 10, 20, 21, 25

Solution: Ask your boss for a roles write-up or a job description for your position. If that is not available, or if you are not satisfied with what exists and you need more detail, then write your own. This is permitted; people are seldom told this, but it is quite acceptable to write your own job description as long as you review and work it with your boss. Start by interviewing your boss, and ask the following questions:

- What are my major job tasks?
- What are my major roles in terms of how this organization operates? In other words, how do I fit in the organization? What is my role relative to my boss and others in the organization?
- Who are the clients who will receive the output from my job?
- What is my output?
- What are your major expectations of me, expressed in terms of, "I expect you to _____"?
- Who are the resources or experts for the tasks associated with my job position?
- What are the names of the people or the organizations I will interface with when I perform my job function?
- What are the priorities associated with my particular job function? What things are important? In what order?

Sit down and think about the answers to these questions. Then summarize the answers and appropriately place them under the following categories:

Job role
Job tasks
Job expectations
Major outputs

Available resources

Job priorities

Major interfaces (names of people, organizations, clients)

A minority individual cannot afford the luxury of not knowing what his or her job is. Once the information is pulled together under the appropriate categories, have it typed and give it to the boss with a note that says, "This is how I view my job role at this point in time. Would you please review this and comment." If there are corrections to be made, then discuss the misunderstandings with the boss and get them resolved; reach a mutual agreement on what your job is. The boss will own the yardstick by which you will be measured. You need to know what that yardstick is as early as possible.

This procedure needs to be completed in the first few weeks on the job.

Problem III: How to set direction in your job. Problem relates to critical issues 1, 3, 4, 6, 7, 8, 10, 19, 20, 22, 24, 25

Solution: After working at your job about a month and after your job has been documented, make a list of the things you would like to learn in the next year. Make the list as specific as possible. List those things that you like to do, that you are interested in, and that juice you up or turn you on. They should be things that make you produce at your optimum level. Try daydreaming about what you will be doing a year from now and what tasks you will be executing when you are feeling good about your job. Write down the thoughts you have from your daydreams. Summarize them in a presentable form.

Bounce your list off a friend, your mate, or a trusted peer for comment. Then use their input to revise your list. Bounce the revised list off your boss for his or her comment. Now turn your list into quantified objectives with this format:

To (action verb) (task) **by** (date).

Example: To learn my organization's basic marketing strategy by September 19--.*

Next, set up regularly scheduled meetings with your boss to take advantage of his or her expertise as well as to resolve any problems you may have with your job. You may also use this time

---

*This is the most simplified form of an objective and will suffice for the Entry Phase. However, if you are interested in more information on how to write better goals, see Robert F. Mager, *Goal Analysis* (Belmont, Cal.: Fearon Publishers, 1972).

to obtain any additional information or training that you need. Remember *all* bosses have some area of expertise, no matter how incompetent they may appear to be. More will be said about direction setting in Chapter 9.

Problem IV: How to handle interpersonally insensitive people. Problem relates to critical issues 1, 3, 4, 7, 9, 10, 11, 12, 13, 14, 15, 17, 18, 19, 20, 21, 24, 26

Solution 1: Ask more questions than you give information. This works because as long as you are asking questions the other person will be concentrating on giving answers instead of getting information from you to use to evaluate you. This works well with people who in the past have displayed prejudiced attitudes. Often this works further in your favor since people tend not to waste time answering questions of people they do not value, so they will adjust their perceptions to a more positive position since they are responding to you.

Solution 2: Confront the insensitive person directly. Say, "After looking at our situation, I'm confused. Maybe you can help me. Can you explain to me why you are behaving the way you are?" Or "Can you explain to me why you are talking to me in this manner? I need to understand in order for us to meet the objective that we have in mind. We are working toward the same end, aren't we?" The person will then have to deal with your "confusion" by looking at his or her behavior and interactions with you.

Solution 3: Sharing your feelings with the person is often appropriate. Say, "When you say that," or "When you do that, I *feel* this way. I wish you wouldn't say or do that." Insensitive people are then made to realize that you will not hesitate to make them face your feelings. They are also put in the position of having to alter their behavior or be subjected to your evaluation. This approach should be used by peers.

To put this solution on less personal terms, which is the best course of action when dealing with a person in a position superior to yours, try this approach. "When you say or do that, I have a problem with it." Then follow up on the response.

Solution 4: There are some people who seem oblivious to others' feelings or who do not care. In this circumstance, your only recourse may be to interact with them only when absolutely necessary. When you do, interact rapidly. Work out the issue or task involved as quickly as possible and move on.

Problem V: How to become more comfortable in social interactions with whites. Problem relates to critical issues 1, 3, 9, 11, 12, 13, 14, 15, 17, 21, 24, 26

Solution: As we previously explained, many blacks feel stress when interacting with whites, whether from lack of experience, lowered confidence, or both. When feelings of stress or awkwardness appear, the black individual tends to do most of the talking. This only causes more stress.

Instead, strike up a conversation and become the listener. Ask questions and listen. Try to find topics of mutual interest, like hobbies and sports. Get involved in the other person's interests in those topics. Stay away from topics that may raise your anxiety or point out how different you may be from the people you are conversing with. Do not position yourself to be left out of the conversation or to be made to feel alienated.

Initially, allow the other person to do most of the talking while you summarize or restate what has been said to make sure you understand. The whole process of restating will help you become more comfortable in talking to the person. It also takes unwanted attention from you and puts the focus on the other person.

To give individuals the impression that you are interested in them and what they are saying, ask them questions about themselves. Ask how they have seen things change over the years in the company, city, or community. Talk more as you feel more comfortable with the person and the topic. Be sure to look the person in the eye. Avoid looking down at the floor or up at the ceiling. You will give the other person negative messages about your interest or self-confidence.

Watch the other person's facial expressions when you talk. If you do not, you may miss 50 percent of the interaction. Avoid talking with your arms folded or hands hidden in pockets. The other person may see your discomfort by these actions.

Problem VI: How to conduct yourself when you are the only black participant (or one of two) in a meeting. Problem relates to critical issues 1, 3, 4, 5, 7, 9, 10, 11, 12, 13, 14, 15, 17, 18, 19, 20, 21, 24, 26

Solution 1: Before the meeting, tell yourself that you are an integral part of the meeting. It is important to remind yourself of this because in most cases whites will tend to dismiss you or not acknowledge you. A solution that works well is to allow the other participants to talk first. Then, when you do speak up, ask a question for clarification. This can also help you get more comfortable in the meeting. Asking questions works to force other participants to acknowledge your presence. It forces the group, even if momentarily, to deal with you by responding to your question.

If the meeting is a decision-making meeting, it is usually best to wait until the group is near closure on the decision. Then ask questions that will cause the group to be clearer about the decision-making process. A black manager can handle him- or herself well in a meeting by taking on a consultant's role. That means taking a look at what was said, by whom, why, and how it relates to the main business of the meeting. Your questions should point up some facts that the others may have missed.

If the meeting is leaderless and you are black, it is advisable that you not be the person to take that leadership initially, because the group will fight you. Since the leadership role shifts during such meetings, it is nearly always best that you assume that role later when the group is in need of your special talents. Instead, let the other participants organize their thoughts and start talking. Do not forget to ask questions periodically to get clarification and people's attention.

As the group gets bogged down in issues, ask questions to help clarify the group's position in the way that a consultant might. The group will then seek clarity as a result of your questions and pay more attention to your input. This will give you an opportunity to lead the group or at least to be heard. At any rate, the group will listen to you more. It is at *that* point that you should switch from asking questions to giving information. This is an effective process for the black individual to use in meetings.

Solution 2: Another option open to blacks in meetings is to just speak up and demand to be heard. If you are a very open, strong, and verbal person, you may prefer this method—it may or may not work. You must be very careful as to *when* you speak up; timing is important. Since you are black, odds are your comments will be dismissed if you attempt to speak up first. If you wait to voice your input until after the third or fourth person has spoken, your chances of being heard are better.

The solutions in the Entry Phase presuppose that you as minority are not the designated leader. If you are, you must deal with some different dynamics. The black individual as the leader of an all-white, or predominantly white, group meeting will be discussed later in this book.

Problem VII: How to prevent being dismissed in meetings.

Problem relates to critical issues 1, 2, 3, 4, 5, 7, 9, 10, 11, 12, 13, 17, 18, 19, 20, 21, 24, 25

Solution 1: In meetings where the boss is present, it is very common for white participants to talk to black participants through the boss instead of directly to them. After this has happened to you once, sit back in your chair, relax, and cross your legs. Wait for the behavior to be repeated. Now place your hand on your boss's arm or hand or shoulder, if he or she is close enough, and say, "I would like to answer that." If you are not close enough, lean forward, put your elbows on the table, and say to your boss, "Jones," or whatever, "I would like to answer that if it is OK with you." It is almost as if you were asking permission. Or say, "May I answer that?" Then answer the question.

If after this someone in the meeting still insists upon not talking directly to you, lean your body forward, put your elbows on the table, touch your boss if you can, and say, "Jones, since this is my area of responsibility, I'm more than willing to [now turn to the meeting leader or the person who asked the question] answer the questions in this area." That should do it, and the meeting will either shut down or people will begin talking directly to you.

This solution is based on the assumption that there are no high-level managers—vice presidents or above—at the meeting. If they are in the room talking to you through your boss, you had better allow them to go ahead without interference. In this case, it is better to try to correct the situation using the indirect method suggested in Solution 2. If the participants in the meeting are at your boss's level or one or two levels up, the above solution works well.

Solution 2: As a variation to Solution 1, you may, depending on what suits you better, choose to be less direct or more direct in handling this situation. Perhaps you would rather let the situation continue without interrupting the meeting. When you leave the meeting, you might say to your boss, "Jones, why didn't you tell those people to direct their questions to me? I suggest the next time that happens you ask them to ask me. There are negative implications associated with their not talking directly to me." Then explain further if it becomes necessary.

Solution 3: If you are more comfortable in meetings and tend to be the aggressive type and if Solutions 1 and 2 did not work, you may prefer this method. Put your elbows on the table, lean your body forward, and say to the person who keeps talking to you through your boss, "Perhaps you didn't hear or understand what I said before, so let me repeat it. That is my area of responsibility, and I'm more than willing to answer any questions that you may have in that area. If I can't, then between my boss and me, we will certainly be able to answer your questions."

Solution 4: Here is a situation somewhat different from the one above. You are in a meeting—it does not matter if your boss is there or not—and you say something. The people in the group disregard your input or act like they do not hear you. Let this go for about five minutes. After this, interrupt someone and say, "That really is a good point and certainly a good piece of input to this issue." Then lean forward and say emphatically, *"As I said a few minutes ago . . ."* and repeat what you had said.

Or you may choose to escalate the situation in this way and make the group deal with their behavior toward you. Get a quizzical, dumbfounded look on your face and say, "I'm confused. I made a statement a few minutes ago, and perhaps it wasn't heard because it certainly wasn't dealt with. I would like to have my comment responded to. Let me repeat it." Then go ahead and repeat your earlier statement.

Problem VIII: How to keep your work experience broad enough to help position you for advancement or increased responsibility. Problem relates to critical issues 2, 3, 4, 5, 6, 8, 19, 21, 22, 25

Solution 1: Keep your energies focused on your responsibilities, and produce good results in your job. When you have mastered your present responsibilities, ask your boss and your peers questions about other responsibilities that relate to what you are currently doing. It is advisable that the peers you approach be people you trust. This helps eliminate the possibility that peers will make unwarranted assumptions about your motivations and gives you some sympathetic support in gathering this information.

Learn more about and get interested in the other areas. Tell yourself, "If I am to grow and develop in my career or job, I need to expand to prevent becoming stagnant." Select new job responsibilities that fit within your general area. Ask your boss if there are additional things you may do—such as helping the boss produce a report or doing some other job in which the boss is involved. If your boss is competitive or hostile in the relationship with you, then it is not a good idea to ask for any part of the work your boss may be doing. In this case, you must find other means to increase your responsibilities. You can do this through your peers or the bosses of your peers who have good relationships with them by simply inquiring and then asking for the work.

Keep adding to your responsibilities as you become proficient with the new ones. At some point, you can ask to be moved to another job area. That point for you may be when both your old and new responsibilities become too simple. Never become comfortable with one area and refuse to move. This is a no-no, a *trap* for blacks.

Solution 2: After having been on the job for awhile, ask your boss about what other jobs relate to your job area. Then ask if you will have an opportunity to work in the other area(s) at a later date.

After getting this information from your boss, turn it into growth objectives and document them. This documentation can be used as a yardstick for both you and your boss to keep track of how well you are setting and meeting your job objectives. It also will indicate to your boss when you should be given more responsibility.

Solution 3: Ask your boss early in the job, "How do I keep from becoming too specialized in a particular area?" Then, with the help of your boss, plan and document a course of action for the future. Make sure your plan provides means to prevent your becoming too highly specialized.

On the other hand, if you already have a job that is highly specialized, if that is what is required of you in your job description and you do not want this, then it is best to consider termination of that job position. Your career movement under these circumstances will be highly restricted. If you see yourself working to climb to upper corporate levels, you will need varied experiences.

Problem IX: How to let your hierarchy know that you are ready for more responsibility. Problem relates to critical issues 1, 2, 4, 5, 6, 7, 8, 19, 20, 21, 25

Solution 1: Set up learning and performance objectives as stated in the solution to Problem III. During your regular meetings with your boss, test yourself against the objectives. For instance, you should have an objective that says that by such and such date you will be able to perform at a certain level. Test this out with your boss by asking if you are performing at that particular level. If the answer is yes, mark off the objective and move on to another one.

As you accomplish each objective, set new ones as suggested in the solutions to Problem VIII. Have your boss participate in the setting of the new objectives. If you follow this process, you will automatically get increased responsibility with the sanction of your boss.

Solution 2: Another option is to ask your boss, after being on the job for two or three months, what his or her criteria are for determining when you are ready for increased responsibility. Document this and give your boss a copy. When you think you have fulfilled the criteria, take out the paper and discuss it with your boss. Then you can legitimately ask for more responsibility. Your boss will be more responsive to your request because the criteria are the boss's.

Problem X: How to translate material from training and development sessions for use by black managers. Problem relates to critical issues 3, 5, 6, 19, 20, 21, 22, 23

Solution: After attending a training or development session, you will have notes and other material from which you can compile a list. The list should consist of the important techniques and action steps you feel may be useful in your job performance. It is seldom helpful to include more than nine good techniques or action steps, because trying to handle too many can cause you to spread your energies too thin.

Now examine each item from your list one at a time using the following process:

- Look at each of the techniques and action steps through the eyes of a white manager, using your knowledge of the perceptions and assumptions of whites about blacks. The white manager represents the system in which you work.
- Imagine the reaction of a white manager upon receiving data about or viewing another white manager performing an activity related to the important technique or action step you are translating.

- Now imagine the reaction of a white manager upon receiving data about or viewing a black manager performing the same activity.
- Compare the reactions—how a white manager would perceive the same action done by a black and a white manager—and look at the differences.
- If the white manager's reaction is neutral or positive when the act is executed by the black manager, then use the behavior suggested in the training session.
- If the reaction is negative, then identify some alternatives to the action suggested in the training session. The alternative behavior or action steps should accomplish the same purpose or desired results but with neutral or positive consequences.

To help clarify this solution, let us look at an example—the "shotgun memo."* A shotgun memo is written as though you are talking to someone. It is short, to the point, and hard hitting. It states in very direct terms what you expect from people. Now be a white manager for a moment looking at a shotgun memo written by a white male manager. The assumption is likely to be, "Wow, this guy is really on top of his job. He knows what he wants. He's hard hitting and to the point. He tells his people exactly what he wants, and he's very aggressive."

If you are a white manager looking at a shotgun memo written by a black manager, however, the perception is more likely to be, "Humm, this fellow has a communication problem. He doesn't write well. He's too pushy and not being supportive of the people." Now you can see that the consequences for a black manager writing and sending a shotgun memo are negative. So, this means black managers must develop some alternatives to the original training material they received in the session. You may still like the concept of the hard-hitting memo; therefore, you may decide to alter it in this manner.

You might use an introductory paragraph stating the problem and the objective you or the company are trying to reach; then write the hard-hitting memo. When white managers see this memo written by a black manager, they will tend to see it in a more positive light. Their response is more likely to be, "Humm,

*American Management Associations' course "Executive Productivity Training," March 19–21, 1979, course notebook, p. 40.

this person really lays his stuff out, knows what he wants, is directing his people well. Although some people may react negatively, at least the objectives are in line with those that I want the people to have."

Problem XI: How to develop and effectively use a psychic support system. Problem relates to critical issues 4, 9, 10, 11, 12, 13, 16, 17. 20, 21, 23, 24, 26

Solution 1: You can develop and use a psychic support system through social interactions at work. Take your coffee breaks with a black friend or any friend whom you trust, respect, and can garner support from to be able to deal with the stress and strain of your everyday work environment. It is helpful to talk about your feelings and reactions to things. Catharsis, that is, the relieving or cleansing of one's emotional self, is very good for your psychological well-being.

Periodically, eat lunch away from the job, if permitted, with a black friend or other associates. At times, have lunch on the premises away from your work group, if you are in the habit of eating as a group, with a black friend to talk privately. Seek out new blacks as they come into your job area and offer to help in any way to be supportive to them. Check in with them periodically. Go on breaks or eat lunch with them occasionally. At these times, make a point of discussing job situations with them. Talk about how you feel about your job and your reactions to it. Seek advice or ask the friend to just listen.

Solution 2: You may be interested in developing and using a support system after work through sports and social interaction. Such a support system has always been a part of the white corporate culture. The golf course is often used for this purpose. White managers tend to play golf with each other, and blacks have tended to be excluded from this. Unfortunately, in many places that exclusion is still operative.

Playing or watching sports with a black friend can be an integral part of a good support system. This is true for both men and women. It gives you the opportunity to enjoy and relax around a common interest. It also provides that important opportunity to talk about the stresses and tensions of the job in a relaxed environment that is conducive to thoughtful and helpful suggestions. Tennis, racketball, golf, swimming, fishing, as well as a myriad of other active and sedentary things, can all be used to stimulate the supportive relationship.

What happens if you are a black in an all-white work environment? Odds are you will have to develop a two-part psychic support system—one part white and the other black. The black support system will be developed after work, and the supporting individual will most likely not be involved directly in your work environment. Sometimes this can work to your advantage in that you may be offered a broader perspective on many of your job situations. The white system will be developed at work. Whether or not this is extended beyond the work environment will depend on the people involved and the nature of the relationship.

The dynamics of the relationship between the black manager and the white support system will be different from the dynamics of the black support system. In one situation, the individuals involved will share a common cultural background that will help in the understanding of problem issues. In the other case, there will be some difficulty in understanding because of differences in cultural perspective. However, astute black managers can use these differences to increase their understanding of the perceptions of the dominant culture.

One thing that is apparent throughout all the solutions in this section is that the black manager is going to have to *speak up.* This is very important. There is nothing that can be said or done to get people to speak up. This has to be done by the individual.

BASIC CONCEPTS USED IN HOW-TO SOLUTIONS

The basic concepts that were applied to solve the specific problems are presented here so the reader can use them to deal with situations other than the ones discussed in the previous section. Many of the concepts found in the how-to solutions may apply to more than one problem. Rather than repeat each concept in each problem as it occurs, only new or different concepts will be discussed.

Problem I: How to overcome reluctance and hesitancy in asking work-related questions of whites.

Concept 1: There is an old adage that says, "When I want to talk to someone nice, I talk to myself." Therefore, we refer to this first concept as Talking to the Champ. Talking to yourself is not the silly exercise we tease each other about. It can be used for a variety of helpful and often healing purposes. It can be calming in stressful situations. In the absence of other people to say the appropriate things you need to hear when you need to hear them, you can do it for yourself. You can provide the factual, logical information you need in order to see a situation as it is. You may discuss things with yourself in private that you would be hesitant to discuss openly with another person.

Talking to yourself can be helpful by giving you the opportunity to dig out, crystallize, and verbalize thoughts and feelings that lie just below your conscious mind. You can look at, experiment with, and examine your thoughts and feelings from various perspectives without having to worry about how you are being perceived by another person. You can give yourself that pep talk you may so badly need at the moment you need it.

Concept 2: Checking Out Both Sides of the Street is the name we have given to the concept of risk analysis and assessment. It is a good practice, especially for the minority individual, to assess the risks involved in any managerial problem. You need to assess the risks to you as a black individual so that you will be able to relax with the decisions you make. The usual result of risk assessment is that you find you have overestimated the risks to yourself. This is particularly true for the black manager in the Entry Phase.

The important method to remember in risk analysis is to ask yourself the question, "In this particular situation, what is the *worst* thing that can happen to me?" Then ask, "What is the *best* thing that can happen to me in this situation?" Now you can weigh the two answers relative to each other and get a picture of what is most likely to be the *real* risks to you. In other words, check out both sides of the street. This method of risk assessment takes you out of the areas of the unknown and of uncertainty.

Concept 3: The third concept used in solving Problem I is Using the Power of the Boss. When you find yourself in a situation in which you have little organizational or personal power—which is typical in the Entry Phase—there will be many instances when you will be empowered by the organization, through your boss, to do certain things. It is appropriate to use that power. In solving Problem I, the power was used by saying to a resource, "My boss said you would be a good resource to me and, if you can't answer my question, I should get back to her." It is correct to use the power of the boss in this case because, if you must interact with someone who displays racist or sexist behavior, it will put pressure on that person to behave appropriately. This is a good concept to use whenever you are in a relatively powerless position and must manage or influence a resistant individual.

Concept 4: Pre-positioning is a useful concept for reducing dysfunctional interactions. People can be positioned by giving them information or messages about what you want or how you expect them to behave. The average person will then work hard not to behave in a dysfunctional manner.

Concept 5: Reverse Psychology is by no means a new concept. It is most recognized as a child–parent relationship concept. However, knowing adults respond to this also, we suggest it can be used effectively in managing people in an organizational setting as well. Tell a person that you expect him or her to feel or react in a certain way, and it is most likely that the person will respond in an opposite manner. People do not like to have their feelings and behavior predicted, especially face to face. Of course, reverse psychology does not work on everyone. Therefore, you must use your own insight about human behavior to pick the personality types on which it will work well. The stubborn person and the resistant person tend to be good candidates for reverse psychology.

Problem II: How to find out what your job is.

Problem III: How to set direction in your job.

Concept 1: This concept is called Publicizing the Yardstick. In a white corporate system, there are built-in organizational cultural norms that get transmitted among the various members of the organization in an informal manner. Whites tend to conform to these easily, as has been previously stated, because these norms are merely extensions of their cultural learnings. When blacks with their different cultural norms are introduced into the system, the informal communications network does not work as well for them. Therefore, blacks must seek means of finding out what the yardstick is that will be used to measure them. White male bosses will tend not to be as comfortable or as informal with blacks as with other white males.

White bosses may also make some inappropriate assumptions about a black manager's ability to get this information. They may think that the information is as readily available to blacks as it is to white males. They do not usually perceive that blacks are often excluded from the activities where information is informally passed. So black managers are put in a position where it becomes important to set up their own measurement device with the sanction of the boss. It must then be legitimized in the organization by making it public.

Concept 2: We suggest black managers use the concept of Collaboration often, particularly with their bosses. This may be difficult in some instances where an adversary relationship exists between the boss and the black subordinate. However, regardless of what the relationship is, the white institution will expect black managers to be able to collaborate with certain people on various issues. This means that in some instances you will have to learn to collaborate with the boss.

Collaboration can also protect the black manager and the boss. In our how-to solutions to Problems II and III, boss and subordinate collaborated on job definition and goal setting. Collaboration protects the subordinate and the boss because the decisions they make are a shared responsibility. The white male boss has the organizational power to legitimize the work done by the black manager, and the black manager does not have to face the consequences of acting alone.

Concept 3: This concept is called Navigation of Your Life. Take a moment and think of your life as a ship and the corporation as the ocean in which you are sailings and you are the navigator—it is your responsibility to plot the course. You cannot assume that the corporation will know in what direction to set the course of your life any more that you would assume that the ocean would know how to set the course of the ship. How would the water and winds know where you wish to go? So do not sit back and expect the boss or the corporation to set your career course. Granted, it is a joint venture and responsibility, but you should initiate it. This is especially true for blacks. Black managers are so new and few to the corporation that the system is just learning how to help these managers set the direction of their careers.

Concept 4: This next concept is called Fantasy and Autosuggestion.* The basic thesis is that, in order to reach a goal, you must fantasize that you have already reached it. You must use autosuggestion to actually see, feel, touch, and taste what you want; doing this will facilitate your setting and obtaining the goals you wish to reach.

Concept 5: The concept of Using Resources can be found

---

*Autosuggestion is a term taken from Napoleon Hill, *Think and Grow Rich* (New York: Fawcett Books, 1960), pp. 67–73, 89–100.

throughout most of these problem solutions. Essentially, there are two ways to use resources: (1) to add to what you already know how to do well or (2) to provide information on what you do not know how to do well. (More will be said about this in Part Three.) The important thing about using resources is to use the *right* resource. This is where your boss, peers, and friends can be helpful in terms of identifying resources for you. First, identify your needs and then the resource to tap for information.

Problem IV: How to handle interpersonally insensitive people.

Concept 1: The concept to use to deal more effectively in some interpersonal interactions is the Questioning–Diversion Technique. This is helpful in avoiding situations where blacks find themselves giving too much information or talking too much about themselves. By "too much," we mean providing information that may inappropriately show another person that you are overly stressful. Running off at the mouth at this point is not helpful. All too often, this is used against you to meet the other person's needs.

Many times blacks may find themselves unwittingly feeding into a white manager's negative racial stereotypes of blacks by offering unnecessary and inappropriate information. Black managers should ask questions of white managers about the issues being discussed in order to get their opinions, feelings, ideas, and so forth. In this way, the interaction can be focused on the issues under discussion or on the white person and will leave little time for the black manager to allow him- or herself to be placed in a position to be evaluated.

Concept 2: The concept of Confrontation is very familiar to most of us. There are some instances when nothing we try seems to work. The chemistry between people is just not right. There may be too great a personality difference between the parties involved. In these cases, you will have to confront the issue. Remember, we said confront the *issue*, not the person. It is very important for the entry-level black manager to confront the *issue* and not the *person* because this is linked to his or her basic survival in the organization.

Appropriate and successful confrontation is not only a concept but also a skill blacks will learn to develop as they grow and mature in the organization. Successful confrontation will be addressed as a separate topic in Part Three because it is a very important job skill needed by the black manager.

Concept 3: The concept of Sharing Your Feelings has some similarities to confrontation but differs principally in that it lacks a menacing affect. That is, your feelings may or may not be presented boldly to the person on the receiving end of the interaction. The sharing of feelings is important to minorities because there will be some instances when you are so frustrated you cannot think of anything else to do. When you get to that point, the simplest thing to do is to share with others how you feel about an issue. That positions people to deal with the issue. It also points out to others that you do have feelings and are being affected by their dysfunctional behavior. In addition, this action demands that your feelings be respected and responded to.

Concept 4: The Avoidance Behavior concept* should be used *only* as a last resort. If all else fails, avoid the person or the situation for the moment. When everything breaks down, leave the scene of action. Here the old proverb "Discretion is the better part of valor" applies. At times, avoidance behavior is quite appropriate. Remind yourself that nothing is solved by unnecessarily subjecting yourself and others to fights and punishments that neither lead to good problem solving nor prove anything. Return when there is a viable plan to solve the problem.

Problem V: How to become more comfortable in social interactions with whites.

Concept: Interest Transference is the concept used to offset those instances when you are in a stressful or awkward situation. This concept can be used to transfer your awareness from your own discomfort to an active interaction with another person. This merely means that you can deemphasize your stress or awkwardness by using your mental energies to get involved in an interaction with another person and his or her interests. You will find that you have little energy left to be wrapped up in how you are feeling at that moment. If you truly involve yourself with what the other person is saying, you will discover that your feelings of discomfort have vanished. The other person will be flattered by your interest and usually will return the favor by a warm response to you. This concept is important for black managers because they frequently find themselves in conversational situations where they feel like outsiders.

*This concept is also suggested in Charles C. Vance. *Manager Today, Executive Tomorrow* (New York: McGraw-Hill, 1974), pp. 1–26.

Problem VI: How to conduct yourself when you are the only black participant (or one of two) in a meeting.

Concept: The concept called Proper Timing means sensing when it is appropriate to carry out some activity or behavior. In many instances, as in the solutions to Problem VI, timing can be crucial. You must learn to sense when it is the best time to act on an issue. Proper timing is like a sixth sense; some people seem to have it naturally, while others must acquire it. It appears to be learned through trial and error. It is essential that black managers acknowledge the importance of this skill and seek to develop it because it is often the critical ingredient that can ensure success. We know of no sure way to teach this skill, but we suggest that finding a role model who displays this ability and copying that person's behavior may help. Watch your role model and ask questions concerning his or her sense of timing. Study what is done and under what circumstances decisions are made. This may help provide clues about what is involved in proper timing.

Problem VII: How to prevent being dismissed in meetings.

Concept 1: After much haggling and deliberation, we decided to call this concept Taking the Critter by the Neck. We really were about to call it Taking the Bull by the Horns but were much too sensitive to that being a sexist cliché; we would not intentionally be guilty of *that*. So we modified the expression to include *all* persons.

Taking the Critter by the Neck means using your sense of timing to determine when it is appropriate to speak up in an aggressive manner to take momentary control over a situation. In the case of Problem VII, the black person senses that he or she is being dismissed in the meeting, does not like it, and becomes angry. This individual does not feel a part of what is occurring in the meeting. The input from the person may be important but nevertheless gets overlooked. It is not only appropriate but essential that blacks aggressively cause their presence and input to be acknowledged by the group.

Concept 2: This concept is humorously but respectfully known as the SSS Syndrome—Sudden Seizure of Stupidity Syndrome. It means that at some appropriate time you choose to affect confusion, misunderstanding, lack of knowledge, or just being dumb in an interaction with someone. You may shrug your shoulders or even say, "I don't understand. You've lost me," or something of the like. Often it helps to frown as though you are really struggling with what is being said.

You may want to use this concept to buy thinking time in a difficult interaction by positioning the other person to give you additional information. Or you may use this concept to place responsibility for some attitude, behavior, or emotional outburst by another person back where it belongs. This technique frequently calms the person who is accusing you of something that you did not do and forces that person to reexamine his or her data. It puts responsibility back on the originator to explain his or her behavior.

Problem VIII: How to keep your work experience broad enough to help position you for advancement or increased responsibility.

Concept: In the concept of Data Sorting, the individual must first use resources. Data Sorting is the idea that you should sift through the mound of information you have collected from your resources and pick out *only* the data that are relevant to your particular case and to what you are trying to do. In other words, keep in mind the objective you are trying to reach and pick out only the information that helps you to reach that particular objective.

Problem IX: How to let your hierarchy know that you are ready for more responsibility.

Concept: The concept of Taking the Initiative relates to some of the other concepts in that the black individual does not sit back and wait for someone else to decide what his or her next move should be. Blacks must learn quickly in the Entry Phase to be concerned and thoughtful enough to initiate some moves to ensure that their needs and concerns are dealt with. If you meet with procrastination on the part of your hierarchy, then be persistent and appropriately demanding. Appropriately demanding here means do not be dysfunctional in your demands and get pushed aside by the system. Be sensitive to when to pull back.

Problem X: How to translate material from training and development sessions for use by black managers.

Concept: The concept used here is called Behold! The Other Side of the Coin. For many people, this can lead to new discoveries and make them more sensitive to people who have differing cultural perspectives. This concept means that in order to make good decisions or to understand another's viewpoint, you will literally have to look at the situation through the eyes of the other person, using what you perceive to be the other person's assumptions, perceptions, and cultural background. This arms you with additional data so you can understand why people do certain things or behave in certain ways in given circumstances, and it also helps you understand your own behavior, attitudes, and motivations in the same circumstances.

Problem XI: How to develop and effectively use a psychic support system.

Concept 1: The concept Seeking Help and Support is similar to the concept of using resources; both embody the informational process of giving and receiving data. However, seeking help and support has the added dimension of emotional encouragement and support.

Concept 2: The concept of Socializing is one that most people are familiar with. It is very important for black managers to learn and understand its significance as applied to the corporate culture. Blacks tend to have a different attitude toward socializing than whites do. Blacks tend to want to have some emotional involvement with the people they socialize with; that is, they want to like the people they are with. Whites, on the other hand, tend to be able to comfortably socialize without that element always being present. They have learned to use socializing for reasons other than being with friends.

It is a normal part of white corporate culture to use socializing to informally gather information, to seek favors, to make contacts that may lead to opportunities, and so forth. Black managers need to be aware of these differences in social attitude in order to take advantage of opportunities to be a part of the informal corporate culture. Be aware that *no one* is demanding that you relinquish any part of your black identity. There is no need to do that. Socializing is an accepted, legitimate tool to use to obtain the opportunities to do the things that need to be done in order to move from a state of survival to success.

Summary of Basic Concepts

This section contains brief definitions of the basic concepts used in the Entry Phase how-to solutions. It may be used as a quick reference.

1. *Talking to the Champ* refers to the process of talking to yourself for a variety of helpful and often healing purposes.
2. *Checking Out Both Sides of the Street* is the name given to the concept of analyzing and assessing risk.
3. *Using the Power of the Boss* is a way to compensate for a lack of organizational or personal power by referring to your boss in a statement to someone; this action empowers you to act through your boss.
4. *Pre-positioning* is a method used to reduce dysfunctional interactions by informing people of how you expect them to behave in a given situation.
5. *Reverse Psychology* is the method used to get people to do one thing by telling them you want another thing; this works well with contrary individuals.
6. *Publicizing the Yardstick* refers to letting people know how they will be evaluated before the evaluation takes place.
7. *Collaboration* is a way of working together to find a solution to a problem or issue by pooling the talents of individuals.
8. *Navigation of Your Life* refers to setting the course and direction of your life.
9. *Fantasy and Autosuggestion* refers to daydreaming about and mentally seeing, feeling, touching, and tasting what you desire to have.
10. *Using Resources* means that you seek out individuals who can add information to what you already know or can provide information about what you do not know.
11. *The Questioning–Diversion Technique* is used to divert people so that they will concentrate on answering your questions instead of spending time gathering information to evaluate you.
12. *Confrontation* refers to meeting an issue head on with another person; stating your feelings and reactions are hallmarks of the process.
13. *Sharing Your Feelings* refers to the appropriate discussion of your feelings in an effort to inform others of your state of being.
14. *Avoidance Behavior* refers to the concept whereby a person will leave the scene of an interaction because an intolerable conflict exists or the person is too uncomfortable to remain.

15. *Interest Transference* is a way to deemphasize your stress by getting involved in an interaction with another person and his or her interests.

16. *Proper Timing* means sensing when it is appropriate to perform an activity or behavior; timing in many instances can be crucial.

17. *Taking the Critter by the Neck* refers to using your sense of timing to appropriately speak up in an aggressive manner to take momentary control over a situation.

18. *SSS Syndrome* means that at some appropriate time you strategically choose to show confusion, misunderstanding, or lack of knowledge, or just to act dumb in an interaction with someone.

19. *Data Sorting* refers to sifting through a large amount of data to select what is relevant.

20. *Taking the Initiative* deals with initiating action on your own to ensure that your needs and concerns are dealt with.

21. *Behold! The Other Side of the Coin* refers to looking at a situation through the eyes of someone else to understand another's viewpoint.

22. *Seeking Help and Support* refers to seeking emotional encouragement, psychic support, and ego support.

23. *Socializing* refers to participation in non-work-related activities in order to make contact with people from the work scene.

3

Adjusting Phase

CRITICAL ISSUES

Attitudes
1. Reality testing
2. Low self-confidence (may run into a lot of criticism)
3. Readjustment of expectations about the company to fit new perceptions
4. Allowing self to see how racial prejudice affects progress (identifies barriers)

Emotions
5. Change in stress level (disappointment in work ethic and disillusionment in company taking care of employees)
6. Frustration
7. Anger or rage

Behaviors
8. Struggling to identify and learn appropriate corporate behavior
9. Linking with informal communications network
10. Learning to identify one's own skills brought to the company
11. Negative reaction to whites (may have a lot of arguments with whites)
12. Becoming more vocal, many times inappropriately

Job Skills
13. More positive perception of one's own competence
14. Struggling to acquire managerial skills
15. Continuing to see white peers get better jobs, more responsibility (the issue of potential versus proven competence)
16. Perceiving little job movement and few results
17. Learning the criteria by which blacks are evaluated on competence

ANALYZING THE CRITICAL ISSUES

Attitudes

The Adjusting Phase is probably the most turbulent period of development for the black manager. In the Entry Phase, black managers are less aware of the issues they face because of inexperience with the workings of the white corporate culture. Blacks will also tend to deny negative activities they begin to see in order to get along well on the job. As they move into the Adjusting Phase, black managers become increasingly aware of all types of issues involved in getting along on the job. The act of denial now becomes harder to sustain as inexperience gives way to growing experience and more understanding of how the white corporate culture operates.

Reality testing is one aspect of adjusting in the corporation. The Entry Phase attitude of acceptance changes to suspicion of the motivations and activities of the corporation regarding the survival and success needs of the black manager.

In the Adjusting Phase, many black managers may still retain an attitude of lower self-confidence about their competence than they will experience in future phases. This is particularly true where blacks experience a lot of criticism in job performance and are not told when they are excelling. However, blacks will see the good results they produce on the job and will compare these results against the results produced by white peers. As black managers experience more and more the discrepancies between how the organization treats them and how it treats their white peers, they will begin to push back on the organization and test it. This testing not only helps build more self-confidence but also helps provide a more realistic picture of how the black manager must operate in order to grow and be successful in the organization.

"I started to overcome my competence problem by showing myself and others what I could do. I could see myself becoming more aggressive."

"When I compared my skills with those of my peers and even some of my bosses, my skills were better, especially my managerial skills."

"I kept looking around for my competition, and I didn't see any. I started hesitating every time I did something because I was so used to getting interference, people bothering me. Whites had been telling me that what I was doing or saying was wrong."

"I was concerned that white people like me. It has become less important. I don't care now. I do care that they behave in a way to let me get my job done."

"I don't use all my energy any more to counteract the feelings I get from whites, that blacks are 'less than.' I now know better than that."

"I got respect even though I can't say people liked me very much. I got results; what could they say?"

"I got a few accomplishments under my belt. That gave me confidence and freed me up some."

"When I realized I had some power and authority over what happened to me, I became more assertive and verbal."

In the Adjusting Phase, black managers realize that the organization is not a benevolent institution and that the same barriers that exist in society exist there as well. The system will not allow industrious activity alone to determine who succeeds. The growing realization of what an organization is all about is coupled with the increasing ability to identify real barriers to a black manager's progress, barriers that white peers do not have to deal with.

"When I looked around at what everybody else was doing, I felt qualified to move up; but I knew that unless I did something about it, no matter how well I did my technical job, it would never happen."

"I began to realize that I was going to have to strategize to get anyplace in this outfit. I'd have to be clever, tenacious, to absorb the punishment and outthink the whites."

"I now know that 'the harder I work, the further I'll go' is not true. There are limitations and obstacles. I began to wonder how far I wanted to go; it may not be worth it, that is, with what I have to go through."

"You have to strategize to just get things done in your job. You have to become a superstar—no less than that."

"Learning the elements of politics goes more for blacks than whites."

"You have to put pressure on the organization . . . 'cause nobody's going to give you anything, no matter how good you are. I'm being more proactive."

Emotions

As the black manager gradually moves from the Entry Phase into the Adjusting Phase, there is also a gradual change in the kind of stress experienced. On much more than the previous superficial and intellectual level, black managers begin to realize that a lot of people in their organization are running to get to the top. Stress results from now knowing that they are also running, but with a handicap that presents barriers to upward movement. At this point in time, black managers are not sure who is responsible for what barriers, and there is great frustration because they do not quite know what to do about the barriers.

More frustration is felt because of the trial-and-error activity required to learn the appropriate corporate behavior and what does or does not work for a black manager. Feelings vacillate from mild irritation to anger and sometimes rage. Expressed emotions vary from anger directed at the organization in general to verbal attacks on specific persons. Black managers often feel anger and resentment over the extra and sometimes excessive energy they must pour forth in order to get simple tasks done when interacting with whites. The anger gets intensified when blacks stop to think about how whites operate with each other in relation to how they operate with blacks.

"People will blatantly lie to you and use you in detrimental *ways. The company won't look out for you. You look out for yourself. The best person won't always get the job."*

"Blacks have to prove competence. Whites can be assumed to have it. Blacks don't fit the white picture of a manager so the company tests blacks. And whites expect blacks to be messiahs around people problems."

"I don't have much faith in the organization because most people around here are insensitive. They just don't know what it takes for me, a black person, to do the job. There is no problem seeing what whites do, but I have to reinterpret everything so the organization can see what I do. My values are higher than their expectations."

"A lot of your energy is used just surviving racist pressures. I have to use energy on whites playing games with me. Blacks can come to the brink of failure because of racism."

"I put everything I did under a microscope and kept all mistakes to myself. I was careful no one else saw them. I have been anxious and frustrated over what it takes to get across to whites that I'm competent."

Behaviors

As mentioned earlier in this section, black managers make concerted efforts in this phase to learn appropriate corporate behavior. In addition, more attention is given to trying to link with the existing informal communications network. If possible, black managers will begin to expend more energy finding each other within the organization and forming their own grapevine for information sharing. This grapevine often leads to support systems for the managers, providing such help as feedback that is more easily trusted and coaching. The coaching from other blacks is very important in identifying one's own skills, building confidence, and providing the kinds of assistance whites get informally from each other but are not able or choose not to share with blacks. Many black managers who have become more vocal in the organization and who are behaving negatively toward whites can learn how to use their anger and behavior in more acceptable ways.

The grapevine is so important to helping blacks adjust to the organizational culture that we suggest that, if a person is totally isolated, that person seek help outside the company. This means making contact and establishing relationships with other blacks who are in similar circumstances and can help in information sharing and coaching.

> "I learned appropriate corporate behavior through trial and error. I used resources both inside and outside my company. I developed a push-and-retreat technique to use on whites. Their reactions taught me a lot."

> "I sought out other blacks to find out how things got done in an acceptable manner. I listened in on white peers' conversations to get information as they talked. Whites don't seek out blacks to share."

> "I'd check out a lot of things with other blacks to see how they sounded before doing something like giving a presentation. We would work out strategies together, so I would come across well and my input would not get dismissed."

> "I did a lot of eyeballing both whites and blacks and doing things through trial and error."

> "At first, I patterned myself after whites but later turned to blacks for help because I wasn't getting what I wanted."

> "I listen in on white peers' conversations to get information. For instance, at lunch, the topics you are interested in are things they may not want to talk about, so you are there as sort of an invisible person. So I take advantage of being a good listener and learn what kinds of things are happening in the organization."

> "I got asked to a lot of parties, and I felt there were consequences for not going, so I'd go and put it on a business basis for myself. I would try to get something out of it and use it as a chance to talk to some people I didn't get a chance to at work."

> "I have found a few sympathetic whites who would sit down and share information and one or two who would look out for me."

"I draw a lot of energy from being around blacks, talking with them, etc. It helps me understand myself better."

"Sometimes I have this overpowering need to get with blacks because I get sick of dealing with white racism. With other blacks I can get new ideas, put my guard down, and relax."

"There's enough of us at my company now to share a variety of experiences, compare notes, look for trends and flaws."

"You have to have a balance. I stay close enough to blacks and some distance from whites to keep from being socialized too much."

"I never got angry in general, but I sure blew up over some incidents and at certain people."

"At first I felt frustration, then anger. Finally I was in a rage as I became more aware of the inequities of the system. I was ready to take on anybody that tried to screw me."

"I'm frustrated and angry. I find myself in a lot of arguments because nobody believes we can come up with our ideas so fast and do as well in our jobs as we do despite the barriers."

Job skills

Competence issues remain a concern until the black manager realizes a sense of success on an intellectual as well as an emotional level. Then, in spite of what else happens, you still feel OK about yourself. Blacks tend to recognize soon after entering an organization that the acquisition of good managerial skills is critical to their success. Whites, on the other hand, often succeed without acquiring these skills. In part, the reason managerial skills are so important to blacks is because the system places so much responsibility for good black–white interactions on the black manager. When communication breaks down, it is usually the black manager who must bear the blame, in people's minds if not publicly.

No matter how hard blacks work at their tasks, they tend to be rewarded and recognized less than their white peers who do the same tasks. The message is, "Prove yourself again and again." In order to prove yourself, you must know what the rules are and by what criteria you are being judged. Many black managers in the Adjusting Phase begin to see that their competence in doing their job tasks is evaluated in direct proportion to how well they are able to manage others. Unfortunately, this is a slow and usually painful realization that nobody warned them about and for which their recognition of racism did not prepare them. The comments that follow provide a disturbing picture of how quite a few black managers see the technical aspect of their job compared with the managerial demands and how their organizations perceive and evaluate them.

> "I'm pretty average at my task performance, but I've lost interest in doing the ordinary task work. I'm seeing that I'm one of the best managers in the company. Few can hold a candle to me, but the company will not take risks on blacks. You have to do the job to get the job. Every time you get moved you get tested again. They are more stringent on blacks than whites. The average black manager will have a difficult time making it. The company thinks I'm good at my job because I can conceptualize. When whites evaluate blacks, they tend to talk about the blacks' managerial abilities; when they talk about whites, they tend to talk about their technical abilities. Even when the black is technically solid, whites reserve their technical strokes for whites. I'm so public, so visible, that whites have no recourse from my results but to praise my work. When whites can't do the job, it's the fault of the system; when blacks can't, the fault is theirs."

> "I know I have survived by doing my tasks exceptionally well. I really didn't want to get involved in interpersonal things. Blacks don't fit into any images whites have of managers. I was already doing this job before I got the title and moved up. Whites get promoted on potential; they don't have to first prove they can do the job. Even though I've been tested over and over, I still get the job done. I have to manage interpersonal interactions; all whites do not. The company has recognized my persistence as well as my ability to get people to do things, but I am not adequately rewarded for what is involved in being a black manager. I can't get honest

feedback from whites. I have to do extra things in my job to offset racism that whites don't."

"I don't question my technical competence any more, and I don't allow anyone else to either. I've shown superior interpersonal skills. My ability to deal with interpersonal issues, direct, guide, and steer people, deal with conflict in a positive manner have all helped me. There is no in-between for blacks; you have to be good in every area. Whites expect excellence from blacks before they can make it. Whites can make it on being average. Blacks will get penalized for making mistakes. The organization can put questions in the system about you to undermine you instead of openly saying something negative about you. Blacks have to manage all kinds of interactions and others' racism. With all the pieces I have handled successfully—a white wouldn't have to do all that and then get underrewarded as I have. A company has no perspective around how much it takes for a black to do the job. I have to face the stereotypes the organization plays out on me. The company will quickly get their negative report if I make a mistake."

"I got a bad performance evaluation, and when I asked for the details on where I was missing the mark, I could see I was not meeting my boss's stereotypes of blacks. Blacks have to amplify managerial skills so much to survive that the task component seems unimportant. Many job tasks get misinterpreted as managerial tasks and then turned into a negative."

"My performance appraisals have always been subject to interpretation by my supervisors. Everything I do is relative to my being black."

The Adjusting Phase is the most active phase in terms of struggle. However, with all of its surface negatism, it is the most positive phase relative to the great learnings acquired by the black manager. Both the Adjusting Phase and the Planned Growth Phase are periods of rapid growth and learning. The two phases differ in the nature of the learning and the methods used. The Adjusting Phase can be compared with the period when a young child learns to become aware of his or her environment and to manipulate it. Much of the behavior displayed is trial and error, and the attitudes are those of reality testing. This development stage lays the foundation for the next great learning period, the Planned Growth Phase, which is more structured and goal directed. The manager in the Planned Growth Phase can be compared with the student who studies in a structured goal-directed manner in preparation for acquiring a job in the society.

In the Adjusting Phase, black managers correct misconceptions and inappropriate assumptions about how the corporation operates. Values are reexamined, and managers begin to crystallize goals and seek a direction in their jobs. They make way for the more structured learnings to come in the next phase. The next great task ahead is to be able to use these learnings by organizing experience and laying out a plan to achieve success. When managers are able to do this, they move into the Planned Growth Phase of development.

A word of caution: black managers will experience many Adjusting Phases throughout their careers. It is necessary to propel a person out of a stagnant period into one of growth. The danger lies in remaining in the Adjusting Phase and thrashing around until you burn out. Remember, the key to moving on is to organize your experience and learn from it.

Now let us return to Jack's story.

"EVERYTHING'S NOT AS GREAT AS I THOUGHT"

Man, oh man! Just stretching and walking around did me a world of good. My muscles had gotten pretty tight just sitting here. Guess I was really into remembering things and got tight.

Yeah, I'm OK. Let's see, where were we? Oh yeah. I was talking about my entry period at my company.

Now you want to know what happened next, what changed me, and how I got into the next period of development. OK. Let's go back to the day I told you about, when I went and told my boss I was going to look for another job, because I didn't feel as though I was growing and developing.

Now the real reason I told him that was because I got angry! I looked around . . . I'd been angry all along, but now I allowed the anger to just seep up, to engulf me, to—to just permeate my every little fiber. That's how strong I felt about it.

So I went to him and told him I was going to quit—and the real reason was because I looked around and I saw some whites who had come in along with me; they had much better jobs than I did. Much, much more responsibility.

I figured, damn! I can't be *that* dumb! So dumb that they're not going to give me some better jobs and more responsibility. It's like they gave me little bitty jobs—to see if I could do them. Then if I could do them, I'd get another little bitty job. And then, maybe, the third time it would be a little bit more responsibility. And it ticked me off!

And also, when I was working with my boss during our weekly meetings, he'd give me, like, some little side job with some little minor problem where I'd have to go and dig up stuff, something that had nothing to do with what I was really doing.

And that ticked me off! Well, it was like I had a private training session. Like I was so dumb that I *needed* a private training session. And it really made me angry. I was just fed up with it because I didn't see myself going anyplace.

Now, my boss . . . just about two weeks passed, and nothing happened. So, I—I figured out how to get a message to my boss's boss's boss. And I did it through a white guy I knew who worked in the office around the corner from me. He was in personnel.

The way I did it was to tell him I wanted to help him in personnel, to help in his office with some of the minority problems. Then the personnel guy, Mike, went to the upper-level boss and asked, "Can Jack help me in personnel?" And the boss said, "No!"

I knew the boss would come looking for me, and he did. We went in one of the empty offices and stayed about two to three hours.

He asked me what was wrong, and I told him that I didn't feel as though I was growing and developing, and uhh . . . I felt that I had talents that I wasn't using. And he agreed.

Then he shocked me! 'Cause he looked at me, and he said, "I'm so glad you feel this way." I almost fell out of my chair! He said, "Well, it finally sounds like you're ready to make some movement." Which implied that that's what they were waiting for. But damn it!! Why didn't they tell me that!

What? What were they waiting for? For me to . . . to, uhhh, get angry. Exercise some initiative. Say, "I want this and I want that." And—and just make some movement. Just get off the dime! In other words, stop accepting peanuts and ask for more. I guess that's what they—

No. No, I don't think the whites were asking for more. I think they just did their jobs, and then the next time they got more responsibility automatically.

Why did I have to make noise before I got better jobs? Why didn't I get automatic increases like my white peers? Now that's a good question! One which I can't answer—other than they were testing me because they didn't think I could do the job in the first place.

Even when I did the damn job, I didn't automatically get as much responsibility as the whites got. Maybe they were asking. But I doubt it. I just don't have any explanation for it.

Anyway, there we were in this room. I was explaining to my upper-level boss that I was upset. And he was shocked when I told him that I had told my boss I was going to quit, 'cause nobody had told him. He didn't know about it.

I was so angry at this point that I looked at him and said, "I don't need you or this *damn company!*" I said, "People are afraid of you, but you're a damn man like I am. You put your pants on exactly like I do, and I'm not afraid of you!"

I know he was surprised, but anyway he said, "I'm glad to hear you say that."

Anyway, the result of that meeting was his admitting they weren't using my skills. He asked me not to quit, and I got the biggest pay raise I'd ever had. That was designed to keep me there. In the meantime, I'd asked to transfer to personnel, so he made arrangements for me to do that.

Now, my second-level boss got into the act. He worked for the boss I had the big conference with. This second-level boss called me up and asked me if I wanted the personnel job and called me "boy" in the ensuing conversation, which further ticked me off. That was adding insult to injury!

I then moved to the personnel office. I now know that this was when I had moved completely into an adjusting period. Realizing how angry I was and wanting to quit my job and telling my bosses is probably what pushed *me* over.

Yes . . . yes, I know it was because I was just so damn angry. I got even angrier when I got to the personnel office and saw the kind of things they were doing—because they were saying, "We can't find any blacks." Well, hell! They were looking in white schools.

"We had trouble orienting the blacks. They didn't respond to the training." I couldn't believe this. There were no black recruiters or black input in the orientation program planning.

So the first thing they did—you're supposed to be in middle management to go out and recruit—they let me recruit without the promotions. I went out and found so many blacks in each of the job areas they wanted that they had to force me to stop.

Nobody in that office understood any racial stuff, so they didn't do a good job. The staff wasn't organized. People didn't know what their jobs were! So I organized the office. I got people to write up their job responsibilities, drew up a chart showing the process involved in the operation of the personnel office and its various responsibilities.

From that, I convinced them to put in a computer management system. But I had to bug the—

Now, see! Here's the difference. If I'd been white, they'd have paid attention to me. But it got. . . . I had to literally bug the *hell* out of them! It got so bad that every time I met with my boss I'd mention it again. He got ticked off—talked to his boss, and he got ticked off.

So finally—just to shut me up, I guess—they allotted some money to study the thing. And the study showed the computer system really would pay off. In the meantime—I had taken some college graduate courses in a nearby city a couple of years past. I guess it was to test myself—to see how I stacked up against supposedly sharp whites. My Army service didn't really count, I felt, because there are a *lot* of people in there who would have trouble making it outside. Now I went back to this school to take courses that related to the computer system I wanted in the office. Finally, they put it in.

Man, I had my hands full. The next step was to upgrade the orientation program, so I got interested in organizational development. I was concerned about what happened to black folks once they got through the doors.

No way! No! My anger hadn't gone away now that I was handling more stuff. My anger was building and building—reaching its zenith. I guess that zenith was when I was so damn frustrated at what I saw happening to blacks coming into the company. I saw the games people were playing— saw racism in action.

Man, it was like—my hands—I was just one person. My hands were tied. I couldn't change the whole thing. So I went outside the company and got some help. I got these people to put on some racial awareness sessions in my organization so they could see for themselves what was happening.

Some of the top-level managers heard about it and wanted to attend. So we started giving some sessions that included managers on every level. Now everybody could see what was going on. The upper-level managers decided to do something about the situation, so they allotted me a sizeable budget and some latitude to do some things that needed to be done.

Now wait! Before you decide everything is OK, remember this is the period when I was so angry and frustrated that I fought every white manager I came in contact with. Just exploded all over them! And I did some inappropriate things with upper-level managers in big meetings. It got so bad that people were saying that I didn't know when to fight or how to fight or, in essence, I didn't know how to act in the corporation—that's what they were saying.

This was happening to other people too—not just to me. For instance, John. You know, I mentioned him earlier. Well, he told me about the time—we can laugh about it now; it wasn't so funny then—he blew up in a meeting in front of a lot of white managers.

We were talking about some of the things we'd learned, and swapping war stories and insights—oh yeah, you can see a lot of things later— twenty-twenty hindsight. But it helps to talk to someone who's going through the same thing.

Anyway, John said he was in this meeting with a couple of his bosses and some peers, and something he had asked to be done for his project wasn't done. He said he started getting all kinds of excuses about why it wasn't done. He was already mad because he had not been able to get cooperation all along. His input was dismissed; his peers wouldn't do what he had asked, and his bosses weren't supportive worth a darn.

John had had it at this point—so he blew his stack! He stood up, and took the papers he had in front of him, and threw them down on the floor. "I don't want this to ever happen again!" And he kept on yelling, letting off some steam.

Well, John said the papers hit the floor, scattered all over, and he had to go pick them all up while everybody sat there looking at him. He said he felt like an idiot, an angry idiot who would have liked to smash some noses. He felt set up at the time, and he just got angrier . . . and was angry at himself for letting them make him lose control. He said he got his point across in that one incident, but it didn't do the kinds of things he wanted for his image.

Course we've talked about those days and realize now that maybe we needed to go through some of this to learn. We know anger is appropriate, but as a tool—not a relief valve.

What was I doing with my anger and frustration? Oh. Oh yeah! One thing I did inappropriately was to get into meetings with upper-level managers and, instead of bringing up an issue and then discussing it, I would sit and watch things happen until my anger just made me explode, and I just kind of erupted. I would just, kind of, uhh—rage! Yeah! That's it! I'd use my black rage.

Yeah, man! It wasn't really aggressiveness—it was black rage! I'd just jump all over people! People who were two and three levels higher than me, because I didn't give a damn any more. I saw I wasn't going anyplace. I wasn't learning anything, so I said, "Just to hell with it." And I pulled out all the stops. OK?

Now what else? Oh! Sometimes I would, uhh . . . yeah, I would see something in writing that I would react to because it would be racist, a racist reaction to something that happened on the job. Like, when they were figuring out minority numbers, they would count black women twice, OK? They'd count them as blacks and as women. To me, this didn't make sense.

I went to one upper-level boss's office to ask about it, and instead of being strategic, I jumped all over him—and he never forgot it. Years later, he still remembers that I did that. And I thought I was being cool and calm.

See, the corporation does not allow for a lot of display of emotion among its members. But blacks are more emotion based than whites. And that's something that usually gets us blacks into trouble.

But man, see . . . whew! I'd got frustrated! I could see what needed to be done, but I couldn't do it because people were too busy trying to *test* me to see if I knew what the hell I was doing.

There were a lot of fights. And they weren't just with white managers above me; they were with white peers also. I just . . . it was just a display of anger! I was trying to make reason out of a maze of confusion.

What things did I see that didn't make sense? Well, uhh. . . . Oh! One thing I could very clearly see was that sharp whites could propose something, and people would listen, ask a few helpful questions, and make plans to try out the idea. If a black manager did that, they would quiz the hell out of the person and then proceed to tell him or her why it wouldn't work.

Also, they'd move blacks from one area of the country to another and assume everything was going to be all right. They'd move black people down South, for instance, and never once give thought to where they would live, how they would get a phone, where they would go to the doctor, where they would get their hair cut—stuff like that.

When we tried to explain that to the whites, they looked like—duhhh! When we tried to tell them to assign a black to a new black person coming into the area, they said, "Why?" Just insensitive—totally insensitive!

Oh! Wait! Another thing! When I got the money to make changes in the personnel department, they put in these silly little controls—like, I had all this money and couldn't sign a request to use it! So to hire somebody to come in to consult—well, I could pick the consultants, but I couldn't pay them. That really gave others veto power over a lot of things.

Now in all this, I still had a white boss who wanted to always take a look at how I was going to solve a problem, even if it was a black problem. And he wanted override authority . . . until one day I'd had enough of it.

So you know what I did? I taped him a message and left it on his desk because I was just *sooo* angry. I just—I knew if I put it in writing I'd lose it, and I knew I couldn't sit in front of him and say it because I'd probably jump in his chest! OK?

And in essence, what I was saying was, "How the hell can you as a white man evaluate what I'm gonna do? You couldn't solve the problem; that's why you got me involved."

That's the kind of crazy things that would happen. Whites would question me to death every time I made a proposal. They didn't do that with other whites.

Whites would use the informal communications network to learn things, but I wasn't privy to that. Why not? Well, it's because they were uncomfortable with blacks; even our bosses were uncomfortable with us.

How do I know? Very simply. They talked to each other differently, spent more time with each other, told each other different things. Offered more help.

Even when I ate lunch with them, they'd share information with each other, but they wouldn't give me any. I'd have to ask, and when I did, I'd get short, to-the-point answers—but no conversation. They'd look disgusted with me. Their faces and voices changed.

When I led meetings and sessions, if a white was doing the session with me, the people in the room would look toward the white individual for leadership . . . including any blacks in the room. Everyone seemed to have trouble accepting black leadership, even the blacks.

I was feeling extremely bitter—crazy at times trying to explain to myself some of the very same things I've been telling you about today. I was looking for an explanation, and—damn it! I couldn't, I had no explanation. How could all this happen? How could you get a budget like this and then not be allowed to sign for anything? That's crazy! Then when I was told to make a major decision, my boss told me I didn't know enough to make the decision.

I had a lot of stress—paranoid type. At times I had a feeling that, after I confronted whites about looking over my shoulder with everything, they'd do the reverse. They let me go out and do stuff without any checkpoints, and if something happened, they'd come back and jump on me.

But I must have been doing something right. Because once every two weeks I had to meet with four upper-level managers, and it was their job to keep me in check.

And that was crazy too. Now, why would you put one black person in a room with four upper-level white managers? It was intimidation. So, what they were trying to do was slow me down by intimidating me.

Man, did I ever need a lot of psychic support, and I got that from other blacks. We'd meet after work. Then we were at a point where everyone needed that support, so we'd meet at work.

At one point if more than three blacks got together during working hours, the phones in the white bosses' offices would ring, and they'd want to know, "Well, what are the blacks doing?" And you'd go in the dining room, and if you ate with each other, you ended up at a table with all blacks, and people would start whispering and talking and asking, "Well, why do you blacks eat together?"

It's very interesting, but none of them ever came over to sit with us. So the same applies to them, "Why do all you whites eat together?"

Hell, yes! A lot of what I learned was from trial and error, and I got into a lot of trouble. I remember one meeting with all upper-level white managers one time, and we were discussing some plans I had laid out for the personnel program. One manager made a comment which to me was stupid, so I turned and jumped all over him—and I got about six messages from six different upper managers saying, "Don't do that again."

Now, they told me don't do *that* again, but they didn't tell me what to do. So there I was, more frustrated—and left out in the cold. Oh, everybody was telling me what *not* to do, but nobody was telling me what *to* do. So I had to learn by trial and error.

We blacks who had gotten together formed a grapevine to keep track of what was going on and to pass information and ways of surviving in the company.

I was frustrated over not having the correct interpersonal skills. Now, in this big meeting I was telling you about, obviously I didn't have the correct interpersonal managerial skills. Right? But I didn't know what was correct. I had nobody to tell me, and . . . and sometimes I couldn't sleep at night. I felt crazy trying to figure out, well, how the hell should I act? I wasn't about to act white.

See, black managers are caught in a chasm. Over here you've got what is so-called black cultural behavior. And over there is white cultural behavior. Now, the black cultural behavior is not corporate based. Obviously, I wasn't, uh. . . . Some blacks like to try and act white—but I wasn't going to. Then there was a third thing I had to develop. Well, what did it look like?

How do you behave? I had no way of knowing that! So I had to learn how to survive and test the system relative to what things I could or could not do.

Obviously, the company could not read black potential and take a risk with blacks, because with me, and other blacks, we . . . we had to display competence and show results, or else we didn't get an opportunity to do more things that required more responsibility. It's like we had to do the job at the next level before we could get more responsibility.

My managerial abilities were questioned. They questioned both my technical competence and managerial abilities. And this is the way the white managers can manage blacks. All they do is create doubt.

See, the trick they play on us is not to say directly that they don't think we can do the job. They say stuff like, "We question if Jack has the right experience." See, that's what they hit you with.

Yeah, they talk about, "Well, I don't know if you have the right background or right experience for that job." Behind closed doors, they decide your future with "haven't had the right kind of experience." Whereas whites don't have to have the "right kind of experience." They'll promote them on, well, based on potential and then provide the experience.

Like I said, during this time, I became a helluva lot more verbal. I told people what I thought, what I felt—'cause I didn't give a damn any more. I didn't have a damn thing to lose. I didn't have anything, so there was nothing to lose.

I became a helluva lot more aggressive, and I was pushed on by the rage—the black rage that I had within me. I had gotten to the point where I said, "This is crazy! I won't tolerate it! I won't stand for it! I'm gonna leave!"

And then . . . I really was going to leave, but then I decided not to because I got angry at that too. I said, "Why the hell should I run away from this? If I run away, then the next black comes along, and they'll do the same thing. I'm going to stay here! I'm gonna dig my heels in, and I'm going to change this organization."

Racism motivated the hell out of me! Now, if whites could understand how to use motivation—Boy! Could you improve the effectiveness of black individuals.

But they don't know how to use all that anger and energy—they're afraid of it, and what they try to do is shut it off! Whites in an organization tend not to attack problems directly. Listen, I know. 'Cause that was one thing that I had a problem with. I'd attack a problem head on—I'd jump dead on it—and whites tended to beat around the bush about what the problem is, who's to blame, what we are going to do about it . . . and "we don't want to upset the organization and change things too fast." And I'd jump dead on it and say, "Let's change things right now." Boom!

White organizations lose opportunities to really use us blacks effectively. How? Because given our cultural style we tend automatically to deal up front with difficult problems—that is, hot issues.

Why? Because that's the nature of our growing up. We've been doing it since the cotton fields: being creative. OK? For example, overseers in the fields didn't want us "lollygagging" and talking to each other, so we developed a system of communication through song. So we've learned to be creative in difficult situations.

I also think it has to do with our emotions. They tend to be closer to our level of consciousness than whites'. We have not been taught to suppress our emotions as much.

Man, one of the biggest issues I dealt with relative to my survival was the managerial piece. You have to get people to listen to your ideas. You have to convince . . . you have to sell yourself and your ideas. And that's not technical competence; that's a managerial competence issue.

During this time I probably threw away the work ethic, because it sure didn't work worth a darn for me. At least I paid a heavy price for what I was given in terms of rewards by the company.

There was a lot of dysfunctional behavior going on, mine and other people's. All this just drives you further into anger and keeps you frustrated. I know why I didn't get that ulcer early on; I was saving it for now.

I noticed a lot of crazy stuff. I noticed a couple of things happened when blacks and whites interacted. One was the verbal, spoken piece, and the other was the nonverbal. And I was missing a lot. I had to learn to notice both.

A lot of managers use intimidation to control people, but it has a different effect on blacks. I'd have to try and sort out the racist piece in the manager's actions, and whites wouldn't. I'd have to try to find out if there was a difference in the way intimidation was used on me versus the whites. The reason it's important to know this is because it would probably have a bearing on how I would respond to the person using intimidation.

Also, another thing I noticed. Uhh, whites can get benevolent sometimes when you take problems to them. They can get into a parent–child mode and try to protect you. They'll say things like, "Well, I'll go and speak to that manager," instead of telling you—or helping you—to take care of the problem yourself. That would be an adult-to-adult teaching mode. That's what a manager is supposed to do. But you get a lot of that crap. And that further frustrates you because you don't learn anything that way!

You know! That makes you angry because it feels like a put-down, like being treated like a child. I'm not a child. I'm an adult, and want to be treated like an adult. Don't take care of something for me—help me understand, so I can do it myself. That's slave–master stuff, 'cause I'm black.

Now, this—this is something! I want to tell you about evaluations before I take another break. I've even seen this happen with my kid at school. The teachers have to tell us about his conduct before they talk grades.

OK! Listen! One day I challenged a high-level manager because, given the job I had, I saw a lot of the performance evaluations on blacks and I noticed something. I noticed that when whites evaluated blacks, the first thing they evaluated, independently of their job role, was style. With whites, it was technical competence. So that if a white had high technical competence, they would overlook some of the negative interpersonal and behavioral things needing change.

With the black, they did the reverse. I felt like this was done from a base of prejudice. They expected blacks to misbehave. Therefore, the first thing looked at was, does the black behave properly?

Nobody was teaching us how to behave. So we all got zonked, automatically, with negative input around our style.

I'd say this happens all over. I'll be that general, that it still goes on. Because we checked it out with a very large number of evaluations, my boss had to give in and say, "You're right." So I say that happens in most institutions, corporate or otherwise. The first thing evaluated is the black's style.

Yeah, that happened to me too. One of my first evaluations started off with, "You've got a communications problem," not with the results I got doing my job. What that meant was, "When people interact with you, they don't feel good." OK!

The funny thing was that this boss had me talk to people he was afraid of. Why would he do that if I had a communications problem? What he was really trying to evaluate was my aggressive style— which may have been rough—and I'll concede that point. But what they tend to do is evaluate you on style and lump it under things like communications problems, or personality problems, and you can't do a damned thing about that.

What I was trying to find out was what do I change if I've got a communications problem? I dug into it, and what it boiled down to was I had a problem because I didn't do everything my boss told me to.

It was also based on his idea of how blacks are supposed to behave in the company, which he wasn't clear about. What he was trying to do was to say, "When *I'm* told to do something, I shut up and do it. Why don't you shut up and do it?" If that's what he was evaluating, he should have said it that way.

Yeah. I am a little tired. I'm going to take a little stretch in a minute. Let me finish up by making a connection here, I mean, uh, put it in some kind of perspective.

When you finally get tired of just sitting there doing your little bitty work tasks, when you get *soooo* angry you want to explode on everything—*then* you'll quit and move on, or you'll start to learn how to adjust to your environment.

In your period of adjusting, you tend to deal the most at an emotional level. You pull out the emotional stops. You don't try to suppress, or try to manage your rage and anger and aggressiveness or initiative. You just let it all hang out, so to speak. OK?

But then what will happen is that you'll discover—Damn! I'm not getting anyplace this way either. It's getting worse! So obviously I gotta do something differently. Let me look around and take in data about what other people . . . how whites make it in the organization.

Plus! Let me translate that into black terms so that I don't become white, and let me get some additional black input from other people that I respect and admire.

So you get to a point where you calm yourself down. You . . . you learn to manage your rage and anger. It's at that point that you begin to plan your own growth and development. You begin to take a look at, OK, what areas do I need improvement in and how can I get it? What are the how-to's, and how can I go about practicing the things I've learned that will work?

You start learning about taking risks. You start being aware of needing and using strategy, using the management skills you've picked up, and increasing your technical competence—all at the same time.

But that whole transition area really has to do with . . . with the black individual realizing that pulling out all the emotional stops is not going to work. So it's the realization that something must be different that swings you over into planning your growth.

Oh sure! I can tell you what did it for me. There was an incident. I had an upper-level boss, and every time I met with him, I felt put down! OK?

So, one day I went to a white manager. Now, this is amazing! I went to a white manager and I asked him, "How do you deal with this upper-level manager?" And what the guy said to me was, "Well, what I do is . . . the guy's whole style is that he appears to know everything and he asks a whole lot of questions of people. He intimidates them. And people shut down."

So right there the white manager was telling me, "Jack, the first thing you've got to do is—you've got to have a behavioral, psychological profile on the person." OK? Then you've got to strategize.

And then he said what he does is to allow the manager to go ahead and roll out his strategy, use his behavioral pattern. And then after about three or four questions, he looks at the guy and says, "Look, you asked me three questions, and the three questions seem to be unrelated. What is it you are really trying to get at?" Or "What is it you really want to know?" And see! What you really do is get on the offensive and not on the defensive.

Now, I learned that from a white individual, but I also learned more of the same from black individuals.

I calmed down after that. And that's when I moved into a period of planning my growth, because I tried it and it worked. It was painless! It was quick! It was to the point! And I didn't turn the guy off. I didn't strip the guy of his dignity. I was strategic, and I got what I wanted!

Look, you think about what I said. And speaking of getting what I want—I'm going for a sandwich. Can I get you anything?

ANALYSIS OF CRITICAL ISSUES

Jack's basic attitude changed drastically in the Adjusting Phase. His confidence was low, but he had fewer doubts about his ability to do his job well. Rather, he began to see and feel that he had little chance of growing, developing, and moving up in the company. Jack began to see certain things regarding his job, such as a lack of increased responsibility, that he seemed powerless to change. So Jack experienced frustration and dissatisfaction, and he became increasingly angry. This anger propelled Jack from his Entry Phase attitudes into Adjusting Phase attitudes.

Jack became so frustrated and angry over what he perceived to be so few avenues to get ahead that he no longer cared if he had the job or not. He decided to quit and look for a job elsewhere. At this point, Jack had certainly readjusted the expectations he held about his company. He came into the organization figuring he would be given a job to do and be left alone to do it without having to interact very much with whites. What he found was that he could not do the job alone and did have to interact with others. He became frustrated because he did not understand the dynamics of what was occurring to him. Jack felt that no matter how dumb he was in relation to whites, he had been with his company long enough to have made a little progress. There had to be some other explanation. So Jack allowed himself to see racial prejudice in action, and he began to see how it was affecting his progress. There were a lot of things happening to him that were not happening to his white peers, and he could not explain it to himself. Therefore, it had to have something to do with race.

Jack tells us in his narrative exactly what led him to angrily confront his upper-level boss about what was occurring to him on the job and how he felt about it. Jack was very surprised to find that his boss had no idea of what was happening. This is a common experience among blacks. When blacks are brought face to face with the realization of how much racial prejudice touches them personally, how hurtful and vicious it can be, the first reaction is to feel as though the perpetrator of the act is consciously and deliberately acting against them. This is of course true in some cases but not in most. Whites tend to be insensitive to how racial prejudice affects blacks.

Jack reacted to his environment in a typical manner once he

realized what was interfering with his development. In the Adjusting Phase, his need was to attack the system rather than inform it because he was now too frustrated and angry to do otherwise. Everything he tried prior to this time did not work; that is, it did not bring him what he needed or wanted.

Now that Jack was more aware of racially based practices acting against him in the company, he began to push back and test the realities of that environment. Jack asked questions about his job environment for which he had no answers. He wanted to know, for instance, why he had to make a lot of noise before he was heard by his organization. How could the organization see what his white peers were doing and not see his contribution, since he was obviously more visible, by his difference, than the white manager? How did he become invisible? The only answer he could deduce was that the organization did not want to see him. Minorities in the professional work force upset the status quo.

In the Adjusting Phase, Jack's emotional state was one of great agitation because he was in direct contact with his black rage. This is the furious anger born out of an individual's blackness and all that means in our society. Jack's reorganization of the personnel office is a good example to help us understand the genesis of his black rage. There were times when Jack could clearly see there was a problem and other people did not seem to see it. He even had some solutions that he could not use because he could not convince anyone that there was a problem. It was as though Jack was standing at a brick wall and trying to get through. All he could do was beat his head against the wall and blow off emotionally. He would pull out all the stops and let go. Jack might have screamed at the white manager, or pounded on his desk, or just walked out of the room—blown his stack as his friend John did.

Jack's movement in this phase was motivated by the rage that had been suppressed, possibly for years. Now these emotions had surfaced, and Jack often had trouble suppressing them, but they also acted to motivate him to boldly explore his environment.

In addition, Jack's stress had changed from the type of stress he experienced in the Entry Phase. It did not come from the fear of losing his job because he was incompetent, but instead it came from disappointment and disillusionment over the values he previously held about the work ethic and people's inherent goodness. Remember, in the Adjusting Phase, blacks turn their stress from inward-looking to outward-looking. However, in the Entry Phase, blacks tend to look into themselves for answers to explain what is occurring to them. They also put a lid on their emotions. They suppress them for all the wrong reasons by focusing on self and whatever deficiencies they perceive within themselves. In the Adjusting Phase, emotions take a diametrically opposite turn, and now everything is focused outward toward the organization and the people who cause the frustration.

Jack had reached an intolerable degree of frustration and now doubted everything he valued and believed in connection with his job. He felt none of these values and beliefs were working for him. This is the point at which the white manager of a black should sense that something is wrong. The display of this attitude signifies that the black manager is well into the Adjusting Phase. It also means, if the company or the supervisors do not do something to make a change to reduce the stress, the black manager will become totally dysfunctional or will leave the organization.

Let us point out here that we said dysfunctional, not irrational. It is a *rational* reaction to the intolerable situation in which the organization puts blacks. In Jack's case, he started to leave the company but changed his mind. His momentary ventilation of anger at his boss and his continuing anger coupled to make him decide to adopt a stubborn attitude to fight it out. He decided not to run away but to stay and somehow force the organization to respond to his needs and those of other blacks. This is the type of positive perseverance that has made it possible for blacks to break down barriers and open previously closed doors. In order to place everything in perspective, let us remember that Jack was not solely responsible for this situation, because the trigger for all of this was Jack's frustration with his inability to manage and deal with the racist behavior that existed within the environment. In the Adjusting Phase, then, situations are jointly caused by the black individual and the corporation.

To recap, Jack came into the organization free of frustration and stated, "I've got it made." He went through the Entry Phase, discovered something, and had to say, "Wait a minute! I don't have it made; something is wrong here!" He then became stressful. As the stress built, he tried to deal with it by rationalizing and justifying what was happening to him as being his fault; that did not work. Then he tried to figure it out logically; that did not work either. So his frustration continued to build to a point at which he just blew up emotionally.

With some blacks, this does not happen. All blacks will go through Jack's experience but will not necessarily behave as Jack did. How they behave will vary even though the frustration is there. Racism affects some individuals worse than others. The sharper, more open blacks will sooner or later publicly display their frustration. Others may not. Unfortunately, many blacks will become bitter and give up. Perhaps they were taught early that there is no point in fighting the system. They may struggle at first and then accept what is happening to them. These individuals spend their job careers in the Entry Phase or on the edge of the Adjusting Phase. Eventually, from length of service, the organization will reward them but never in the way that their more aggressive brothers and sisters will be rewarded.

Viewing the Adjusting Phase from this vantage point, we can see that although Jack was filled with negative thoughts and feelings, he had embarked on what could be considered one of the most positive stages of his development. This development phase should not be feared, because it is the doorway to reaching success. Jack was now highly motivated. Whites who can see and capitalize on that motivation can help the black manager shorten the adjusting period and move more rapidly to the Planned Growth Phase. This is where structured learning takes place at a rapid pace and higher results are seen with a greater payout for the organization.

As Jack continued to test his environment and use his trial-and-error behavior, he began to realize that he was not powerless to change his organization. Through outside contacts and consultants, he learned there were things that were being done by other blacks to manage racism and effectively get their jobs accomplished. Jack had the initiative to use these resources to acquire some of the skills he needed to do his job; many of these skills related to identifying and learning appropriate corporate behavior. This was an area of difficulty for Jack, as it is for most blacks.

The angry feelings at this stage often push the black manager into snap reactions but at the same time also force reactions from the environment. This is not the best way to learn, but it is *a* way, and it may be the *only* way when the environment is totally unresponsive. Jack tells us about his friend John and John's reaction to the uncooperative staff. Jack also tells us about how he told off an upper-level manager in a meeting and was instructed through notes from his boss's peers never to do that again.

There were valuable learnings about corporate behavior associated with these experiences for both men. True, this was learning from negative responses, but it *was* learning! The men began to realize that losing their temper and putting themselves in embarrassing situations was not the answer either. They must search elsewhere. These types of experiences often form the basis for sharing information and exploring options among blacks. This process becomes necessary because the white organization tends to feel little or no responsibility to inform blacks of what *is* appropriate but merely criticizes what is not appropriate.

Jack was still struggling to become a part of the company's informal communications network, where relevant corporate behavior can be learned. Because blacks rarely fit into this system, it is extremely difficult to sort out the mixed messages they receive from the organization. Jack and his friends were caught between the proverbial "rock and a hard place." The company chastised them for their misbehavior but presented few avenues to learn how to behave. The grapevine continues to be the system through which black managers can piece together corrective measures.

The grapevine helped Jack identify the skills that he brought to the organization. It is often used, in addition, as a pressure relief valve for the type of frustration Jack encountered as he attempted to use his creative skills. Jack moved to the personnel office and accomplished some things no one else could. No one in his hierarchy acknowledged his creativity, but supervisors often criticized him or tried to talk him out of his ideas.

In the Adjusting Phase, it is extremely important for a white supervisor to give strokes or verbal rewards to blacks. Jack identified his skills, put them to use, and did not get any strokes for them. It is important for blacks to get strokes because they have been positioned by the organization to struggle with issues of competence. When they develop skills to use on the job, they expect some external reinforcement and verification of their competence. They are still questioning their skills, and when they find a few they can use, they expect someone to say, "Hey, that was great!" Whites can inadvertently negatively manage blacks by *not* stroking them by withholding positive information. This will create further stress, confusion, and doubt. As the black manager moves to the Success Phase, stroking comes more from within. In the Success Phase, blacks are able to provide internal reinforcement. Their successes are more obvious to them and to the public.

Jack saw that he possessed some skills to offer in the personnel office. He put in a computer system, developed an organization chart showing task responsibilities, and had the staff define their jobs; but even then he felt insecure. So Jack went back to school to ensure his success with his projects. He did not want to look bad or to fail.

In the Adjusting Phase, blacks tend to underrate what they do and the results they obtain. This is a consistent theme seen in their behavior and attitudes. To Jack, what he did was simple. He saw a problem and took the initiative to correct it head on. This, too, is typical of minorities in the Adjusting Phase. They will take the initiative in one area, and, if they are humiliated or receive negative feedback, they will not do that any more. They will then initiate action in another area, and if they obtain success there, they will do more of that. If a person is consistently humiliated over a long time period, the person may stop taking the initiative. Remember that anger is a motivating force and constant humiliation can act as a weeding out process. Out of fear or stress, blacks may make a decision that they will no longer take risks and will stay where they are. This is a major decision that affects the black manager as well as the corporation. This manager is now stuck in the Adjusting Phase—angry, hostile, and dysfunctional.

Throughout Jack's narrative, he lets you feel the negative reaction he had toward whites and tells you about the arguments he and his friends had. He became more vocal in expressing his needs and feelings and especially his anger. He wanted others to know somehow that he was in pain and, since whites were perceived to be the source of that pain, they were the recipients of that anger. Jack was now having less of a problem with his feelings of incompetence. He was moving toward a positive attitude about his job skills because he was able to handle difficult problems better than his white peers and in a creative manner. Part of this ability resulted from Jack's lack of socialization in the white culture. This gave him a freedom to think of and try ideas that whites might not try because they know much more about the rules and corporate norms. In this way, Jack's lack of knowledge often worked to his benefit. But in the Adjusting Phase, Jack was neither aware of this nor able to take advantage of it in the strategic manner he would be able to in the Planned Growth Phase.

Jack was struggling to acquire managerial skills in an unplanned, unorganized, catch-as-catch-can manner. He picked up some skills by discussing his trial-and-error activities with his friends, some from consultants, or wherever he could. Most of them came from other blacks, but Jack tells us that at least one piece of management data came from a white manager, and it was instrumental in pushing him into the next stage of development. It became a turning point because he was forced to recognize that both he and the organization had a responsibility for his attainment of success.

At some time in the Adjusting Phase, black managers learn the organization is not going to take any chances on them. The better jobs and more responsibility will not come until they have proven competence in the job. This is not true for white peers. They will be given jobs and responsibility on perceived potential. Jack tells us proving your competence once is not enough for blacks. Your track record will not hold, so you must prove yourself over and over with each new responsibility.

Again, this is a very common experience for blacks. Today, they still have to disprove the "inferior black" concept of the dominant culture. This is reality for blacks whether it upsets people to hear it or not. Black professionals need to be aware of and understand this reality and plan for its occurrence because this too is a source of great frustration and anger. When blacks enter a white organization that operates under the rules and norms of the white culture, the majority of the whites will automatically assume that the blacks are not competent. Therefore, whites will overquestion, overtest, and withhold needed strokes from blacks.

Blacks are further frustrated, as Jack was, at finding in the Adjusting Phase that they are evaluated first on style, while their white peers are evaluated first on task performance. Again, this relates to the assumptions of the dominant culture, one of which is that blacks do not know how to act. The trap for blacks in the Adjusting Phase is that they usually display behavior that confirms what the whites thought in the first place. Although this is a danger for blacks, they must go through it to reach success because the Adjusting Phase cannot be circumvented. As we have said repeatedly, this is a time for testing the environment much as children test theirs to determine the limitations. After this has been done, the black manager is prepared to accept the planned structured behavior required in the Planned Growth Phase.

DEVELOPMENT OF HOW-TO SOLUTIONS

The following solutions cannot help you skip your adjusting period but certainly can help you alleviate some of the sting or prevent some of your trial-and-error mistakes and embarrassment. If you are a fast learner, perhaps the how-to solutions can help shorten your period of adjusting. Again, we are faced with the dilemma of more problems to deal with than space to write about them. Therefore, we have chosen the ones we feel are key to the interest of most minorities surviving the Adjusting Phase.

Problem I: How to bring various problems to your boss. Problem relates to critical issues 1, 2, 4, 6, 7, 8, 11, 12, 13, 14

Solution 1: A key to this solution is to hook your boss's interest around organizational issues. Go to your boss and lay out the organizational issue, not the problem. Now connect the issue to the high-priority work items or the organization's goals. For example, John had to get some people to do a job for him, and they would not do it. Let us say that John's people had to get him information to help put together a means to reduce operating costs. John could have gone to the boss and stated, "As you know, one high-priority organizational item we have is operating cost reduction." Then the boss would have said, "Yes, that's right." John could then have replied. "Well, I have a problem that relates to that," and then have stopped talking. The boss would have said, "Well, what's the problem?" At this point, the boss would have been hooked!

The second key to this solution is to stop talking and let the white boss ask you questions about the problem instead of doing all the talking yourself. It is a simple three-step process:

1. Mention an organizational issue and connect it to a high-priority goal to establish the importance of your problem. This reduces the risk of your continuing to talk without getting any results.

2. Say that the problem you are having is associated with the organizational issue.

3 Now stop talking, and wait for your boss to ask you to state the problem.

Solution 2: This is a variation of Solution 1. If your organization has not set clear goals and priorities for the major work tasks, you may have to do it for yourself.

Sit down with your boss and ask, "What are our high-priority work items?" Now make a list of about five to seven items. Have the list typed and keep it in your desk. If you are having a problem bringing up work issues to your white boss, take out the sheet and relate the problems to the items on the sheet. Proceed as in Solution 1.

As an example, let us look at John again. John's people did not follow through on getting the cost reduction information he needed. If John had his high-priority work list, he could have gone to his boss and stated, "I'm in charge of these people and the project. It is important that we complete this project on time and at cost or under." The boss would have agreed. Then John could have responded with, "I'm having some difficulty, and I need your assistance." Then he could have stopped talking, and the boss would have *asked* "What's wrong?" John could have stated the group's reluctance to do their tasks—you need *not discuss race*—and then John could have stopped talking again. The boss would have *asked*, "What happened?" Now John could have presented what had occurred. After this, it would have been appropriate to look at solutions, not before. John could have asked his boss to meet with the group or to produce a letter; or he could have gone back and told the group he had met with the boss and discussed their problems.

Solution 3: What if your problem is not associated with a high-priority issue? Use the same general method.

Go to your boss and say, "I need your help on a problem I'm involved with." Stop talking and wait for your boss's question. When you are asked about the problem, lay it out. If the boss attempts to convince you that your problem is *not* a problem, then begin to express your anger, which is near the surface in the Adjusting Phase. Say, "It is a problem for *me!*" Now slowly escalate the emotion. At some point, the boss will have to concede it is a problem to *you*. Do not be afraid of using your anger occasionally in the Adjusting Phase. It is a part of the learning and developing process.

Problem II: How to manage meetings with your boss. Problem relates to critical issues 1, 2, 4, 5, 6, 7, 8, 11, 12, 13, 14

Solution: You should have regularly scheduled meetings with your boss. If you are in the Adjusting Phase, we suggest these meetings should be weekly and last one to two hours. Bear in mind, even if these meetings are in your boss's office, they are still in part *your* meetings. Meetings with your boss give you an opportunity to update the boss on what you are working on. You may discuss any problems you are having and also use some of the time as a growth and development session. It can be a planning and organizing session to allow you to make use of your boss's expertise. Remember, no matter how incompetent your boss may appear to be, he or she *does* have some expertise that you should use.

One way for you to manage the meetings so you get what you want and still leave room for your boss to get what he or she wants is to go in with an agenda. We propose using the format shown in Figure 1.*

Notice there are three categories. This forces you and your boss to exhibit structured behavior. Everything you discuss should fall within these categories. List the items you want to discuss under the categories in outline form. You may have additional detailed information, such as drawings, an expansion of your outline, or references.

Item I on the agenda, Information Exchange, should include the topics about which you have information to give to your boss. Your boss needs only to ask questions about the subject for clarification or understanding. All you want at this point is to share information, not solve a problem.

Under Item II, Consultant and Resource, list topics about which you want your boss to share information and experience. This will indicate to your boss that you want information that will help in solving a problem or accomplishing a task. In other words, you are

---

*This agenda format was shared with Floyd by Eugene Weinshenker, an engineering manager at Procter & Gamble Company in Cincinnati, Ohio.

FIGURE 1. Suggested agenda format.

Agenda

Date _____

Meeting Time _____

I. Information Exchange

II. Consultant and Resource

III. Decision and Agreement

using your boss as a consultant and a resource. Therefore, your boss will be positioned to give you advice.

Under Item III, Decision and Agreement, write down topics on which you need to make a decision or get closure. Also write down topics on which you need your boss's agreement. This will place your boss in a position to make a decision, help you make a decision, or agree with a plan you have outlined.

Problem III: How to successfully interact with whites when you are angry. Problem relates to critical issues 1, 2, 4, 6, 7, 8, 11, 12, 14

Solution: The first thing you must do is ask your self, "Why did I choose to get angry?" Or "Why did I allow myself to get angry?" You must be able to answer that question before you can successfully interact with whites when you are angry, otherwise the interaction will not be functional. No one can make us angry against our wishes.

Make a quick mental list of the things that caused you to get angry. If you are away from the interaction at the time, make a list on paper. This will help you easily visualize the issues and also give you an opportunity to dissipate some of the anger onto the paper. Push the list aside, and think about or write down what you want to get out of the interaction you are about to have.

Base whatever you do in the interaction on a *need*—one that you have, the other person has, or you jointly have. Open the interaction by telling the white individual what you want and asking what he or she wants; that is, what is the business need? Each individual must be able to state a need in acceptable organizational terms.

As much as possible, deal only with *facts* related to the issue, not with the emotions involved. Wrap the facts around the need you are trying to fulfill. This will minimize emotional outbursts. Be willing to ask questions and give explanations. Avoid blaming each other in the interaction and personalizing the issues and needs. If the interaction escalates emotionally despite your efforts, feel free to disengage. Say, "Perhaps this isn't a good time to work on this issue. Let's drop it for now and continue later."

Problem IV: How to sell ideas to your boss. Problem relates to critical issues 2, 3, 4, 5, 6, 7, 8, 10, 11, 12, 14

Solution: Blacks will encounter varying degrees of prejudiced attitudes against them, so this process is important in general. It can eliminate the need to ascertain how open your boss is to your input. Whatever the boss's attitudes, you are more likely to sell your ideas using this method.

As soon as you get an idea and are comfortable with suggesting it to your boss, solicit input from others. They can help you fill in any gaps you may have overlooked.

Try to view the situation through your boss's eyes. Guess at how he or she may react to your idea based on the kind of relationship you have with the boss. (You may want to review the solution to Problem X of the Entry Phase for the exercise on imagining being the other person.) Select a time when your boss is at ease and not agitated or under pressure. Hook the boss's interest by connecting your idea to high-priority organizational issues or work tasks. (See the solutions to Problem I of the Adjusting Phase, in this chapter.)

Tell your boss you have bounced the idea off others and have solicited their input. If your boss exhibits racist behavior, this approach is particularly effective because it will minimize the consequences of your boss's negative attitude toward you and your idea. Your boss will be able to say, "Oh, it's not *all* your idea; others had input." Do not worry, you will get credit for it, because your boss will have to admit you developed the idea.

Expose the facts and share your thinking about the idea. Focus the conversation on the idea and not on yourself by minimizing any personal references, such as "I," "my," or "me." If your boss tends to exhibit racist behavior, such references will have a negative impact and easily be interpreted as bragging, and you will be negatively evaluated.

Assume your boss will accept your idea. Then analyze the risk. Is it high or low? (See Entry Phase Problem I, Solution 1.)

There may be things you did not think about. Relax and be prepared to compromise when necessary—the idea is still yours. Compromising is often a problem for blacks in the Adjusting Phase. They tend to think that an idea should be all theirs without change. When a compromise is made, they fear that the idea will be credited to someone else.

Be confident that your idea will work, *but always* have a backup or contingency plan.

Problem V: How to get cooperation from others. Problem relates to critical issues 1, 2, 3, 4, 5, 6, 7, 8, 9, 10, 11, 12, 13, 14

Solution: The first thing to consider in getting people to cooper-

FIGURE 2.   Form for schedule of tasks.

Task (what)	Date (when)	Responsibility (who)
1. Prepare May forecast	4/13	Doug Fisher
2.		
3.		
4.		
5.		
6.		
7.		
8.		
9.		
10.		

ate with you is to connect their cooperation and the task to a business need. Sometimes you may be able to connect the cooperation of others to their self-interest. Plan their cooperation by scheduling the various tasks associated with whatever you are trying to do. Your schedule should show what is to be done, by whom, and when. The *how* is best left with the individual worker. Document the schedule, and send copies to the people involved and their bosses. You should set up milestones and check back with people to see if they are on schedule in accomplishing their tasks. Figure 2 shows a simple way of making your schedule.

It is important to document the tasks so everyone will have the same information regarding who is responsible for what and by when. This documentation makes everything public and legitimizes agreements. It considerably increases the odds that the tasks will be accomplished on time, because no one wants to be seen as the one who dropped the ball. It gives you a way of going back and checking with people before the end date to make sure they are on the track to complete their tasks. If they are not, you then have the opportunity to help work out any problems they may have. If they become hostile with you, the documentation legitimizes your going to their bosses. This method increases your span of managerial control over people who will attempt to resist cooperating with you.

Problem VI: How to tap into the informal communications network. Problem relates to critical issues 1, 3, 4, 5, 6, 7, 8, 9, 10, 11, 14, 15

Solution: This is a touchy problem for blacks in the Adjusting Phase. They tend to exhibit hostile behavior toward whites at the smallest provocation and to be least inclined to socialize with whites during this period. However, when the need for information far outweighs the need to avoid social interaction with whites, this solution will work. The solution is broken into two broad areas: the social-related area and the work-related area.

Under the social-related area, there are several types of activities blacks might choose to engage in to tap the informal communications network. One is sports. You may join some existing company team—bowling, baseball, basketball. Or you may engage in a one-on-one sport, such as tennis or racketball, with co-workers. While you are having fun, you will at some point talk about work-related items and therefore have an opportunity to get information otherwise not available to you. A second type of activity may be hobbies you share—model railroading, building, woodworking, hooking rugs, and so forth. You may arrange to get together to work jointly on a hobby. Or you might accept some invitations to attend parties or take advantage of an informal get-together, something as simple as helping someone with a home repair job like painting or repairing a driveway. A great deal of business information is "dropped" at parties.

Under the work-related area, one activity would be to go on a five- or ten-minute coffee break with your white peers. Go to lunch, either on or off the premises, and have an informal conversation about work issues. Have an after-work rap session on the work premises. Go to someone's office after work, sit down, and ask how things are going. Steer the conversation to the areas you want to discuss. Perhaps *occasionally* drop by a white worker's office during working hours for a brief chat. Be careful with this last one because since you are black, people will tend to think you are wasting time socializing and not doing productive work. As a black, you will have to weigh the need to avoid whites against the need for information.

Problem VII: How to manage your stress (making use of cultural paranoia). Problem relates to critical issues 1, 2, 3, 4, 5, 6, 7, 8, 9, 10, 11, 12, 14, 17

Solution: There are three main keys to dealing simply with this problem. This first is discussing your stress with someone you trust and respect. Relief by ventilating can have a cleansing or unloading effect for you. Second, talk to yourself about your stress. This is very helpful. Third, understand that the phase you are going through is only temporary and you will pass through it. Stress is an eliminator for minorities. If you do not learn to manage stress, you will avoid those situations that are stressful, and some of those situations may have benefits for you. You will then essentially eliminate yourself from a fast track for growth and development as well as from the mainstream movement that leads to success. Understand that you cannot eliminate all stress; you must endure some of it. The trick is to manage it. Some stress is helpful in heightening awareness to solve problems in a creative manner. Here is a process for managing your stress.

1. List those things that cause you stress. For example, you have to give a presentation and you are anxious about it.

2. List reasons for having stress around the particular situation, such as the presentation.

3. List what you think would remove the stress. After looking at your list, you will probably discover you are being unrealistic about the situation—it's not all that bad.

4. Look carefully at the list of things to do to remove the stress and pick several to work on. For example:
   - You have a presentation that you feel stress about.
   - One reason for the stress is lack of stage presence or smooth delivery.
   - One way to remove some of the stress is to appear as though you have done this all your life.
   - So practice your speech before a mirror and then in front of a couple of good friends who will offer corrective feedback until you are more comfortable with it.

5. Discuss your list with one or more people you trust, whose input you value. They may have some helpful suggestions. Use them as resources.

6. Talk to yourself throughout your stressful situation. Remind yourself that cultural paranoia can be a healthy and helpful response to your environment that prepares you to handle situations creatively. Tell yourself stress heightens your awareness, which helps you prepare yourself enough to ensure success. Also, remind yourself you are probably overreacting to the situation and that all this will pass.

Problem VIII: How to use anger as a motivator. Problem relates to critical issues 1, 4, 6, 7, 10, 12, 13, 14, 16, 17

Solution: The Adjusting Phase, as we have stated repeatedly, is a period of high stress, frustration, and anger. You can learn to use the energy associated with these emotions to your benefit instead of your detriment. Use the energy by remaining angry. It is virtually impossible not to be angry in this phase if you are black. Try practicing feeling, almost touching, the anger. *Feel* what it is doing to you; then *understand* what it is doing to you.

Now mentally brush the anger aside and focus on the energy left. Say to yourself, "I will use the energy that my anger has produced to change or remove the source of my anger." For example, you became angry because a peer did not do what should have been done to allow you to perform some task, and it made you look bad. Feel the anger and savor it; now push it aside. Focus your remaining energy on determining how you will *not* let that situation occur again. In essence, you will be using the energy from your anger to replace the anger with a stubborn determination to change events so that the situation will not recur in the future.

As we have stated, blacks tend to be closer to their emotions than whites are. This also explains why blacks are apt to jump onto a problem and attack it head on. Anger tends to drive blacks to remove the source of anger. Being aware of and appreciating this tendency can help you direct the energy specifically to the area to be changed. Awareness keeps you from inappropriately dispersing the energy in directions that are not important or where no change can be made; it also keeps you from feeling guilty about being angry. The white corporation will tend to tell you that you should not get angry. Historically, the white middle-class cultural norm has been not to get emotional or angry. Therefore, at times, we as blacks will deny our anger, which means we deny a source of our energy that will help us strike at a problem head on.

The use of anger is an *overlooked cultural skill* that blacks bring to the white organization. The skill is to be able to get angry quickly, then channel the energy from the anger into creative problem solutions or into attacking the problem and forcing swift resolution. That is how you can make anger work for you.

Problem IX: How to resist intimidation from whites. Problem relates to critical issues 1, 2, 3, 4, 5, 6, 7, 8, 10, 11, 12, 13, 14, 17

Solution: Blacks and other minorities tend to be more sensitive to the moods of people in various situations; that is, they can easily read where people are and what is happening with them. When blacks are interacting with whites who are attempting to intimidate them, blacks get a visceral feeling from the interaction. Not only do blacks recognize the power of others, they can feel it. When this happens to you, say to yourself, "I am *feeling* the intimidation the other person is emitting." If you think of it in terms of a radio, the black individual is the receiver and the white individual is the transmitter. Now you can say, "What I feel is being picked up from the other person, it is not being generated from within me. Therefore, I am not and will not be intimidated." Your receiver is picking up what the other person is transmitting, and that transmission is intimidation.

It is important to be aware that the feeling is not yours. As a result you will be less likely to accept the feeling and subsequently feel fear. You can now sit back, relax, and think about an appropriate response to the intimidation without the accompanying barrier of fear. One type of response can be a question. Use the questioning technique we discussed in the previous chapter. Or try a thought-provoking response designed to grab the other person's attention so that that person will drop the transmission of intimidation.

It takes practice to negate intimidation. Remember, *no one* can intimidate you unless *you* allow that person to do it. Historically, blacks have been managed through intimidation and are particularly sensitive to it. Here is a PS: You can *always* leave the scene of the action if it is real physical intimidation!

Problem X: How to help reduce time spent in the Adjusting Phase. Problem relates to critical issues 1, 2, 3, 4, 5, 6, 7, 8, 9, 10, 11, 12, 13, 14, 15, 16, 17

Solution: The first thing you need to do is acknowledge that you cannot circumvent this phase. You need to say to yourself, "I will stay in this phase until I have fulfilled my need to publicly express myself emotionally and have acquired the learning I need to move into a more structured direction." Although you cannot skip this phase, there are a few ways to help shorten it.

Take a really big piece of paper, say, the size used in flip-charts, and write down as many things as you can think of that you want from your job, such as:

1. I want a promotion.
2. I want learning opportunities.
3. I want etc.

Now post this on your wall.

On another large piece of paper, write "I can move into the Planned Growth Phase when I. . . ." Now make another list. For example:

1. Become more aware of how racism is acted out.
2. Learn how to manage my emotions.
3. Learn more about corporate norms.
4. Etc.

Each day look at these sheets of paper and use them as reminders. If you keep a work diary of your learnings, you may prefer to enter these lists there and periodically go over them as checklists to see where you are in terms of your growth and development.

White managers need to understand that blacks go through an adjusting period in the white organization that differs from that of their white peers. White managers can offer assistance to blacks in the Adjusting Phase by taking the time to discuss needs relative to information gathering and help with difficulties. A white manager can open doors for blacks by introducing them into the informal communications network. The manager can see to it that blacks are included in work activities where corporate information is discussed.

A very important point for the white manager to remember is: *Do not take the black manager's behavior personally and overreact to it.* Instead, try to understand why black managers behave the way they do. White managers may be able to provide an additional perspective by sharing their interpretations of the behavior. By understanding the dynamics of the Adjusting Phase for blacks, white managers can take their cues from this and be creative in assisting the black manager through the period.

Problem XI: How to manage the process used to evaluate you. Problem relates to critical issues 1, 3, 4, 5, 6, 7, 8, 9, 10, 11, 12, 13, 14, 16, 17

Solution: There are five key precepts involved in this solution.

1. Involve people other than your boss in the evaluation process.
2. Test against prior criteria established by you and your boss. This is to be used by all people giving feedback or input.
3. Use written, not verbal, responses for input.
4. Always set up an evaluation system that gives you ongoing feedback rather than a once-a-year shocker.
5. Use "step-level counseling" with your boss's boss. That is, take the opportunity to talk to your boss's boss and use his or her experience. This is not an opportunity to tell on your boss but rather an opportunity to discuss your career development and to tap into and use the experience of your boss's boss. For example, you might ask, "What kinds of things were you concerned about when you were at my level?" And "What did you do about them?"

Here are the how-to's connected with the precepts.

1. Very early in your job, develop criteria for evaluation. Do this with your boss and then document the criteria.
2. At evaluation time, you and your boss should select the people from whom you want to obtain feedback. These people can be peers, subordinates, and superiors. This protects you, because you get a balanced perspective.
3. Use a written format and ask individuals selected for written feedback.
4. The boss will collect the feedback and share the written information with you.
5. You and your boss *together* can develop a mutually agreed upon summary signed by the two of you. This is where you will have an opportunity to discuss directly with the boss what people have said about you.
6. The signed summary will be passed along to the boss's boss for review and for a face-to-face meeting with you. This session can be used for step-level counseling.

BASIC CONCEPTS USED IN HOW-TO SOLUTIONS

Problem I: How to bring various problems to your boss.

Concept 1: The first concept used here is called Hooking Interest. Before you bring a problem to your white boss, first plan to hook his or her interest. You can do this by relating the problem you have to an important organizational issue or objective or a personal objective of the boss. This approach is important and works because the boss is there to solve hot organizational issues or to meet organizational goals. Also, the boss needs to know immediately that you are bringing an important problem.

Concept 2: We call this concept State and Wait. One way for a black manager to ensure a successful interaction with a white boss, regardless of whether that boss exhibits racist behavior or not, is to make a statement and then stop talking. The statement should be designed to elicit a question from the boss. This approach works especially well if the statement relates to an issue of concern to the boss.

This technique works because whites tend to listen to blacks better when the whites are asking questions than when the blacks are giving a lot of information. When blacks give a lot of information, sometimes whites tend to discount it. This is especially true if the information is something they do not want to hear or to deal with. They can tune out the black who is giving all the data unless they are asking questions and are actively involved in the interaction or feel a personal stake in it.

Problem II: How to manage meetings with your boss.

Concept: The concept here is called Structuring. This is the use of an agenda to improve the odds that you will have a successful outcome when interacting with your white boss. This process does just what it states. It structures the interaction so that it follows a predetermined course and improves effectiveness and efficiency. You will know you are talking about the right things and spending the appropriate amount of time discussing them. For blacks, this concept will eliminate the dysfunctional pieces of the interaction that can occur between blacks and whites. When a black must meet with an upper-level manager, structuring is essential because there is an even greater need to get in, take care of business, and get out. Upper-level managers are very busy and must conserve their time.

Problem III: How to successfully interact with whites when you are angry.

Concept: The new concept given in this problem is called Dealing with the Need. This means when you are angry and emotionally upset and you know you are going to have difficulty interacting with a white person, you will need to approach the situation from a factual standpoint. Dealing only with the facts will help subtract the emotionality from the interaction. You can place the interaction on a logical, intellectual level, which means you must be clear about the business need involved. Stick to that business need as much as possible by dealing with the facts.

Problem IV: How to sell ideas to your boss.

Concept: This concept is very simply called Compromising and is extremely important to blacks. If your boss is the kind of person who is threatened, intimidated, or made uneasy by blacks or exhibits racist behavior toward them, you may leave yourself open for automatic rejection of an idea. If you attempt to sell an idea to your boss and the boss senses that it is solely your idea, he or she may try to pick holes in it or evaluate it in a negative manner. White bosses of blacks are more likely to accept an idea if they can add to it. You need to become comfortable with and accept this, because the idea will still be credited to you. Once you can accept the boss's addition, the boss will accept your idea. Some people, for whatever reasons, feel they must contribute to any idea formulated by a subordinate, and this is especially true for a black subordinate. Do not make an issue of it. It is usually not worth it.

Problem V: How to get cooperation from others.

Concept: Responsibility Charting is the concept used here. It is important because it documents task agreements between people. It shows what, when, and who on a document that becomes public. As a black manager, you can use responsibility charting to protect yourself and improve your effectiveness. Unfortunately, there are many instances when it becomes necessary to cover yourself because, as we stated earlier, blacks tend to be easy targets for blame when something goes amiss.

Problem VI: How to tap into the informal communications network.

Concept: The basic concept used here is Socializing. See Concept 1, Problem XI of the Entry Phase for a discussion.

Problem VII: How to manage your stress.

Concept: Listing is the only concept used in this solution not previously reviewed. It involves writing down those issues that are important to you so you may stand back and look at them. This process is important because it helps give you a clear understanding of what is occurring. Once you are able to get the information out of your head and onto paper, where you can look at the data in black and white, you will often find things do not look as bad as they did when you were thinking about them. Your mind tends to expand problems, whereas writing them down tends to narrow their focus. Listing is a good habit to form in problem solving. It helps to clarify things and to put them in proper perspective and in a form that facilitates your taking action or sharing with others to solicit their input.

Problem VIII: How to use anger as a motivator.

Concept 1: Sensing is a concept used to get in touch with feelings from within. In sensing you focus intently into yourself and force the anger and other feelings to the surface of your consciousness so you are totally aware of them on a physical level. It is similar to a process used by actors before a performance. This concept is useful in preventing denial and in converting the vast amount of energy produced by recognizing and drawing upon intense feelings.

Concept 2: Converting Energy is a concept closely linked to sensing. It is particularly useful in the Adjusting Phase because, if you are black, you will find you are angry quite often. The energy produced from that anger can be converted into something help-ful, as described in the solution to Problem VIII. Converting en-ergy can be used for any strong emotion that generates energy, not just anger, and where it may be inappropriate to openly express the emotion. The energy from excitement, for instance, may be converted into a drive to rapidly accomplish something rather than be displayed in a more direct form.

Problem IX: How to resist intimidation from whites.

Concept: The new concept found in this solution is called Readin'. Readin' will be a familiar concept to many of you. It is a black term given to a process we like to call "high-speed calcula-tion of interpersonal data." It is the ability of one person to per-ceive information from another person by observing the nonverbal behavioral cues the other gives about him- or herself in an inter-action. This process usually takes place below the level of awareness of the observer. To put it more simply, all of us tell others about our personalities and about the kinds of people we are by the way we speak and move our bodies. People who can "read" others will translate this into responsive feelings about the person they are observing. Many of us grew up hearing about how well our grandmothers, other relatives, or neighbors could read people. If you wanted to know about some stranger you met, "Go ask yo' gran'ma; she's good at readin' folks." This merely meant grandmother was skilled in observing nonverbal behavioral cues.

Problem XI: How to manage the process used to evaluate you.

Concept 1: This solution contains two new concepts. The first one is Step-Level Counseling. This is used by subordinates to talk to bosses above the level of the subordinate's immediate boss in the same hierarchical chain to get the benefit of their counseling, experience, expertise, and perspective. This is extremely helpful to blacks. It also provides blacks with the much needed exposure to important others in the hierarchical chain. For those all-white organizations that are concerned about the growth and development of blacks within the company, this concept could be a valuable addition to any program that may be instituted.

Concept 2: The second concept is called Checks and Balances. This is very helpful to blacks because more than one person is included in such processes as evaluations, feedback sessions, or whatever information sharing is done with a black by members of an organization. This concept can also be used in conjunction with other concepts, such as responsibility charting. When a black manager makes copies of a task schedule and sends them to the person responsible for the task and the person's boss, that is an example of using checks and balances in connection with responsibility charting.

Summary of Basic Concepts

This section contains brief definitions of the basic concepts used in the Adjusting Phase how-to solutions. It may be used as a quick reference.

1. *Hooking Interest* is used to get the attention of someone else. A person's interest may be hooked by expressing a problem in terms of an organizational issue or objective.
2. *State and Wait* refers to an interaction by which a black makes a statement designed to elicit questions from a white manager rather than offer a lot of information that may get dismissed.
3. *Structuring* refers to the use of an agenda so that an interaction follows a predetermined course to improve effectiveness and efficiency.
4. *Dealing with the Need* instructs you to deal only with logic, facts, and business needs when you are angry, thus reducing emotionalism in an interaction.
5. *Compromising* is used in selling ideas to your boss by allowing your boss to add to your idea and making concessions for the sake of having it approved.
6. *Responsibility Charting* is used to document task agreements between people. It clearly shows who will do what and by when.
7. *Listing* refers to writing down issues that are important to you so that you can analyze them before taking any action.

8. *Sensing* is used to get in touch with your internal feelings about an external event. This is accomplished by intently focusing into yourself and forcing your feelings to the surface of your consciousness.

9. *Converting Energy* refers to the process used to channel the energy from any strong emotion into something useful.

10. *Readin'* is the process used by a person to perceive information from another person by observing the nonverbal behavioral cues the other gives about him- or herself in an interaction.

11. *Step-Level Counseling* is used by subordinates to talk to bosses above the level of the subordinates' immediate boss in the same hierarchical chain. The discussion centers around counseling and sharing experience and expertise.

12. *Checks and Balances* is a process that prevents blacks from becoming victims of racism and sexism when information is shared with them. This is done by involving more than one person in the information-sharing process.

4

Planned
Growth Phase

CRITICAL ISSUES

Attitudes
1. The need to be a superstar becomes apparent (prepared to expend more energy than white peers)
2. Taking a serious look at personal style (removes barriers to style)
3. Understanding the need to get more black input

Emotions
4. Acquiring a sense of determination
5. Building a feeling of pride
6. Using anger as strategy

Behaviors
7. Consciously acting to remove barriers under one's own control
8. Using strategy more to position people and company to meet one's needs
9. Seeking sponsors
10. Learning to effectively use white resources
11. Using protective hesitation
12. Learning to make proper demands on the corporation (plotting career)
13. Setting and meeting goals

Job Skills

14. Learning and using multicultural management skills
15. Making continued use of communications network

ANALYZING THE CRITICAL ISSUES

Attitudes

By the time the black manager is well into the Planned Growth Phase of development, the need to be a superstar is very apparent. This will be more or less true depending on the number of blacks holding professional positions within the white organization. Black managers see themselves having to expend much more energy on the same job tasks than their white peers to obtain the same results. Whether black managers will admit it openly or not, the truth of the matter is that, with every job task carried out by a black individual in an interaction or transaction with a white person, there is a racial component that must be dealt with effectively if job performance is to be maximized. As black managers move into the Planned Growth Phase, they are more likely to accept this fact, stop fighting against it, plan for it, and move to manage it. The extra expenditure of energy becomes the price one pays to succeed if one is black working in a white setting.

> "I have to spend energy doing black–white activities that whites don't have to do, but I don't get any extra reward for it."

> "I spend a lot of extra time fighting the effects of racism. Whites in the development mode can make mistakes, but I can't. Whites tend to believe what other whites say about blacks, so you have to work with a racist listening to a racist."

> "The thing that tires me out is having to overexplain why I want to do certain tasks in certain ways. I have to exert greater influence than whites around issues."

> "I'm always trying to find an appropriate balance between which are the important racist behavioral issues to fight and which to let go."

> "Sometimes you get into situations on the job where it becomes important to expend some extra energy in identifying

white peers and supervisors in terms of where their racism
will hurt you or help you."

"There is tremendous time my organization asks blacks to
put in on black–white activities besides our regular jobs.
They don't ask whites to do that. And I spend lots of time
justifying myself to whites—trying to sell my ideas and
viewpoints, and they question you to death about details."

Although black managers are no longer willing to bear the
whole burden of their inability to behave in the correct corporate
manner, they are willing to systematically make those changes
under their control. Personal operating style tends to be one of the
most problematic interpersonal issues for the black manager. Successful managers will understand that they are not locked into any
kind of behavior and will seek the personal style that best facilitates the most effective and profitable interactions with others.

"Overcoming my own low-key interpersonal style was a
problem for me. I'm a quiet person. But I knew I'd continue
to get run over if I didn't learn to speak up and be more
proactive. You can say I've become quietly assertive."

"I didn't look or act competent and that's the way people
treated me, like I was incompetent. I had to relearn how to
dress and walk and carry myself."

"I learned how to be more intellectually aggressive and less
emotionally angry."

In the Planned Growth Phase, black managers know the value of
their black resources and do not hesitate to use them. They have
identified the learnings reaped from other blacks' expertise and
draw on them for help in a variety of areas, such as (1) interpersonal and behavioral strategies; (2) personal feedback; (3) the
understanding of the effects of racism and how to use strategy to
get around those types of barriers; and (4) the gaining of insight
and the development of reflective observation.

"I often go out of my way to find blacks who will help me
with management problems. I don't do that with the technical problems because there are always plenty of whites who
will help with that."

"I was a slow learner, but I have finally turned to other

blacks to get the quality help I need in coaching, strategizing, and support."

"If you want to get the real scoop on promotional information, a black has to ask another black who has access to the data."

"I couldn't get along without bouncing ideas off of other blacks, thinking about stuff and how to use it, etc. We all help each other learn how to strategize."

Emotions

The Planned Growth Phase is characterized by determination. It is as though blacks, facing and passing through a wall of flame, are not going to let the sight of an erupting volcano stop them now. With each barrier overcome and accomplishment made, there is a growing sense of pride. Confidence in one's competence and abilities is built from practicing the newly learned behaviors and skills. Old dysfunctional behavior is discarded or else incorporated into the black's growing repertoire of strategies. The anger that was so prevalent in the Adjusting Phase is now more controlled and is usually employed as a last-ditch effort when all else fails. Even then, the use of anger is generally well thought out beforehand and its consequences anticipated.

Behaviors

Now black managers consciously seek to identify the various barriers to progress and remove those within their control, rather than ignoring them as in the Entry Phase or angrily complaining about them as in the Adjusting Phase.

"I suffered too long from a lack of self-confidence. I decided it was time to stop buying into racist beliefs and recognize the effect it had on me. I sat down and laid out some changes I would make. Things looked a lot clearer written down. After that, I wrote out a whole self-improvement plan."

My own arrogance and denial of being black in a white environment slowed me down. I refused to see how racism blocked my progress, and I made no use of my black peers and any role models to learn about how to succeed. When I saw my black peers getting bigger jobs and more responsibility than I, I had to face myself and my denials."

"One day it hit me. I had too much emotional involvement and energy in fighting racism on my job. I had to pull myself together. I started allowing business relationships with whites to help me."

"I wasn't proactive enough. So I adopted this rule for myself: 'If you don't make things happen for yourself, you'll be a long time succeeding, if ever.'"

The realization of the need for strategy for both survival and success in the corporation is very apparent in many of the statements made by black managers throughout the different phases of development. We consider strategy of such monumental importance for blacks in attaining success that it will be handled as a separate topic in Part Three.

Seeking sponsors is a big step forward for blacks in the Planned Growth Phase. Sponsorship for whites in the organization is a very accepted and usually known procedure to give bright, up-and-coming young managers that extra boost they need to beat the competition in moving up. Older, more experienced managers will pick younger managers who they perceive have potential and will coach, guide, and act as advocates for their protégés. Often a social relationship develops between them, and the young managers get special grooming for their career paths.

Rarely do black managers get picked for sponsorship; if they do, it is almost never in conjunction with a social relationship and special grooming. If a black manager has a sponsor, it is usually because that person has sought out and adopted one. The black manager must then establish a relationship with the adopted sponsor and work to, at best, develop a real alliance or, at the least, affect one.

One very big problem for blacks getting sponsored is that white managers are still often not able to recognize minority potential. Blacks tend to bear little resemblance to how the white organization thinks its managers should look and behave. Establishing a social relationship is difficult because the pressures of differing cultures, differing expectations of each other, and personal and institutional prejudices are always there to interfere. We are not saying the situation is impossible, because it has worked, but we are saying it is difficult.

"I went out and accessed a sponsor and affected a relationship."

*"I identified some key people in the hierarchy who are pow-
erful and got on their good sides. I received some help—
coaching—and used that to move on."*

*"Blacks have to get real close to a white to find out things,
one who is committed to moving them on."*

*"I got adopted by a white manager in the hierarchy early in
my job. I tried to be white and emulate the white managers,
so it was easy for someone to relate to me and help me in the
organization."*

*"I thought you'd need someone who feels he can give you a
helping hand, who would reach down and pick you up. That
was my first type of sponsor and that was a 'one-down' type
of relationship. Since I've closed the gap between us, I've
been dropped. Now I'm looking to find a sponsor type who
will help me because he respects my competence and abilities."*

*"You have to identify someone for yourself, get established
with him or her; someone who is viewed as a valuable con-
tributor and who will go to bat for you."*

Using white resources is a perplexing issue for black managers.
They are ambivalent about seeking information from whites.
Black managers want to use whites as resources but are concerned
about how that will be viewed. Initially, what black managers lack
is an effective how-to approach to get information from whites.
There tends to be a lack of trust on the part of the black individual
toward the white resource and an inability to sense and properly
react to racism. In the Entry Phase, blacks are cautious about the
use of whites as resources because blacks are dealing with issues
of negative self-concept. In the Adjusting Phase, blacks often have
too much anger to effectively use or listen to whites as resources.
When a black manager does use white resources, it tends to be for
technical assistance, that is, questions about the job task. This
kind of assistance requires less trust. In the Planned Growth
Phase, blacks have learned the value of strategy and will use it to
make more effective and frequent use of whites as resources, and
for a wide variety of other purposes.

At this juncture, we would like to reintroduce two of the concepts we defined in Part One, Chapter 1—*cultural paranoia* and

protective hesitation. We must treat them together because they are interrelated. We think it is appropriate to define them here because one of them is highly refined and used strategically by black managers in the Planned Growth Phase.

Cultural paranoia is a sociological and anthropological concept that refers to a protective hesitation or suspicion, a group coping mechanism that has evolved to deal with the consequences of racism. It does *not* refer to the psychological concept that implies individual mental disorders.

Protective hesitation is the behavior associated with cultural paranoia in which blacks hesitate in order to protect themselves from possible psychological assault before interacting or preparing to interact with whites. This behavior is also used in an attempt to avoid reinforcing any negative stereotypes that whites may have about blacks.

Blacks are taught early in their lives to be suspicious of whites in general. Historically, this has been necessary for the preservation of life for blacks. A swift death could result for a black person if he or she stepped too far out of the bounds set by the dominant society. This attitude has been handed down through generations. Today, although the law has changed regarding private citizens meting out their personal forms of justice or injustice, cultural paranoia still prevails. It exists for real, if somewhat changed, reasons. Blacks are still subjected to psychological assault by whites. Therefore, the natural hesitation most blacks display when approaching whites can be used in a strategic manner in the Planned Growth Phase. This can be done by preplanning or prethinking an idea before approaching and interacting with a white individual.

> *"Every time you use a resource, it's a risk. . . . You run the risk of being evaluated negatively. Before I use a white as a resource, I think over carefully what I'm going to say and how I'm going to say it."*

> *"Whites hear part of what they expect to be said and part of what is actually said by blacks; so I preplan my interaction before I speak so I can be sure to state things clearly enough to be understood correctly."*

A great deal of activity in the Planned Growth Phase is directed toward career planning and setting and meeting goals. In this way, black managers are able to appropriately notify their organizations that they are ready for more responsibility and that they have career goals. Both the organization and the black manager can be clearer about expectations of each other. (Personal and corporate planning will be discussed in detail in Part Four.)

> "I attended a seminar on career planning that my company paid for me to attend. I was very excited about it. When I returned to the job, I spent some time planning a career path for myself. I committed it to writing and had it publicized within my hierarchy."

> "I do more planning now, more discussing my career with my boss regarding the types of jobs I get."

> "First, I get the idea of what it takes to make a person promotable, then I take the information and write up a plan. I take it to my supervisor and say, 'I want these things.' We form a training program. I get input from other people about the key points of my program and how to accomplish them."

> "I've had to play catch-up. I got tired of being the underdog."

> "Now I can look at interpersonal pieces I can bone up on since I finally refuse to believe in my incompetence."

> "I've learned how to make my boss accountable for my training."

> "I see my job as a career, and I try to influence some of what happens to me."

> "I was disappointed about losing a possible position; so with the help of a black resource, I strategized, planned, and even retrained in another technology to get another management position. I now am more demanding of white supervisors, making sure they give me the right data, lay out formal criteria for getting ahead in the organization."

> "I've set up a training program tailored to my needs, not just some standardized program. I'm learning skills around my job and forcing data from people."

> "I try to be more visible in my organization. I continue to try to understand what an organization is all about. I try to find out what I'm in store for beforehand."

Job Skills

The Adjusting Phase was a time of exploration for the black manager. As a result of moving through the adjusting process, the black manager learned, out of necessity, many management skills that can be viewed as being somewhat different from those learned by the white manager. More correctly, we might say that some of those management skills are the same, but in practice they contain an additional component—the skill used to neutralize the racism or sexism of others. This skill, which falls within the area of multicultural management, must be mastered by blacks in the practice of effective management. In the Planned Growth Phase, the black manager learns to become an effective multicultural manager.

"I have to use energy figuring out how to—or planning how to—communicate with my boss when I feel there is something racial in the interaction that is affecting me."

"In many cases whites will ask for input, then go check with a white to check your data. They claim they didn't understand. You have to anticipate such behavior and put data in writing. They will pay attention and can't forget it then."

"Whites avoid telling you where they see you, so what I do is try to find out where I am by just talking instead of having regular performance reviews. I focus on positioning myself on the placement scale and giving data to help the supervisor see me."

"In meetings with whites you are either on the offensive or the defensive. I stay on the offensive."

"In dealing with whites you have to be always two steps ahead of their thought processes to make up for the extra stuff you have to deal with, never be thinking on the same level."

"Blacks must be friendly to whites. Whites are easily turned off by hostility or unfriendliness by blacks. Blacks have to operate more smoothly than whites in interactions."

"Whites are allowed to be dysfunctional in a behavioral sense with each other, but blacks are not allowed to be dysfunctional with whites."

"Blacks must confront a situation in a way that the white does not lose his dignity. Whites can do that and get away with it, but a black will receive very negative feedback."

"To keep my input from being dismissed on important issues, I preplan. I sit down and plan out everything myself, then check it with another black, and more if necessary, and make sure all the bases are covered. Then I try to anticipate what all the comebacks will be from the people I'm presenting to."

Lastly, the challenge to make effective use of the communications network continues for the black manager in the Planned Growth phase.

"Whites take care of whites; they don't worry about it. Blacks have to piece things together, or they may have a sponsor who will share information with them. I got a lot of information from my white supervisor, who got it from other whites. I've been fortunate."

"Blacks are not privy to whites' mainstream informal network, which is social, so they do not get information as fast as whites do. That always keeps blacks in a one-down position."

"Whites don't discuss many organizational norms, criteria, etc. with blacks. I got a lot of my data from a black who was promoted above my level and who had access to more information. Part of his day was spent tutoring, counseling, and developing blacks who weren't even reporting to him."

Now let us continue with Jack's story.

"IT WILL BE A COLD DAY IN HELL BEFORE THEY DEFEAT ME"

Ahhhh, that was good! OK, we'll get started again. Let me put my feet up and stretch out. Yeah, that's good! I've got to get my mind back on what I was saying.

Now, going into this next period of development was *really* exciting. It was exciting because I had an opportunity to get out of my old mode of operating. The way I had been doing things—uh, I guess the last period where I was trying to adjust to things was highly active, but it was also very depressing because that's when I really discovered . . . well, when I *allowed* myself to see racial reality.

It was depressing. I felt down a lot. I felt as though I was going "off," as though I was crazy. I felt nothing I did was right. I got negative input from all directions, all quarters, even though I *knew* I was making progress.

So at some point I had to go back and recall that I had decided to stay with the company and make it, so I had to get rejuvenated. And the thing that rejuvenated me was the discovery that the harder I fought with whites, the slower I was going to progress. So I knew there must be another answer. My job now was to start out and seek and find the answer. OK?

The way I did that was to take a look at what was going on with me and set some goals and objectives. What was going on with me was that I was being asked to slay a giant with a switch or a pea shooter. That was a pretty big giant, too!

Man, what I was doing was running all over the place, being a fire fighter—consulting with groups here and there—making people feel good . . . but I wasn't accomplishing a hell of a lot in terms of moving the company ahead in the area of recruiting and good affirmative action.

This kind of thing went on until I ran into a friend of mine who had been doing some consulting on the side. He took me aside one day when I was groaning and complaining and said, "Why're you running around like a chicken with his neck wrung off when you ought to stay in your office to plan and organize your work? You'll get a heck of a lot more done." That brought me up short, and so that's exactly what I did.

So what I'm saying to you is this new phase of my development was a period in which I, uh, stopped momentarily long enough to see what was happening to me—both in terms of within myself and outside. Internally, I had very high energy because I was starting to learn how to use strategy and how to manage my emotions. I really was just wrapped up in my job, because I really wanted to make it go well.

So I *was* running around like a chicken with its head wrung off, and when this black friend said this to me—it kinda hit me between the eyes and I really *did* slow down.

I slowed down and thought about what the devil I wanted. And there were about three or four major goals that I wanted. One was to develop a smoother style of interacting; two was to plan and organize my work; and three was to change the organization. So that's what I set out to do!

And to do that, I decided that probably what I needed to do was to get the heck away from the work environment and go to some management training function—to really try and see how I fit. How did I fit in relative to other people?

Where did I stand relative to people from other companies? Was I being crazy because I was only looking at my company? I was looking at myself only in the context of my company.

The first session I attended was in another state and was an eye-opener. Most of the people there were high-level whites. No blacks other than me were there—and one woman—a white female. We had two work groups. Both minorities were in the same group, and from the first day I arrived there, I intuitively knew what had happened.

See, before I went to the session, on one hand I felt like, "Crap! I'm really making progress!" On the other hand, I'm getting steadily beat up by whites. So I went to this session, and after the first day, I said to myself, "Damn! I'm a whole lot further along than I thought I was." And what was happening is the whites at work had started to see me make movement, got threatened, and gave me even more negative feedback.

Then I went with these strangers, who had never even seen me before; they just heaped strokes on me like, "Damn! Where did you learn to do that?" So what I discovered was—Shoot! I've got some sharp skills here that I, uh, I didn't even know I had. That was very helpful to me; so that was helping me take care of my first objective, which was to develop a smoother operating style.

And I worked hard in those workshops. Just testing and trying new behaviors, which I could easily do because I was away from my work environment. I think it's damn important for minorities—women, blacks, and so forth—to go to sessions like that away from the company environment because you'll get more accurate feedback. It will be more realistic.

So each time I'd come back from one of those training sessions, I'd be in good shape. 'Cause I'd just . . . I felt stronger; I felt enthusiastic. I would be really ready to attack my job—and just—I was *determined* to have a smoother style!

Each time I got back, people would see an increasingly obvious air of confidence about me. But after about a week, the same crap would start again, in other words, giving me negative feedback! But now, it didn't take. I got to the point where I'd question the feedback. I got sick and tired of people telling me I wasn't any good, when I knew I was taking care of business!

So when I'd get a negative piece of feedback, either from—well—anybody, I'd quiz them about it. When I got some from my boss, I'd quiz him about it, too. He'd get mad about that! So what I would say is, "Look, when you get feedback on blacks you've got to probe it to weed out the racist pieces."

So, even though I was in a relatively calmer phase, my boss expected me to fight with him like I did before—but I wouldn't do it!

I fought differently now!

I now fought strategically instead of totally emotional and open all the time.

So, one thing I told my boss I was going to do—because the workshops had helped me wrap my mind around the fact that I did need to get organized—so I told him, "Look, I'm going to stop fighting fires. I'm going to plan and organize my work. I'm going to become a fire marshal and prevent fires instead of a fire fighter."

I pulled together a budget for my office and a plan for my personnel responsibilities.

The budget was fairly easy to sell because of some outstanding results we'd been getting, but it was harder to sell the new plan, which included some affirmative action programs. But I did sell it to my hierarchy after some heated discussions.

We kicked the training programs off. I brought in some outside people to work with us. And with the first session . . . all hell broke loose!

And really! I had cleaned my desk out, because I was ready to go! I *knew* I was going to get fired!

Because about three of the upper-level white managers in that session complained bitterly, and what happened was—uh, was their—we had tapped into their racial attitudes in the session. And they, uh . . . they angrily reacted to it.

What we had to do was meet with them separately and calm them down. I did it—and here I was, at the lowest level in a room with three upper-level managers—but I was *dealing hard*, because I was *determined* that I'd just be damned if they were going to shut down this good thing we'd started.

We finally got permission to go ahead and do another session. Now, the second one came out better because the . . . I got together first with my outside people, and we strategized this one better, did some new things like changed the—the sequence of events slightly so we'd take responsibility off us and put it onto the participants, where it really belonged. We made the highest-ranking manager responsible for the goals and objectives for each session—and it worked beautifully. Now, that was being appropriately strategic! OK?

Throughout this time period, I began to feel better and better about myself, took pride in what I was doing . . . and I started to get respect from people, especially from whites.

And that happened because I was less harsh with whites. I still confronted them and pushed them, but I did it in a way they could handle. I stopped stripping them of their dignity, the way I used to do.

I was really excited these days and felt better about a lot of things. I could see myself making movement, smoothing and ironing out things—planning and organizing and filling in gaps. I felt like I had faced the giant and tied his hands . . . tied them by strategy, planning, and organizing.

The next step was to trip the giant and get it off its feet. The way I did that was to publish a report of the activities, findings, and results of the personnel office relative to our recruiting efforts, training procedures, and the new affirmative action programs I had instituted. I gave background information, analysis of where we were and what we needed to do, and then a broad conceptual plan.

When I presented this to my boss, he thought it was great—but he was a new boss and hadn't read the organizational norms and cues yet. But his boss just blew up!

He said, "What do you mean doing this? We didn't tell you to do this!" In other words, one norm I had violated was that I wouldn't shut up and draw—or . . . I didn't—I didn't only do what I was told to do. I was learning how to be a manager, and this really threatened some people. I was taking more initiative and being creative. Yes, I was making some decisions on my own because of outside feedback. It was more realistic than the inside feedback.

Well, the report was approved, and I got what I wanted. Oh no! I didn't get everything, but I did get a lot more responsibility—a new position and a subordinate—and a whole new ball game.

Man, oh man! Now the giant's hands were tied; we tripped him, and we were on the verge of getting him under control. OK?

What I continued to do was to refine my personal style so I could be even smoother, learn how to be even a better manager, learn how to delegate things—uh, how to keep people informed, and uh . . . just how to generally operate more smoothly. I looked around and identified a new concept.

It was the concept of how to deal with hot issues. I mean, find things that were important to the company and that people were having trouble doing—and jump dead on them. I handled a couple of these. I found out *that* was important for me as a black to do. It made me visible and positioned the company to take more notice of my skills.

Exactly how did I operate differently? OK. For instance, if I were in a meeting with a white individual and I said something which elicited an arrogant, nasty, or inappropriate response from the white person—well, instead of jumping back at the white individual like I used to, instead I would calm down, sit back, and cross my legs . . . relax and look at the person and say, "I really don't understand your comment. Can you help me understand it?"

In other words, instead of jumping on people and deluging them by preaching, I would take their logic and use their data and dissect it, bit by bit, so they could see what they had said to me. Half the time they'd end up saying, "Oh, I didn't realize I had said that."

People will accept that kind of interaction much more than they will accept a black manager jumping on them if they're white.

OK, another thing I discovered was that some white managers were uncomfortable around black managers—especially if the black manager could speak up and talk back and, uh, show signs of really being able to outthink some of the whites. So I found that before I went into a meeting with a white and started working business things I had to put the white individual at ease.

I'd talk about baseball, mowing the lawn, or uh—I'd spend five minutes or so just shooting the bull. OK? Then I'd wrap the conversation . . . or initiate the conversation by wrapping it around a business need. I had learned that when you do that you can neutralize an interaction by sticking strictly to, uh, the business needs.

See, whites tended to operate with blacks by personalizing things—by giving personal feedback, or feedback about their personal behavioral style. If I got to a point where a white would start to do that, I would really take the white's information. I didn't get *defensive*, I'd get *offensive*!

For example, my boss once said to me, uh . . . he said that he'd gotten feedback from a manager that said, uh . . . how did he put it? He said I was difficult to—uh, interact with. Oh yeah, that's it.

I asked my boss if he had explored the information and what the feedback meant. He said no. So I said, "Well, don't you think you need to go back and find out exactly what was meant? Otherwise, it's possible that you have become a messenger—carrying inappropriate racist messages."

What? Oh, yeah, he understood what I was saying. So then he went back and talked to the individual. He discovered that the white manager had given him negative information about me because the white individual had discovered that, uh . . . on a particular issue, I had the ability to outthink him—probe, find out, and uncover flaws in his thinking.

Again, even on one to one, I tried to use the other person's information and put that in front of him instead of using a "give-the-black-the mike" technique—which is talk a whole lot in the hopes that along the way you'll convince a white individual of something. What that tends to do is further alienate the white, and it gives him more information to use to beat up on you.

Let's see. Oh! We're rolling along. I was given this new position—subordinates, learned how to manage them. Uhh . . . I immediately became aware that a lot of managers did the daily work tasks, performed maintenance functions, but didn't do any development of their people. So! I developed my people, in a creative manner, and I—Oh! Wait a minute! I forgot to tell you about this. It's an important piece to my development.

Before I got my new position in the personnel department—now realize, I didn't really know what I was doing at the time—but I went out and acquired three white sponsors. I figured I needed that many to institute my plans, and I inadvertently did it by asking three people if I could—upper-level managers—if I could meet with them and learn some management techniques, things like budgets, how to delegate, managing various situations. And as a result of doing that, I ended up with three sponsors. And they came in handy for me.

How did I do that? Aha! First of all they were identified as resources in one of the training sessions for the new-hires. They had expressed interest in the newly proposed affirmative action plans and wanted to help blacks. So I took advantage of that. I seized an opportunity!

I remembered what they said, and looking at my goals and objectives, I made a list of the things I needed and wanted to do a better job of. Then, I looked around at the upper-level white managers, and I said, "Who does this well?" and I put some names beside my list.

Then I picked up the phone and called those people and said, "Look, you said you wanted to help blacks; I need some help in this area, and I really think you're an excellent resource in that area."

And they were just flabbergasted! They just . . . awwww man, they just jumped at the opportunity, even though they were three or four levels above me. Other blacks didn't try that—if they had, then I guess they would have gotten the same response.

Man, it got to the point where I had set up a situation whereby, if an upper-level manager wasn't talking directly to a black, he went out and found a black to talk to because he figured that was the thing to do! It was also rewarding and fulfilling. So I inadvertently started a trend, but at the same time, I learned a *tremendous* amount of information . . . and it really paid off in terms of helping me do a better job.

Another thing I learned, going to those outside training and management sessions, was that you can unlearn negative behavior—or replace it very quickly with positive behavior—if you use behavior change. All that means is be aware of and understand what the negative behavior is, the effect it has on people and what you should replace it with. OK?

Now! What I did was, I looked around and found some white managers with . . . with a very smooth style in an area that I wanted to develop, such as delegating, for example, or such as, uh . . . managing subordinates—and I learned to pattern myself after them in terms of their behavior in managing.

And you know? This is a critical issue with blacks, because you have to separate that from becoming white. I did not use their specific speech patterns. I did not throw away my blackness. What I *did* do was duplicate the process they used to manage certain things. And, being around upper-level managers, I was able to identify their positive behavior and duplicate it. Now, that's one way a black can change very quickly.

The other issue I had to face was how do you separate . . . how do you interact with racists—understand and realize they are racist, but separate some of the good skills and techniques they use? Now I was able to learn how to do that in this part of my development.

For example, this one individual, well, displayed obvious negatively prejudiced behavior toward blacks. He took pride in trying to out-maneuver blacks. But I was able to spot some positive skills in that person and duplicate them, even though this individual kept trying to keep me in a slave–master context—like trying to position me to have to humbly ask for everything I received from him. Oh yes! I always managed to maneuver around him instead.

A lot of people were amazed at how fast I was learning, including me. It was as though I had discovered some keys to learning. I've read a lot of behavioral stuff, so let me see if I can articulate what it was.

Let's see, it was like . . . like the keys were behavior modification—uh, behavior duplication—and getting information from outside the existing organization. And the remarks I received were that I was on an upward vector and people couldn't understand how I could change so fast and so much.

I'll tell you something else I did, too. As a result of my inappropriate behavior and a remark to an upper-level manager in a meeting and the subsequent negative feedback—then followed by a training session with some of those same managers—well, I tell you . . . I got all kinds of input about some things I should do. And, uh, it came so fast, I . . . I decided after that high-level meeting and the training session to sit down and write up what I remembered from the comments and put a date on it.

When I did that, I discovered, "Wait a minute! If I do this from now on, I'll have a wealth of knowledge in my own handwriting, dated, and I can tell who I got the information from." So I started a personal development file, which has been *invaluable* because I can periodically go back and read through it and it'll refresh my memory on certain things.

Now! Man, I'm really growing fast and just getting into it—and just lovin' it because I'm feeling, uh . . . I've got a sense of pride—uh, now using my anger as a strategy. People can see I'm making progress—but!

There was a negative side! And the negative side was, for those whites who used to have you under their wing, some of them retracted the wing! For now, I—and they—found I was able to do some things they couldn't do. And this is very threatening to some people, especially being in levels above me.

Sure—you're darned right! I was doing a lot of things differently. When I had an idea, I would document it and go in and discuss it with my boss. I'd take it in early, before I had put details around it, and that way my white boss could feel a part of making the idea come to fruition—but I'd still get credit for the idea. It would help make both of us feel more like we were working as a team and not as competitors.

Here's another important piece for a black to learn. When you're in an interaction—especially with a white individual—there're two things going on: the content of what you're discussing, and then the process of the discussion. That is, who says what to whom—body movements, reactions, and things like that.

So for a black, the process of an interaction is just as important as the content—and in some cases, maybe more important because it allows us to utilize our skill to read situations; with some of us, I think it's an inherent cultural skill.

But there're also a lot of good books out on the subject of watching the physical dynamics in interactions. Most of them are written only with whites in mind—but with a little translating and a little adding to, you can learn a lot.

In this phase of my development, I used my readin' skills to their maximum. In essence, as they say, I'd learned how to snatch victory from the jaws of defeat. Now, you want to know what that means. For example, if I received some negative input from a white on an interaction—in one case I was told I was formal—and after digging into it, I discovered that I was very organized, not formal. I went in with an agenda, had my plan clearly laid out, and uh . . . when I discussed it with the person, he said, "Well, that's . . . well, that's not . . . I see what you mean. That's not formal; that's organized. But it's too structured." Then I asked the person, "Did I ever come in here with an agenda that you had a problem with, that I didn't listen to you and refused to change it?"

"Well, no you didn't, because you were flexible." That's the purpose of an agenda: to reflect what one person wants, and if that's not what the other person wants, then collaborate, compromise, modify, and change the damn thing. Anyway, that person had to withdraw his complaint.

Another big problem I had during this period was the standoffish reaction I got from whites because I was learning so fast. I had become smoother in conducting meetings; the way I did it was threatening to some people.

When I got negative feedback, I now had the ability to dig into it, dissect it, and make people own some of their own stuff. And I'm not saying all of the feedback was wrong! Some of it was right on and very helpful. I don't want to give you the wrong impression—I wasn't doing everything right!

When blacks take charge of meetings with whites, you always run the risk that someone is going to try to take leadership from you. So what blacks—and I—will usually do at first is to hold on to the leadership . . . overcontrol the participants. But when you get smoother, you can relax, allow people to take control and, when it's appropriate, take it back—but smoothly. You can do it by being the person who writes on the board, or who runs the agenda.

What did all this do to me? I'll tell you. I moved so fast, gained so much managerial skill and knowledge, that at times I'd go into a situation and be overstressful. My self-concept, or what I thought I could take care of or handle, had not caught up with my skill attainment. I was capable of doing more than I thought or believed I could do.

So sometimes when I'd go into a meeting, my stress would show—the white individuals would pick up that stress from me without knowing it, and we'd end up fighting when there was no need to. I had to learn to relax and trust my black intellect.

Aha! That's what it is! That's what has been pulling at the back of my mind—*black intellect!* This is the period when a . . . a black individual will start to develop a high level of trust in black intellect.

Now what is that? Black intellect means that, uh . . . as a result of slavery, the words *black* and *intellect* are antithetical in this country. Man, I mean for blacks and whites! For some people, black intellect doesn't even exist as a concept!

Man, I'm smiling because of the feelings involved here. When you discover that you *do* have intellect—that you can strategize, that you can adroitly handle a situation, that you can be extremely logical— conceptualize in every sense of the word that you *thought* all whites could—

Oh man, I don't mean just in your head. You might have been saying that for years. But did you believe it—with every fiber of your being? Or were you quick to say, "Look at that black person showing off. Who does he think he is? He's no better than the rest of us."

In this phase of development, blacks can learn to truly believe in and trust black intellect, your own as well as others. You begin to lose the need to see all blacks as the same . . . to accept our common experience, but—but respect our differing intellects. Yeah man! That's it!

It was during this period that I made closer contacts at work, talked more deeply about what happened to us, shared information, talked strategy, developed our own black heroes and black role models, and . . . and we—we just helped each other. We helped each other, not only to survive, but to—to grow and develop.

We not only learned to trust our black intellect but the intellect of other blacks, and that's why I feel so strongly that it's important for a company hiring blacks that they don't go out and hire just one or two. They need to hire blacks in larger numbers—what is called a *critical mass*—which will vary from company to company depending on company size.

At this time in our history there are some things that only blacks can help other blacks learn. [Jack fell silent for a few moments.]

It was during this phase that I discovered I needed a way to resist power, and I guess that's one thing I didn't master until much later.

No. No man, I guess the broadest concept to crystallize in my mind and that hit me between the eyes was the concept of *black development*. There are some areas black managers need to develop that white managers don't have knowledge or skill to help them with. These are the kinds of things that only other blacks can transmit, as I said before.

See, it's like being in a big family . . . and, like having a father hand down certain information to the sons, or the mother to the daughters. You know, like that.

What kinds of information am I talking about? Well, uh, like how to resist power is one. Another is how do you keep a positive psychological attitude about yourself as a black, uh, and . . . how do you sharpen and refine your skills to read a situation with racial components and be OK with using your skills?

See, because we blacks bring skills to the white corporation from the streets, so to speak, we tend to throw 'em away as being out of place or not important or not useful. So what we have to do is learn to reach back and pull those skills out from our experience and history and use them in today's atmosphere. OK?

The other piece of black development that's different from whites' is how to manage the racist behavior or attitudes of others. What does that mean? It means that given racism in the corporation in America is not going to change at this point in time, and . . . and yet I still had to interact with all kinds of people and be successful. I had to learn how to manage some people's negatively prejudiced behavior toward me.

The first thing I had to do was not be reactive to it. There was no sense reacting to it, because the person was not going to change instantaneously or overnight—or even next week. But yet I had a responsibility to be successful. So what that means is that a black is going to have to carry an extra burden, whether you like it or not.

So you have to identify the behavior, learn how to control or neutralize it, and be successful in spite of it. *That's* what you can learn in black development from other blacks.

There is also the management of conflict, because now there is a different kind of conflict than in the previous phase. This is the kind of conflict where whites want to take me on around my black intellect. They want to know what skills I've developed, and they'll question them. Oh yeah! What they'll question is whether or not they are *legitimate* skills.

I had to learn how to manage that. If it's a peer, you might be able to verbally kick 'im in the behind; if it's an upper-level boss in a meeting, you'd better not or you're in trouble.

We often cause a lot of problems during this period. For instance, a lot of blacks on occasion buy into the slave–master concept. The way we do it is by positioning whites to *protect us!* And when we give them that message, that's exactly how they behave: in a way to protect us. Then at some point we get angry about it, but we have to take responsibility for that.

You know, thinking back . . . I generally felt so good about myself during this period. I didn't wait for people to give me feedback—I went out and sought it!

How? I sent out a one-page questionnaire asking people about my area—about how they evaluated the service they received and whether or not they had any additional suggestions.

I really calmed down from that last phase. I thought a lot—planned, organized, systematically proceeded to carry out my plans. I really learned how to effectively run a meeting—not Uncle Tomming or shuffling or screaming and jumping on people; neither fighting the system full time nor being totally socialized.

I learned how important it was to have sponsors to keep some whites from withholding helpful information from me when I started moving fast. I had to watch out for that.

What else can I say about this phase of my development? I did a much better job of separating those barriers to my success that I owned from those that the corporation owned. That was a major difference too between this phase and the last one. I feel competent and confident enough to own . . . to feel OK in owning the negative things I've done.

The concept of protective hesitation took on a new meaning for me. I would now take more of what you would call a calculated risk. I would expose more information about me, but I'd be careful as to who I would expose it to and what I exposed. Before, I felt I'd go into a meeting not knowing the outcome, not knowing if I'd still own my shirt afterwards. But during this time, I felt I could go into any meeting and come out with my shirt intact as well as my dignity.

I used protective hesitation, not to hide myself or shut down, but to anticipate what would happen—plan my behavior—organize my thoughts and respond in an appropriate manner so that I got what I wanted. Yeah.

OK, what other questions do you have? That's about it, unless you want to hear some more war stories about this period. I haven't even mentioned some of the similar stuff my friends went through. But really, I'd just as soon move on to the next period.

Oh! Wait! There's the phone. Will you excuse me for a minute?

ANALYSIS OF CRITICAL ISSUES

The Planned Growth Phase, representing the critical turning point for blacks, is the beginning of an exciting uphill climb. Jack became aware that he could no longer continue in the same vein as in the previous phase because it required too much energy for too little results and was too depressing. He was tired of feeling crazy and having negative thoughts about himself.

Jack identified his next phase as calming and one in which he could focus his energies on something concrete that he could both understand and do something about. He started taking a serious look at his personal style, which prevented him from getting what he wanted, and took serious strides to change it. In the Planned Growth Phase, blacks put a lot of emphasis and energy into modifying personal style and identifying and removing barriers in addition to handling the normal work tasks. Jack also put more energy into using black input, and he told us why it was important. He leaned heavily on his resources, both black and white. However, he realized that those racially sensitive skills—managing conflict and managing the racial attitudes of others—must be learned from other blacks.

Jack does not say he is a superstar, but it is apparent throughout his narrative that it is a position he sees himself in. He brings to our attention that he is aware of the extra burdens and responsibilities he as a black is willing to bear in order to become successful. When you join an organization in the Entry Phase feeling like "I've got it made" and then discover you don't, you become angry. For example, you see you are not moving as fast as your white peers, and then you will make a decision. In the Adjusting Phase, you will try to change things so you can grow and develop—or you will slip back into the Entry Phase. One thing is for sure: You will not stay in the Adjusting Phase and remain with your present employer for very long. The pressure will be too great, and your company will not tolerate your dysfunctional behavior forever. You will either go forward, or backward and out.

Jack chose to go forward, not backward and give up. Therefore, he knew that in order to overcome some of the difficulties he was having, he had to be a superstar. He had to be prepared and be able to expend much more energy than his white peers to accomplish the same task because he had to fight against a system that is inherently against his being there. Of course, we all hope someday this will change.

When whites opened the doors of industries and other institutions to blacks, many whites wanted to show that blacks could make it. As a result, whites ferreted out the superstars, not the average blacks. Blacks in the first wave, unlike the one or two—here and there—of the 1940s and 1950s, entered the newly opened institutions and were rapidly weeded out. The first group that rose into the hierarchies of industries really were superstars; they had to be in order just to survive. When Jack took on the challenge of moving ahead, he became a superstar. He had to be able to take on the demands and pressures that are unique to blacks in white organizations. He also had to accomplish outstanding job results that would make him competitive with his white peers.

As the second, third, and fourth waves of blacks enter white organizations, there should be sufficient numbers scattered throughout hierarchies so that various procedures can be changed from within. For example, as a result of blacks and women entering industry, it is easier for white male managers now to formulate career development plans; minorities caused this to happen. Minorities can influence personnel policies, which in turn can change an organization as a whole, benefiting both the white and minority employees. Therefore, it can be expected that in years to come blacks may not have to assume superstar roles to become successful. One of the objectives of affirmative action programs is to change the employment situation so that the average minority can work and be successful in the same way the average white male employee can. At this time, we are not at that point.

As we have seen, Jack is a superstar because he chose to go forward, but what of the blacks who chose to give up and slipped backward into the Entry Phase? What can be done in their cases? Let us take a friend of Jack's, Ansel, and see what happened to him. Ansel came into the company a couple of years after Jack. He was in another area of the company but saw Jack regularly because they often had to collaborate on job tasks. They also had socialized outside the company on a number of occasions.

Ansel had two degrees and, to most people, was obviously sharp, but he had been beaten down so much that he moved into the Adjusting Phase furious and highly resentful. He became dysfunctional with everyone and rejected a lot of the information sharing from other blacks. "They didn't understand," he told himself. Ansel became increasingly difficult to work with. This increased his organization's negative reaction toward him so much that it scared Ansel half to death and he went running back to his Entry Phase level and gave up.

At some point Jack realized what had happened to Ansel and started to work with him, pulling and prodding him back to his Adjusting Phase level. Jack had to go to Ansel's managers and try to calm them down by telling them that, by helping Ansel through this period, they would learn something and so would Ansel. Jack's hope was to get Ansel past his anger and disappointment and move him into the Planned Growth Phase, where Ansel could then deal with himself and the system.

Now, what if Jack failed or there was no "father" to help the "son" back on track. Perhaps Ansel would be locked in because the system beat him down or frightened him too much. There may now be information in his evaluation file that marks him as a "troublemaker" or "uppity" or "militant." In this case, the company has lost a valuable resource; Ansel has met many negative expectations and has failed. The best that Jack can do is make a new opportunity for Ansel, not hold his hand. Jack can also fulfill his need to give back to someone the opportunity he received— but Ansel must accept it.

Jack acquired a sense of determination in the Planned Growth Phase. He changed his mind about leaving the company; they were not going to chase him away, and he was determined to make a success of his job. Again, this speaks to the superstar status of Jack, a status without which Ansel was unable to make it at this point in time. Jack's determination was often at the root of his creativity, and he often stumbled into it rather than reached it by design. For example, Jack went to his first management seminar, not because he *knew* it was going to provide him with such valuable learning opportunities, but because it was a chance to get away and find out what was happening outside his company. However, Jack discovered the advantages of these seminars and used them to facilitate his rapid growth.

Jack's determination and subsequent creativity brought him a sense of pride. He could see for himself the quality of his results.

This pride and self-evaluation based on results ultimately makes it possible for blacks to slowly become less dependent on external strokes. The pride Jack took in his results showed him he need not expend his energy fighting inappropriately with whites, that it cost him nothing to allow others to keep their dignity, and that he could still perform his job and achieve his goals. His anger was managed; it was used only as a strategy when absolutely necessary. The energy from the anger was consciously turned into creative output.

In the Planned Growth Phase, white managers will see a big difference in the behavior of black managers. Whites are apt to be confused and sometimes upset because they have come to expect one type of interaction and will see another. Black managers struggle to smooth their style and to be more effective. Hopefully, white managers will sense this and feel free to openly discuss this subject with black managers, because white managers can be a tremendous help at this time.

This can also be a great learning opportunity for white managers. Since blacks do not tend to become as socialized into the white corporate culture, whites can learn to expand their managerial repertoires by having blacks share information. Research in the behavioral fields has shown that blacks and women bring a more humanistic form of management to organizations. We believe one reason for this is that blacks and women have a more highly developed level of sensitivity toward people resulting from the role status they have been historically assigned. Here, then, is an opportunity for white male managers to take advantage of a different management style and to use it to everyone's benefit. The key to doing this is for white managers to first admit to themselves that something *can* be learned from black managers. Second, they must decide *what* is to be learned, and third, they must be *open* to learning.

This is an important time in the professional life of a black manager, and white managers can help. However, if a black is the subordinate of a white manager who is highly threatened, then this is going to be a rough period for that white manager, because the black manager will be learning a lot of positive new behaviors and skills at a rapid pace. Instead of allowing the black manager to share and use those skills, the white manager will tend to react negatively to the changes. The white boss will inadvertently or even deliberately try to slow down the black manager. This reaction, if strong and persistent, can frustrate black managers enough to push them back into the Adjusting Phase.

In the Planned Growth Phase, the black manager develops a hard skin. Jack, for instance, could now listen to both negative and positive input and was strong and astute enough to deal with it by ensuring that it was proper and accurate feedback. He asked questions about it and accepted it when he thought it was correct. If he thought the feedback was not correct, he weeded out the inappropriate pieces and kept the helpful ones. Because he had learned about the corporate culture during the Adjusting Phase, Jack was now able to identify and separate various information and place the pieces where they properly belonged.

To sum up, blacks develop in the Planned Growth Phase the refined skill to weed out negative racial and sexual data and to determine if a barrier is organizational or personal. Not only will blacks welcome and listen to feedback, but they will tend to go out and seek it from any appropriate person, white or black. Jack was even willing to expose himself and his shortcomings in training and management seminars so he could get the right kind of information to move ahead. This action showed how much he valued the input, because public exposure is risky for most individuals, especially for blacks. What Jack and other blacks try to do in this phase is refine those things that turn them on, juice them up, and cause them to do a good job.

Jack did not go into any detail about his discoveries in the interactional processes, but we know from his narrative that he worked very hard to improve the manner in which he approached people to give and get information. Jack noticed, both at work and away, that there are some differences in the dynamics of the interactional processes between different groups of people. The impact of this was important because it had implications for how Jack would approach different people and what he could expect the nonverbal and often hidden issues to be. Figure 3 diagrams and explains three of the most outstanding issues—power, control, and trust—in the interactional process between three different racial dyads. Of course, there are other dynamics and hidden issues involved in these interactions, but those shown are basic in the corporate culture.

Because of his understanding of interactional processes, Jack

FIGURE 3.   Three dynamic issues involved in the interactional process of three different racial dyads.

Interaction:

Power

- Characterized by persons seeking to identify job positions for mutual beneficial contact and/or to establish one's place in the pecking order.

Control

- Persons display intelligence or seek level of intelligence of each other.
- Persons show and discuss material goods and comforts, clubs joined, neighborhood lived in, trips, etc.

Trust

- Initially little display of trust.
- Lack of personal or emotional display in conversation.
- Trust established after positions in the pecking order are identified.

Interaction:

Power

- Centers around and is held by the white person, who is a member of the dominant culture.

Control

- Some fear by the white person of loss of control.

Trust

- Little trust, because there is no common base of cultural experience and may be little common base of personal experience.

Interaction:

Power

- Persons tend to establish respect independent of job position.
- Characterized by a display of mental prowess and/or street sense, education, and sometimes material goods.

Control

- There tends to be an absence of control issues.

Trust

- Trust is established very quickly and often assumed because of common cultural experiences.
- Personal or emotional affect is displayed in conversation.

could see the value of the warm-up conversation before getting into the business at hand. He knew when and why it was important, what purpose it should serve, and how to use it strategically to position people to listen and seriously consider his needs. Jack could now easily put both blacks and whites at ease and anticipate their needs and concerns in order to move to meet or reject them. During the Planned Growth Phase, blacks tend to focus very quickly on the differences in the dynamics that occur when individuals from different cultures interact.

Jack took advantage of an opportunity to develop and use sponsors. He chose people in the hierarchy who not only would act as advocates for him but were willing to be used as coaches and resources. That action helped Jack move faster because he could learn through the experiences of others. Anyone who expects to move up the hierarchy needs the extra help of sponsors. As we have already stated, competition is keen and the pyramid narrows rapidly as it reaches its apex. Blacks cannot afford to wait until someone sees their potential to advance; that may never happen. Minorities must be aggressive enough to make their desires known to someone who is willing and in a position to help. We cannot repeat this too often or state it too strongly to the minority manager.

Jack also lets us know how important it is to set goals. The setting of goals is a main indication of when a black has moved into the Planned Growth Phase. These goals provide a road map to success in terms of attaining some of the things that the black manager wants. However, this is also the phase in which the acquisition of skills and new knowledge and the setting and meeting of goals occur so rapidly that the black manager's self-concept always lags behind the level of managerial skill that can be used to handle complex situations. This is illustrated in Figure 4.

At this point you may be asking, "What are the implications of this gap for blacks?" Let us look at an example that will point out the implications. Take the case of a black manager who has to attend a meeting that will involve the discussion and resolution of hot organizational issues. The black manager knows that meeting participants will debate various points. A manager in the Planned Growth Phase will tend to go into the meeting with a great deal of stress, anxiety, and concern. Usually, shortly after the meeting starts, the black manager will discover that he or she is handling

FIGURE 4. Managerial skills acquired and improvement of self-concept over time for black managers.

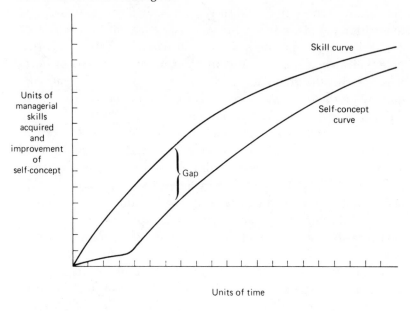

him- or herself very adroitly in the ensuing debate and may even wonder afterward why there was so much stress and worry before the meeting. Unfortunately, this scenario will be repeated again and again.

A gap will always exist, as shown in the graph. As a black manager moves toward the Success Phase, the gap will decrease significantly. For some individuals the gap reduces fairly quickly; for others it may take years. This depends on how rapidly the individuals can change their self-concepts in a positive direction.

In summary, blacks usually develop managerial skills at a much more rapid rate than they develop positive self-concepts. Although all of us sometimes have doubts about our ability to get the results we want, the primary difference is that whites are concerned over whether success will be achieved, whereas blacks are concerned about whether total failure can be avoided.

DEVELOPMENT OF HOW-TO SOLUTIONS

The how-to solutions tend to be more complicated in the Planned Growth Phase. They are, as we have said, more structured and more strategic than those in the two previous phases. Some of the solutions are very involved, and we choose not to go into them at this time. Therefore, we will give rather simplistic solutions to some of the problems here and refer you to another part of this book for the more involved explanations and problem solutions in that specific area.

Problem I: How to manage conflict. Problem relates to critical issues 1, 2, 4, 5, 6, 8, 11, 14

Solution: This solution can apply to conflicts between black peers and white peers and between white bosses and black subordinates. Successful confrontation will be discussed in greater depth in Part Three, Chapter 7. This solution has seven steps and is especially useful with people who tend not to be open and candid in interactions. It also works well with people who tend not to confront others. Figure 5 illustrates the confrontation process.

1. Spend three to five minutes discussing subjects designed to help relax and reduce stress in both you and the other person involved in the conflict. The subjects could be sports, hobbies, the latest home project, or some funny event.
2. Bring up the subject of the conflict by placing it in terms of factual data. Describe the problem relative to what happened.
3. Agree on the facts—nothing but what actually took place—because a confrontation cannot be resolved if the two parties cannot start from a common base. However, if there is disagreement about the critical facts, agree on a method to get the data. Reconnect and resume the above process when you have the data.
4. Probe each other by asking questions. Ask how the other person felt about the incident. Find out what the person actually had a problem with in the situation, or why it gave the person a problem. You need to understand the other person's thought processes. One reason conflicts arise is because people use different thought processes, and you need to find a common way of viewing the situation in question.
5. After you have asked sufficient questions and are comfortable with the information you have received, comment on the information. Then give your reaction, such as, "When

FIGURE 5. Steps for successful confrontation.

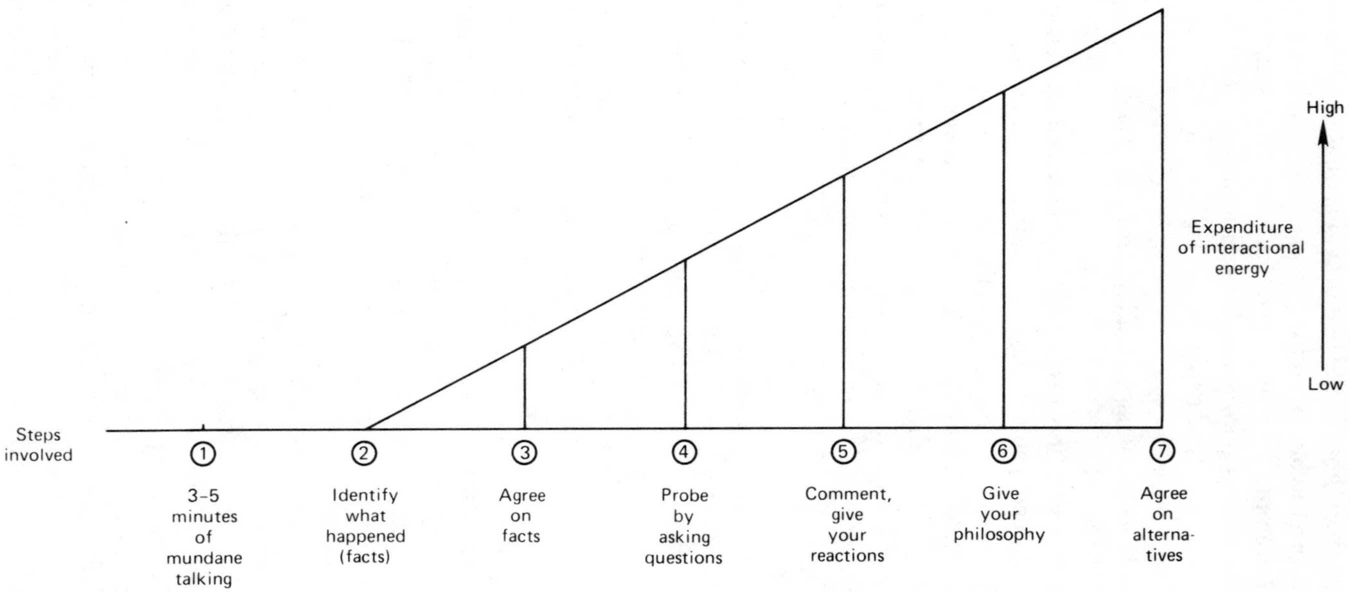

you do things like that, I react in this way," or "When you say something like that, I tend to get angry." Explain, "When I get angry, I may get dysfunctional" or "I get angry and find it difficult to cooperate with you."

6. Give your philosophy about the incident. For instance, "My general thoughts are," or, "My general feelings on that are," or, "My philosophy about that kind of issue is this."
7. The last step is to agree on some alternatives to resolving the conflict. Pick one, and use it to resolve the issues between you and the other person.

Problem II: How to develop a smoother style of interacting. Problem relates to critical issues 1, 2, 4, 5, 7, 13, 14

Solution: We are presenting one solution to this problem. For more discussion on effective styles, see Part Three, Chapter 6.

Be aware of your need to develop a smoother style; this is half your battle. Your level of awareness and ability to accept the responsibility for changing your style will determine how much energy you will give to the task and how successful you will be in accomplishing it. If your interactions with people tend to make them react negatively rather than respond positively to you, then that is a clear signal that you need to develop a smoother style.

Define the specific areas you feel you need to change or want to change. For example, perhaps you have been given feedback that you tend to be aloof with people and as a result they will not share information readily with you. You may see that you are awkward in conducting meetings and people get impatient with you. You may see another manager handle conflict in an effective manner you wish you could duplicate. Be clear about what you desire to change or improve.

Pick a role model who exhibits smoothness in the areas you are concerned about. You may choose several different people as role models for various changes you wish to make; their ethnic group or sex does not matter. A good argument for picking several role models is that it is harder to generalize from one case. Seeing several people who are skillful in one area helps you ignore individual mannerisms and concentrate on the key processes involved in the skill area. Use the listing concept to identify and describe the processes the people use that produce the smoothness of behavior in their interactions with others. For instance, you may see that one manager has a great deal of charisma with people and as a result people eagerly share information with that person. You may see that another manager is quite skilled at running meetings, and people leave full of energy and ready to do their tasks. Still another manager may have the ability to confront conflict and resolve it leaving all parties satisfied. You need to describe what you see and understand how it is done—that is, pull out the process.

Duplicate the process used by the role model. Again, we want you to understand that if your role model is white, you are not attempting to become "white-like." Your delivery and mannerisms will be your own and within the personal character that is comfortable to you.

Role play the interaction to be changed or improved in your mind, or with a friend, or with your mate. Practice the behavior you want to use, such as being more personable, leading a meeting, or confronting conflict. Picture yourself in the situation, integrating your words and mannerisms into the process of your role model.

Practice the new behavior in actual situations. Greet people using a more personal affect; lead your next meeting using the role model's process; or deal with conflict by operating in a smoother manner. You probably will not get the new process and behavior 100 percent correct the first few times, but that is OK. You should realize that you are learning, and change does not happen overnight.

Make corrections and refine your behavior and the new process if you make a mistake. Keep doing this until you are satisfied with your behavior in that particular area. Do not get discouraged if people do not immediately react differently to you. They will have "old tapes" on you that they will need to erase.

Problem III: How to probe negative feedback. Problem relates to critical issues 1, 3, 4, 5, 7, 8, 10, 11, 12, 13, 14

Solution: First, let us take a broad overview of the entire process. Position your psyche, or put more simply, set a positive mental attitude. Make sure you understand the negative feedback. Look at the perceptions of others as well as your own. Now look at ownership and then develop corrective steps. From this overview, let us discuss each specific step involved.

To position your psyche you must talk to yourself. Use the concept of talking to the champ. Being black and getting feedback from a white person is stressful. You become tense because you face these questions about the feedback: "Is it racist, or isn't it?" "Is it sexist, or isn't it?" Another question blacks commonly ask themselves is, "Is this person trying to be helpful by sharing feedback, or is the person trying to degrade me?" Try not to react too quickly to the feedback. Try not to get defensive, even though it is natural to do so. Say to yourself, "I should not react negatively or be defensive yet because there may be some constructive pieces in the feedback. If so, I need to listen and find them. I can use them for my benefit."

Some of the feedback may not be valid or may not apply to you. It may apply to the person who supplied the feedback; that is, the person may be attributing his or her own faults or feelings to you. Therefore, you must prepare yourself psychologically to receive the information.

Make sure you understand the feedback. Ask questions for understanding, such as: "When does the behavior occur?" "How does it occur?" "What does it do to people?" "What are the implications for me?" Also ask questions to find out the implications of your behavior for others. "Why is my behavior seen as negative by you or others?" "Why do you think I behave as I do in this situation?"

Look at ownership. Is the feedback valid as it pertains to you, or is it someone's projection onto you? Is someone reacting to you because of something which that person owns or which is an attribute of that person? People's perceptions of you can be influenced by your affect as well as your verbal communication. People may react negatively to your mannerisms as well as to what you say. Test this by asking yourself, "What portion of this feedback actually resulted from my behavior'" "Do I behave in this manner?" "What portion of the feedback applies to the other person as well as to me?" "Am I reacting to the person or to the situation and its becoming a reciprocal interaction?" "Does this feedback really apply to the giver because this is his or her behavioral style?"

Now analyze the information you have about ownership and other people's perceptions of you and discuss it. Sift through it. This is where you will throw away the irrelevant data and keep the constructive data. Probe to see if others misinterpreted your behavior. Also, check to see if you were unaware of how your actions impacted people.

You are ready to develop some specific corrective action steps at this point. The feedback may not apply to you, however, and if it is a case of inappropriate data, then correction is unnecessary.

Problem IV: How to recognize hot organizational issues. Problem relates to critical issues 1, 4, 5, 7, 8, 10, 12, 13, 14, 15

Solution: People tend to be successful when they focus on and resolve hot organizational issues. A hot organizational issue is an existing condition that poses a barrier to effective operation and that an organization is willing to put monetary and human resources against to eliminate. The speed at which you gain success is directly proportional to your ability to recognize and resolve hot issues. All organizations have hot issues. These issues are dynamic and may change often. Some examples are: how to increase production, how to increase efficiency, how to reduce operating cost, and how to reduce employee turnover.

List those issues discussed at the highest levels in your organization. Do this by tapping into the informal communications network, for instance, by listening to the bosses at lunch and on breaks and listening carefully to company speeches. List issues by reviewing organizational goals and pulling out the high-priority ones. Ask your boss if you may see the organizational goals for the next year. Extract key messages or issues from various pieces of correspondence. Read memos and letters written by bosses at the highest levels in the organization.

After you list the issues and extract the key messages from the correspondence, you can discuss them with your boss to get his or her input. Also, bounce them off your peers, other supervisors, and your sponsors. Do this to ascertain whether you have chosen the correct issues. Once you feel comfortable with what you think are the hot organizational issues, the next step is to work to resolve them in addition to attending to your normal work tasks.

Problem V: How to take initiative in your job. Problem relates to critical issues 1, 4, 5, 7, 8, 10, 12, 13, 14, 15

Solution: Start by clearly identifying a hot issue or a problem that your boss needs to solve. Subordinates become very valuable to their bosses when they can focus on and solve or help the boss solve some of his or her problems. Make sure the problem is clearly stated.

Develop a very rough plan to resolve the issue or problem. Do this by trying to sense what upper-level managers want in terms of a resolution. Use resources by seeking their advice on the issue or problem and the rough plan you have developed. Allow your ideas and your plan to be shaped by input from others.

Identify the barriers involved in executing your rough plan. Identify the personal risk involved for you. There may not be any risk, or there may be a very low level of risk. Identify any other risks to resolving the issue or problems. Then decide if you are willing to take the risks.

Develop a "battle plan." This is an action plan that you will use to resolve the issue or solve the problem. Plan and organize in order to make a unique contribution to the business.

Then executive your battle plan.

Problem VI: How to acquire a sponsor. Problem relates to critical issues 1, 4, 5, 7, 8, 9, 10, 12, 13, 14, 15

Solution: Sponsors in an organization act as teachers, coaches, and advocates for others who are at lower hierarchical levels in the company. Sponsors give inside information relative to important company norms, share experiences, and tell what to watch out for as well as share information about appropriate and useful organizational behavior. They can also empower you to do certain things, such as asking your boss questions you might otherwise not feel free to ask. Sponsors can be used as both technical and managerial resources. They may, in addition, have an opportunity to speak up for you, recommend you for something, or defend you for some reason.

Basically, there are two ways you can acquire sponsors. One way is to seek them out; the other is to allow them to seek you out. First, let us look at how you can seek a sponsor. Most blacks acquire sponsors by seeking them, because it is not as easy for whites to identify black potential and interest as it is for whites to spot other sharp whites. Look around in your organization and identify those upper-level managers who are movers and shakers and get things done. You may need more than one. They should be at least two to three levels above your level in the hierarchy. Select people who are seen by a large number of people in the organization as sharp and powerful.

The next step is to make contact with the sponsor you have identified. Contact can occur as a result of being in a meeting with the person, hearing a speech by the person, or being in a social setting where you had an opportunity to talk with the person. You can call the potential sponsor's office and ask to meet to further discuss some item of mutual interest. You may have an idea or rough plan worked out that you can share and ask for input on from the potential sponsor. Use the first meeting to assess the potential relationship and begin to develop it. Do this by asking some general questions, such as: What principles are important to success in the organization? You can also ask questions about the event at which you made initial contact with the person.

Do not use the first meeting to ask the person how you can get to the next level, because that may be too forward and presumptuous on your part at such an early stage. First you must develop the person as a sponsor before he or she will give you inside information—such as how to get to the next level. Ask whether the person would be willing to meet with you again. If so, mention what you would like to discuss. For example, you might say, "In the future I would like to discuss with you the principles for successful task execution." Or "How do you properly delegate?" You might also ask, "How do you lead a meeting smoothly?"

At the second meeting, you want to further test the person's willingness to be a sponsor. At the end of this meeting, ask if you can have a monthly meeting to discuss various subjects; have a prepared list you can pull out and show. Throughout the sessions, be sure that you document the learnings, but *do not write down confidential information* or inside information of a sensitive nature. Use your discretion about this, because there may be data your sponsor does not want passed around. However, *do* take notes on such things as the principles of successful task execution.

Continue to meet as long as the meetings are profitable. As you meet, your relationship will grow and the sponsor will begin to take you into his or her confidence and provide you with the assistance you need. Allow your sponsor to get to know you, because this relationship will also be a test for you. The sponsor will test your competence, listen for the logic of your thinking, and test you to see if you can handle confidential information in a professional manner. The sponsor must have enough information about you as an employee and an individual to act as an advocate for you if the need ever arises.

The second way to acquire a sponsor is to be sought out by a person in the hierarchy. This happens less frequently, but it does happen, usually as a result of a presentation or an impressive contribution you made at a meeting, or as a result of a conversation with someone at a social event. If for any reason you are approached by an upper-level manager who strikes up a conversation with you, you need to listen very carefully for the organizational cues or indirect hints and suggestions that indicate the person is willing to work with and develop you. Listen for such things as a suggestion that you drop by sometime or that the two of you continue the discussion at a later date. *Follow up on this.* Call the person's office to set up a meeting and say you would like to follow up on a prior conversation. Allow the potential sponsor to direct the first meeting. Let the sponsor start talking first. Be prepared, however, with a couple of key questions, such as: What are the principles for successful task execution? What are the important goals of the organization?

After the first meeting, review the results. If you are satisfied, then ask for a second meeting. In fact, if you feel satisfied during the course of the first meeting, then ask for a second meeting before you leave. Use the second meeting, as we said before, to further test the willingness of the person to be your sponsor. Make sure you stroke the person and thank him or her for taking time out of a busy schedule to talk to you.

Make sure you understand what sponsorship means. It does *not* mean your sponsors will bypass your hierarchy and completely dismiss your bosses. Nor should you use your sponsors for that purpose. Sponsorship *can* help maximize your potential and offer you a means of public exposure.

Problem VII: How to document and continue to use your personal learnings. Problem relates to critical issues 3, 4, 5, 7, 13, 14

Solution: Document your personal learnings by developing a personal development file. Your personal learnings relate to both the technical and managerial aspects of your job. Documentation is important for the continued use of your learnings.

There are a couple of ways you can conveniently start your file. Purchase an expandable file folder, which should be kept at home, not in the office, because these are personal learnings. Jot down the things you learn and be consistent; use 8½″ × 11″ pieces of paper instead of a lot of scraps. (If you happen to be a paper napkin artist or writer, transfer your notes later to something more readable.) Work out your own filing system, so information is readily available when you need it. We can attest to the extreme annoyance that occurs when you cannot find that important note to yourself right when you need it most.

Another option is to purchase a large notebook and keep sheets of information there. You may want to get sophisticated and index the notebook by technical learnings and managerial learnings. You may choose to break those categories down to suit your own individual needs.

Across the top of each sheet, write the subject of the learning, the date you acquired the information, and the source, which will usually be the name of a person. This is important because when you refer to the learning in the future and it is not clear you can always go back to the source for clarification. Jot down as much information as you need to ensure clarity of understanding for future use. You may wish to include how the learning can be used. Read through the material every two to three months to refresh your memory. You will be surprised at how much useful data you forget when there is a large volume of learnings.

Problem VIII: How to use constructive feedback. Problem relates to critical issues 1, 2, 3, 4, 5, 6, 7, 10, 11, 13, 14

Solution: This problem differs from Problem II in that that problem dealt specifically with style development. This solution is geared more to general feedback, because feedback also covers such issues as task execution and decision making.

First, always be clear about the feedback. Ask questions for understanding and try not to be defensive or reactive. Remember to test the feedback for racist and sexist content and to use your resources, peers, friends, and spouse to help you. Sometimes we are too close to the information to see it clearly. Ask yourself and others what would happen to a white manager in similar circumstances: Would the feedback and the data be the same? Are there extenuating circumstances surrounding the data?

After exploring the feedback, develop a rough plan to make changes in your behavior if the feedback is legitimate and genuine. Again, use a resource to test and refine your plan. The most important thing to do in using your corrective plan is to employ a behavioral change model; that is, alter your behavior while working on your attitude. To facilitate this whole process, say to yourself, "I did this thing the way I did because this is a new situation for me, and I have not had the opportunity to learn how to act appropriately or correctly." This is a *positive* learning model. Do this instead of saying, "I did not know how to proceed because there is a hole in my educational background." This is a *negative* learning model, and this model is used too often by blacks. Sometimes white managers will inadvertently cause blacks to use this negative model. When that happens, it merely raises the black manager's stress level and anxiety unnecessarily. As a result it makes the black manager less open to receiving and using constructive feedback.

In sum, using constructive feedback ceases to be a problem when you are able to listen without reacting, probe the data, check its validity with resources, develop a plan of correction if needed, change the behavior, adopt a positive learning attitude, and lastly practice.

Problem IX: How to present ideas to your boss. Problem relates to critical issues 1, 4, 5, 8, 10, 12, 13, 14

Solution: In the Adjusting Phase, we offered a rather detailed solution to how to *sell* ideas to your boss. This solution will speak to how to *present* ideas to your boss. The difference here is that we are talking to individuals who are in the Planned Growth Phase, and presenting ideas is best done by people who are about to step over into the Success Phase. The ideas we are referring to here are more conceptual than those in the Adjusting Phase and border on new developments or new directions. They are more risky or radical and may deviate from the norms of the organization. These are also ideas that you need to get your boss's endorsement on before proceeding to develop them further.

You should present the idea to your boss in the very early stages of its formulation, before you use other resources. Rough out your ideas and put them in a tight format. Place the words "Blue Sky Thinking" at the top and bottom of each sheet. This will signal to your boss that this is a very rough idea and you are using the boss as a resource to help further develop it with thoughts, comments, and reactions. Ask your boss to give you the names of other resources to consult on the idea.

Problem X: How to discuss racial incidents and the effects of race on an issue or situation with whites. Problem relates to critical issues 1, 2, 4, 6, 7, 8, 10, 11, 12, 13, 14

Solution: This is an important issue to deal with because most blacks sooner or later will encounter a work situation where race will affect the dynamics. At best, this is a difficult problem for both blacks and whites to deal with because there is normally some confrontation associated with the resolution of the problem. Racial prejudice is a sensitive subject, packed with emotion, threat, guilt, power, and so forth.

When talking about racial incidents with whites or the effects of race on an issue, the important thing to keep in mind is that people behave on the basis of their perceptions of the world. These perceptions may or may not be correct; that should *never* be the issue, since it leads down a one-way street going nowhere. It also diverts attention away from dealing with the issue at hand. That kind of discussion of right or wrong perceptions is best left for parlor room debates. Whatever the perception, the person's viewpoint and behavior will be affected by it.

When you discuss racial incidents in the work place, stick as much as possible to the facts as you perceive them. For example, you are trying to accomplish a task and you have to work with a person who is displaying racist behavior toward you. It has gotten in the way of performing the task, and you need to discuss this with your boss. Open the session by clearly stating what you want from the boss. He or she needs to know if you want to be merely listened to or if you are asking for some action to be taken. Describe the incident as factually as possible. Then tell your boss the effect it has on you. If your boss reacts negatively to you, for whatever reason, say that you are not dealing with the boss's perception of what happened or how the boss perceives or interacts with the other person, but rather with how *you* see the situation and how it makes you feel. The least your boss can do is respect your different view of what occurred. The boss may not have noticed the other person interacting in an interracial situation.

If the discussion comes to a confrontation, and the boss attempts to shut you down, then you should relax and let the boss blow off steam. *Do not* allow yourself to become intimidated or to react hostilely to the boss. This can be accomplished by not responding when the boss blows off steam. When he or she has finished, look the person in the eye and ask, "Can you share with me why this makes you angry?" This simple question offers the boss an opportunity to share discomforts and feelings about the situation and, once these are dealt with, the boss is freed up to help you with your problem.

If the problem you are experiencing is deep, complex, or extremely upsetting, you may not be able to help the boss face his or her difficulties with the racial content of the situation. If this is the case and you need immediate assistance, you may prefer to say to the boss, "I don't know why *you're* upset, but let me tell you again what the situation did to me and how it is interfering with my accomplishing my job." Then repeat the incident. Give the boss another chance to deal with the problem, because it *is* a legitimate employee need.

The next thing to happen, in most cases, is the white boss will feel a need to take care of the problem and will become alarmed. Let the boss know you would first like to discuss what needs to be done. Maybe you as a black can handle the situation better than the boss can. Perhaps you do not want the boss to do anything except listen and be apprised of what is going on. You may need the boss to help you resolve the issue or to sanction some strategy you have developed. However, remember to state this before the conversation begins.

BASIC CONCEPTS USED IN HOW-TO SOLUTIONS

Many of the concepts used in the how-to solutions of the Planned Growth Phase and the Success Phase are concepts previously discussed in the Entry Phase and Adjusting Phase. In the Planned Growth and Success Phases, blacks learn to use these concepts in conjunction with others to broaden their ability to solve problems. For this reason, fewer new concepts are needed to formulate solutions. For example, in Problem I of the Planned Growth Phase— how to manage conflict—the concepts used were confrontation and sharing your feelings from the Entry Phase in addition to dealing with the need and a broader application of compromising from the Adjusting Phase.

The concepts discussed in the Planned Growth and Success Phases will be new concepts not previously discussed. As you read the solutions in the how-to sections, you will be aware of the varied uses of the concepts. At some later time, you may find it interesting and helpful to go back to these how-to sections and see how many concepts you can find in each solution.

Problem II: How to develop a smoother style of interacting.

Concept 1: Role Modeling is the idea of selecting a *specific* behavioral skill, characteristic, or quality that you admire in a person and want to acquire. You may find many different people, regardless of race or gender, with some one quality or skill you would like to possess. It is extremely rare that one person will embody all the traits and skills you are looking for. This concept is very important to blacks. Use of role modeling can free you from the fear, intimidation, anxiety, and stress that occurs when you want to do something but prevent yourself from doing it. If you can handle the situation the way you have seen another person do it, then it frees you from your inhibitions.

Concept 2: Role Playing provides you with the important step of practicing the behavior you hope to acquire. This can be done in private or in front of someone you trust. Role playing is based on the same principle you used as a child when you played mama, papa, teacher, or cowboy to practice the grown-up behavior of the adults around you. It was preliminary then for your taking a place in the adult world; role playing can be preliminary now for more effective performance as a manager.

Problem III: How to probe negative feedback.

Concept: The concept used here is *Probing.* It directs you to explore and thoroughly examine information for clarity and understanding and to extract additional information.

Problem IV: How to recognize hot organizational issues.

Concept: Assessing the Organization is the new concept used here. It means that you need to look at the organization and pull out the most important problems and issues that the company is wrestling with at the time. As a black you need to be aware of the importance of doing something in the organization that will place you in a position to make a unique contribution. The easiest way to do this is to deal with a hot issue. Resolving problematic issues for the organization will definitely set you apart from your peers and create the exposure you need to get ahead.

Problem V: How to take initiative in your job.

Concept: The concept in this solution conjures up images of generals poring over maps and plotting strategies because this concept is called Battle Planning. This is an action-oriented concept in that it is used to solve hot organizational issues and implies that you will have to battle with some existing norms and perhaps some people in the organization. Strategy is used in close conjunction with battle planning.

Problem VI: How to acquire a sponsor.

Concept 1: We call this concept simply Seizing an Opportunity. But using it is not necessarily simple. You will have to take what may appear to be a casually made comment and recognize in it an opportunity to acquire something you need or want—in this particular case, a sponsor. Blacks need to be especially aware of casually dropped suggestions, hints, or other information. When you feel there is something you can use to your benefit, then follow it through. It may lead to an opportunity for both you and the organization.

Concept 2: This one is called Testing. It is used often by blacks in a variety of situations and can be found in many of the solutions throughout the phases. Testing is used in any situation where there is a lack of clarity about where people are on issues or needs. It is a way to ascertain whether the assumptions you are making are correct. In the case of acquiring sponsors, you need to test for sincerity by the second meeting. Making and acting on assumptions can be detrimental to the survival and success of blacks in an organization. Therefore, testing becomes a critical action step for blacks.

Problem VII: How to document and continue to use your personal learnings.

Concept: Jotting It Down is one of the best habits to acquire and one of the most widely and consistently used concepts. Very simply it refers to the old cliché "A short pencil is better than a long memory." When you jot things down, you capture the essence of your learning for future use and it is always at your disposal.

Problem VIII: How to use constructive feedback.

Concept: Since we could not think of anything catchy to name this concept, we thought a straightforward title would do: so we call this Positive Is Better than Negative. This concept means what it says, that when you are in a situation where you must evaluate yourself it is much better to *choose* a positive viewpoint than a negative one. All situations can have a negative aspect and a positive aspect; we have control over which we choose to focus on. When we choose to indulge ourselves in the negative viewpoint, we inhibit our growth. When we choose to view things from a positive viewpoint, we are more open to input, change, rapid growth, and development.

Problem IX: How to present ideas to your boss.

Concept: This concept has a rather romantic title, Blue Sky

Thinking, but it has serious content. Blue sky thinking is a non-threatening way to introduce new and innovative ideas into the organization that may not be very receptive to creative change. It is safer because it is low risk. By using it you get your idea sanctioned or disapproved by your organization early on. You may still go forward with your plan regardless of your boss's reaction, but at least you will know where you stand and what you are up against.

Problem X: How to discuss racial incidents and the effects of race on an issue or situation with whites.

Concept: This concept is called the No-Response Response. This may sound like double-talk, but it is a very useful concept. Many times we use it without realizing that we have done so. A no-response response is simply refusing to acknowledge some dysfunctional comments or behavior. For example, we may tell our children when teasing starts, "Just ignore it," or "Do not respond." The other person will be forced to cease the unwanted comments or behavior. This works well when adults temporarily lose control. Fuel is not added to the emotional fire by responding and giving a person additional cause to continue the unwanted interaction. This concept can be used to stop many unnecessary arguments before they begin. It does, however, take emotional control on your part to successfully use this concept.

Summary of Basic Concepts

Here are brief definitions of the basic concepts used in the Planned Growth Phase how-to solutions for your reference.

1. *Role Modeling* is selecting a specific behavioral skill or characteristic that you would like to acquire from the total behavioral pattern of a person.
2. *Role Playing* is the practicing of the selected specific behavioral skill or characteristic.
3. *Probing* means exploring and examining information in depth.
4. *Assessing the Organization* refers to identifying the most problematic issues of the company in order to seek resolution of those hot issues.
5. *Battle Planning* is an action-oriented strategy used to approach hot issues or other difficult problem-solving tasks.
6. *Seizing an Opportunity* is taking advantage of any chance,

however, casual, that comes your way to make a unique contribution to your job.

7. *Testing* refers to scrutinizing persons or situations until your assumptions are proven correct or incorrect.

8. *Jotting It Down* means capturing the essence of your learnings on paper for future reference rather than trusting data to memory.

9. *Positive Is Better than Negative* means just what it states. It is often more useful for you to focus on the positive aspects of a situation rather than the negative.

10. *Blue Sky Thinking* refers to a low-risk way of introducing new creative ideas into an organization that may be resistant to innovative change.

11. *No-Response Response* is refusing to react in any way to the dysfunctional comments or behavior of another person in order to reduce or stop the interaction.

5

Success Phase

CRITICAL ISSUES

Attitudes

1. Accepting the additional burdens of a supervisory manager or first promotion
2. Realizing making mistakes or failing is not an option
3. Using protective hesitation as a strategy
4. Being aware of one's own blackness and its impact on an organization and various situations
5. Continuing awareness of how subtle prejudice operates
6. Being more sensitive to the work environment
7. Seeking fewer strokes; being results oriented

Emotions

8. Sublimating emotions
9. Feeling high confidence

Behaviors

10. Using communications networks effectively (formal and informal)
11. Continuing to refine and smooth personal style
12. Confronting whites in a way that leaves them their dignity
13. Continuing to set and meet goals
14. Producing high-quality results
15. Displaying a success affect

Job Skills

16. Using higher interpersonal and behavioral skills
17. Using skills to resist power
18. Continuing to develop multicultural management skills

ANALYZING THE CRITICAL ISSUES

The criteria for determining success vary among individuals. We will be discussing the Success Phase from the standpoint of a promotion; therefore, if you have different success indicators in your organization, you will need to make that translation in your mind as you read this chapter.

Let us reiterate; in the Success Phase, black managers reach a plateau that is the culmination of all the learnings and experiences from the Entry Phase through the Planned Growth Phase. This becomes a cycle that begins again with each major job change throughout the career life of a black manager. Each time the growth pattern is repeated, it should take a shorter time to complete, and the learnings will be more sophisticated. Black managers become successful when they adopt productive attitudes about the job, learn to properly use and control emotions, display more than adequate job behavior, and learn the appropriate job skills during the Entry through Success Phases.

Attitudes

Black managers who become successful are aware of additional burdens that their white peers do not have to contend with. Moving up in the white corporation, some blacks become concerned over how they are viewed by others of their cultural group. They fear that they may be seen as part of the establishment, having deserted the brotherhood or sisterhood. This is especially true in situations where a black is the first black to be promoted or if there are only a few blacks represented in the hierarchy.

There is also the added burden of feeling responsible and obligated.to other blacks in subordinate positions. Some blacks attempt to help pave a way for those other blacks who aspire to move up in the organization; this draws extra time and energy from the successful black manager. While some whites may also want to help blacks move up, a major difference is that a black manager feels a responsibility and an obligation to ensure that the black subordinate succeeds. If the subordinate fails the successful manager usually has some feeling that he or she has also failed. This is especially true when there are few blacks in the organization. The success of one black (regardless of level) has a carry-over effect to other blacks. Conversely, and even more significant, the failure of one casts a stigma on all. If successful managers ignore their cultural group, they often feel guilty that they have not paid their dues, that is, turned back to some other black the opportunity and personal help to also become successful.

"I spend time talking with blacks about the management role I play and what it's like so I won't be out there alone. I am careful not to get on an ego trip and lose touch with reality."

"I avoid being too much 'in' with white peers. I maintain some closeness with blacks and some distance from whites so as not to be socialized too much."

"Being way up in the hierarchy is a lonely place to be. I think about it a lot. It's a strange existence."

"As you are promoted, you advance deeper into an all-white environment. There are fewer black peers and different interactions—it creates internal stress."

"Upper-level black managers are in a bind from having to give training to other blacks. You must never be on a fence about anything. I must make the brotherhood feel I'm a part of it, tell the brothers what I've done, but mostly keep in contact."

"I spend time talking to most blacks, especially the new ones. I spend extra energy and effort to keep in touch with other blacks; I try to keep pulling other blacks along and pushing those above me. I feel the lowest black is me."

"I feel obligated to spend time justifying myself to other blacks, mainly at the lower level, to dispel the thought that as blacks move up, they collude with whites and lose sight of their blackness and the problems blacks have because they have a little bit of power."

"You're always being expected to work people problems.

*I've gotten some criticism from my boss's boss for not shar-
ing my black–white interpersonal skills with my organization."*

*"I have to spend extra time and energy doing black–white
activities that whites don't have to do, and I don't get any
reward for it."*

One of the most important attitudes of the black manager in the
Success Phase is the knowledge that making mistakes or failing is
not an option. With every failure, blacks know they reinforce the
expectations of some whites. When a white male manager fails, he
fails himself. "He couldn't cut the mustard," it is said. When a
black manager fails, he or she fails for the group.

*"A white manager found a couple of holes in my presenta-
tion, so now I make sure there are no mistakes in my work."*

*"Blacks feel under a microscope and can't afford to make
too many mistakes because we will feed into whites' negative stereotypes."*

An attitudinal result of the desire not to fail is the development
of protective hesitation as a strategy. Successful black managers
tend to accept this attitude as a way of life in the white organization. They remain cautious in interactions with whites, prethinking before speaking or making a move. Smart successful black
managers have by this time learned that openness in a white organization is a luxury afforded only to whites by whites. They are
cautious about identifying and using resources. Preplanning is
now a normal part of the protective hesitation process and just
doing the job.

*"You cannot be open with whites. You cannot say, 'I would
like that job a level above mine.' Rather, you must say you
want to learn—using terms that apply to all the attributes of
that job level."*

"I give a lot of careful thought before I make any input."

In the Success Phase, most black managers realize that their
success is in part a result of their being constantly aware of their
blackness and how this impacts the white corporation; that is,
they know their success depends on their remembering who they
are and how they are seen by the organization. Therefore, black

managers must have a good understanding of how their blackness impacts the people and the relationships in the corporation. It is not too strong a statement to say that to forget these factors is tantamount to a *loss of survival instincts.* Black managers who forget may find it quite easy to be brushed aside and forgotten.

In the Success Phase, black managers know they must be aware of the prejudiced behavior around them and have peripheral vision in interactions with others. In other words, they must continue to be sensitive to the many cues in the environment but not respond to them all; however, they must be able to respond to those that may threaten survival or that may offer an opportunity for growth.

Successful black managers have more positive attitudes toward themselves. Blacks in this phase can look outward at the events that happen instead of turning inward and perceiving failure. They can make the system own more of the failures while they own fewer. By now, blacks seek fewer strokes from other people or the organization. Since they have become more results oriented, the strokes come from within by knowing that a job has been particularly well done.

> "I'm not dependent on organizational rewards or strokes, because they are few and far between; so I make my own."

> "Sometimes, the way whites tell you you've done a good job, it's two days later before you figure out you got a compliment. I don't depend on that kind of begrudging reward any more. I know when I've done an outstanding job."

> "I know my job better than most. When I finish a job, I don't give a darn what whites say. The result shows for itself."

Emotions

By the end of the Planned Growth Phase, black managers have learned to sublimate their emotions. Anger and rage have been made to work as part of the overall acquired strategic skills. These feelings get channeled into something that helps produce better results; managers do not allow emotional displays to present barriers to productivity.

Behaviors

As black managers move up the hierarchical ladder, they have more and more access to both the formal and informal communications networks. Since they know by now how important those networks are, there is little hesitation in tapping them, even when the source is obviously discriminatory.

"I take what I can even though I know blacks aren't privy to the real in-depth, inside info which equips many whites for progress."

"To reverse black exclusion from the communications network, I seldom pass up a chance to eat lunch with whites or stop with them for a drink on the way home. It's my chance to penetrate their data."

"Even though I keep my ears open, I find we still don't get information until something is almost at hand, and that kind of exclusion keeps us always in a one-down position from our white peers."

As black managers reach the Success Phase, they have generally smoothed their problematic personal style. Development of personal style continues as the environment helps shape that style. They discard behavior that proves dysfunctional and develop behavior that works well. The real crux of the shaping of personal style is that black managers find they must use more influential behavior than their white peers do. In working with whites, they have at their disposal more charismatic power than real power recognized by the organization, no matter what hierarchical level they occupy. As part of that developing style and use of influential behavior, black managers in the Success Phase have learned to confront whites in a way that does not strip them of their dignity. The dangers of hard confrontation have all too often become apparent in the face of illogical responses from whites and the prevention of closure on issues.

Black managers continue to set and meet goals. Their focus is on high-quality results. Black managers in the Success Phase behave in a manner that conveys confidence, knowledge, and the appearance of being in charge. They have now forged a track record. They have produced outstanding results and gained respect from others. However, blacks also know that to keep that record they will have to prove their competence again and again.

"The company moves cautiously with everyone, but with blacks they have to be sure."

"You find yourself having to establish credibility each time you shift jobs."

"Blacks get tested over and over on each job, often having to spend extra time sorting out the racial pieces, then figuring out what to do about it."

Job Skills

Everything has become important to the black manager in the Success Phase—dress, style, and timing. Blacks see themselves as having to develop a higher level of interpersonal and behavioral skills than white males do. As we have said, the corporation will allow whites, as part of the normal corporate system, more latitude to be dysfunctional than blacks, who are a relatively new entity in the system. Overall, strategy is a very important component of success to blacks in the utilization of their job skills. All of this is important because external forces work on black managers but not on whites, to reduce their impact on the system.

"You have to know about the interpersonal–behavioral aspects of working with people just to survive as a black, and you must understand it to succeed. You have to be strategic."

"Strategy and high visibility are what count. Whatever I get from the organization in terms of a reward won't be because it was right for me to get it but will be because I helped whites to see that I deserved to be rewarded."

"You have to strategize around everything, do more of everything, and be darn sure about how you as a black are coming across. Whites have negative stereotypes about blacks that they may consider to be positive in other whites."

"No matter what level you are on in the hierarchy, blacks are faced with not having their input accepted by whites. And you'd better have your interpersonal skills together, because blacks are always having to use whites to get things done. Whites can have potential and make mistakes, but blacks have to prove everything and can't make mistakes. You'd better learn to strategize well too, because blacks have to do a lot more of it than whites to get to the same place."

To become successful, black managers have to learn how to resist power under some circumstances. This is necessary to offset the slave–master relationship that can potentially build in a white boss–black subordinate relationship.

"White people in organizations seem to be comfortable in allowing power to be used on them. As a black individual, I didn't like it. I didn't like it because I didn't know if power was used on me because I was black and seen as less than or because I was just another person in the organization."

"I got to the point where I automatically reacted every time I felt power was being used on me by a white manager."

"Blacks have no other choice but to challenge the boss, because things that are effective for whites are not necessarily effective for blacks. If a black has to go away and do exactly as the boss told him to do, a lose–lose situation sometimes results, especially when the black person's experience tells him to do something different. Whites very often do what the boss wants them to do. Whites are very hierarchically oriented; they can feel the pressure of power very easily."

"I challenge the boss and have no fear because I'll give him three options: (1) I'll go home, (2) he can send me home, or (3) I'll go back to work. Most whites tend to compromise because they're the bosses. What whites don't understand is that, even though they are boss, what you are really challenging is not them and their ability to reason, but instead you are challenging whether or not we have looked at all the data and options. Whites tend to get tunnel vision."

"Blacks will challenge the boss; whites tend not to. Blacks will react to power, not being able to separate the boss's directions from his racism, and will act in a strong independent manner to show what they can do."

Now let us return to Jack's story.

"I DID IT, DIDN'T I?"

I'm sorry; that was my wife. She said she was running a little late; it'll be another hour before she arrives home from the city. We should be finished by then, don't you think?

Now, where were we? Oh yeah. It's kind of hard to say just when I went into the next phase. There's really no clean cutoff and start-up point for any of this. There are a lot of indications that you're operating differently and that past behavior is refined, that you're handling things with more proficiency and without a lot of conscious thought. When you know you're operating at a different and higher level, that's when you know you've moved on to another phase in your development.

It's like I told you before; I was doing my thing, learning fast, everything was exciting, challenging. I was learning rapidly—got to apply a lot of techniques, made some mistakes, slipped a little, uh . . . had to go back and refine some more of the things I was doing.

I didn't realize it at the time, but as I became more refined at managing, the racism got more subtle. Before, people would openly challenge me. Now they challenge in more subtle ways.

Like what? OK! I put together a program whereby the black and white managers had an opportunity to have open dialogue between them, get their problems out on the table, and work to iron them out—you know, the difficulties they encountered in working in a multicultural environment. One white upper-level manager wanted to know, "How do you know your program is going to work? People can't just sit and talk about those issues. They're not going to learn anything."

It was a direct challenge. OK? The unspoken message was, "You don't know what the hell you're talking about, nigger!" That's one example!

Another thing people would do—instead of asking you questions, they'd just take an opposite viewpoint. "You can't do it like that; you have to do it like this!" In meetings, for instance, people would openly challenge you by simply saying, "I don't believe that." I'd make a statement, and they'd say, "I don't believe that!"

After I had established a successful track record, then . . . then when I rolled out creative things like my program, people didn't say, "Prove to me it'll work." They'd say, "How are we going to implement it? How will it work?" Not, *if* it'll work—and that's a more subtle difference.

As my public track record got better and better, they'd say, "Yeah, I hear what you're saying. I'm not sure that will work." See the difference? There was still negative prejudice operating, but it had become more subtle. The message was still, "I don't think you know what you're talking about, nigger," but it was said politely.

"Man, I'm not readin' nothing into nothing. Hear me out. Let me run it down to you. I had to strategize and outthink a lot of people in the hierarchy to get my program over. I knew it was good. I had a lot of support from the ranks. People were begging me to help them with a lot of issues they were dealing with. I'll tell you what happened, and you tell me if I'm seeing something that wasn't there.

When my people had workshops, one upper-level boss in another department of the company wouldn't let me give workshops in his area because he figured the stuff wasn't going to work. But as soon as we started to develop a track record—as soon as I pulled together a small bunch of other upper-level managers who had tried the program and results were shared—then this guy wanted to jump on the bandwagon.

Oh, yeah! We had a lot of managers who were reluctant to attend the workshops. I sensed it, sensed an undercurrent of negatism. OK? Again, a lot of the negatism was racially based stuff that was subtle. But by now I had my act together, so I decided to take the initiative and seize upon an opportunity, so to speak.

What I did was to put on a half-day session for upper-level managers using my consulting team to discuss our program. I used both black and white consultants, and everybody had a story to tell. So we told what we had done, how we had done it, and what the results were—how we, uh . . . how we used questionnaires, which were completed before and after the workshops. And it was in company language and terms, presented in a way the upper-level managers could understand. They didn't realize that we were evaluating and documenting what we had done—keeping track of results, assessing the value to the company and in terms used by the company—*and it blew their minds!*

So at that point, they all wanted to jump on the bandwagon because they had visual proof that there were a lot of positive results. There was nothing I did or said that had made any difference before this. There had been just a few white upper-level managers who had believed I could deliver the right results. The rest couldn't believe a black manager had the potential to handle such a large project before they could see it.

Oh, in terms of how I felt about it . . . I felt damned good about it, because I felt I'd had a gem of an idea. I used my creativity, I planned, I organized, and I implemented something—and got outstanding results. That turned me on; the more I got, the more I wanted!

See, in the last phase I was telling you about, it was like being on a roller coaster. You'd be up some days, and you'd be down some days when you didn't do things right and people were telling you that you had screwed something up. It was up and down.

Whereas now it felt more like a steady climb. I'd go up, and things wouldn't drop out from under me as before. You have some plateaus, where you'll flatten out. You'll go up again—but you won't drop.

You know? During this time when you experience success, if you don't have a continuous challenge, you feel, uh . . . like—blah! It's because you've been running and charging hard, and then you have to slow down or stop.

So, I guess one of the effects of being successful on most black managers is it will cause you to ask for more responsibility.

Yeah, that's what I did! I asked for more work and was given some additional personnel programs along with the people who administered the programs. Oh! Well, that meant I got a promotion. I got a title that I had deserved, which essentially—well, uh . . . I had been working with these people in the background anyway, even though they didn't report to me.

Sooo, it's as though I had already been operating at that level long before I got the title and official responsibility. I'd been managing a budget and doing some other tasks.

You know what? It got so bad, people would come up and ask me, "Well, when are they going to promote you? You're already operating at the next level." Yeah, man! Even some of the secretaries said that; they could clearly see it.

You know, it finally dawned on me that organizations make blacks operate at the next level before they sanction it—and they do this to protect themselves. That way they can ensure that they don't have any blacks who will fail.

What it did was to make me angry; I was very angry over it. It was a different kind of anger from what I had experienced before. I could see my results and successes and . . . and I was angry because I didn't get rewards for my work.

But I sublimated that anger and used the energy instead to position the organization so it became embarrassing to them to not give me a reward. How? By getting unique results. Outstandingly unique results, such that nobody could deny that they were outstandingly unique results.

Since I had done that several times, the company had to do something to show they recognized my outstanding contribution—more money, a title, a promotion, or something! You almost have to force organizations to see your results! You have to strategize because your results can easily get dismissed, or the organization might not attribute a . . . uh, lot of expertise to the obtaining of the results.

You—you have to show the results in a dramatic way, so that it's undeniable that you got *good, unique, outstanding* results. You've got to strategize about who you're going to show the results to or how to position people so they can see the results.

That's what I did when I had the half-day session for the upper-level managers. And the most important thing I did was that—that *I* didn't put the results in front of them, other people did. The experts. And some of them were white. You had whites listening to whites about something that I was responsible for. See, I didn't blow my own horn; other people did. So anyway, I got some people working for me and a title, and . . . and the thing that really bothered me was the first day I had to look at a subordinate's salary and give input on how much I—I thought the person should get. And it hit me all of a sudden that here I was in a proper position, that I could dictate somebody's life-style.

I guess what ran through my mind was, "Does this mean that I am now on the other end of the stick—the power stick?"

See, at one time I was on the receiving end. And I'm now on the giving end! So the first thing that hit me as a black was, "Oh, my God! Am I leaving a group?" It was a strange feeling. Like, am I leaving one group—familiar, comfortable—and going to another group—alien?

I guess that was the beginning of my, uh . . . uh being stressful around, "Are you giving up your blackness? Have you now been absorbed by the system?" I really had to think through and deal with that.

The same thing happened when it came time for me to evaluate a person. The first thing that hit me was, "Wait a minute, am I going to be guilty of doing the same to other managers that I felt was done to me?" That was a struggle.

I had to think that through, too, and just deal with it. Do you understand? All of a sudden you're a supervising manager, and what does that mean to a black? Have you been absorbed by the white system? Or does it mean you're still black, or—or? You have to think it through. That's a confusing feeling even though you feel good about the results you've gotten and proud of your successes.

OK, now where was I in terms of all of this? I had people working for me and a wider span of control. That had an effect on me because, even though I had gone through this last structured growth period, now what I did was to reach back in my mind and implement more of the things I had learned to do in terms of effective managing because I now had more latitude to do it.

For example, now I had to think about subordinates, their evaluations, about, uh . . . their pay, about vacations—uh, planning, organizing, coordinating! What it meant was that I had to do a better job of using whites as resources.

Some of them kind of reacted to my getting promoted. What do I mean? "Well, it was confusing to some of them and a little threatening, because now I had more power in the organization. Some couldn't figure out how I got promoted.

The only answer I've got is that it was their racism. I don't know. Well, it may not make sense, but—let's see. How can I explain? Let me see if I can put it in words. Let me go back and see if I can put the *feelings* in words.

When I got promoted, a strange thing happened. People would step back and let me walk through the door first. They would hold the door for me. Sometimes on the elevators, they would step out and hold the door for me to come in and then they would reenter—whereas before they wouldn't do any of these things. It was strange to me as a black to have whites do that.

It was just . . . a funny feeling. I guess what it was related to was the fact that, uh, growing up, I'd never seen blacks in a power position before. That was a new phenomenon to me.

You see, it's as though you stop long enough to catch your breath and say, "I really do have it made this time. I didn't when I came in—but I do now—because the people are showing respect for me—like opening doors and letting me pass first and so forth." *That felt good!* Man, oh, man!

But then—you—you get hit again with the day-to-day negative prejudiced behavior of people.

For example, if you've got white subordinates and black subordinates, you've got to treat them differently. You can't manage them the same way. A white manager has to consider a person's blackness because it is part of the person and must be responded to. Most white managers say, "I treat all people the same." And they work hard to do it, too. But all people aren't the same, you know. People are different—they have different needs which must be responded to differently.

What the white subordinates will do is to immediately challenge you. Their whole behavioral pattern is one of "I know I'm smarter than you, and I'm not going to do what you tell me." Your immediate reaction is to get angry and say, "Damn, you can't act that way with me because I'm your boss." But then you don't quite know how to deal with their attitudes. You know what's behind it.

Oh no, man! Don't just take my word for it. Let me tell you just one of a lot of little incidents. I know you're gonna smile, but this really happened to me. Not that long after I'd been promoted.

I had this white subordinate who had worked for me for just two days. So he came in and told me, "I don't like that picture behind your desk. It looks depressing, and I don't see how I can be comfortable trying to have a discussion with you while looking at that." OK?

What I did was to look at him and . . . you know, I kind of shrugged my shoulders and went on and worked our meeting agenda. At that point, I knew he was trying to pick a fight with me—he *had* to take me on in a fight because he was white and he's supposed to be smarter and quicker than me, and he had to see if he could win. Except, I didn't fight him. I went on and worked our agenda.

Then when I finished the agenda, I went back to his first issue and said, "Now let's work—let's deal with your response about my picture."

I said, "This is my damn office, and I will decorate it the way I want to. If the picture is too depressing for you, then I guess you'll have to look in another direction or place your chair where you can't see it." I said, "Why did you feel the need to tell me that?"

He said, "Well, I thought maybe you'd want to know, because you might want to change the picture."

I said, "Hell, no! I'm not going to change my picture. I like it. That's why I put it there in the first place." What he made me do was verbally smack him, and when I finished he couldn't wait to get out of the room.

I've had more bizarre incidents than that happen, and most of my black friends have, too. What I'm trying to tell you is black managers get tested by *everybody*. Not just those above them in the hierarchy, but subordinates, peers . . . [sigh].

OK! OK! I'll give you another example! One of the white managers working with me was responsible for setting up programs to meet the different needs of women in the company. And he set up a group of managers to just . . . kind of be a resource to him. And he tried to keep me out of it. Yet he had some white outside consultants sitting in on the group. And I blew up at him! Because I asked him, "How can you *not* have me in this group?

See, all along the guy had been potshotting at me anyway because I was getting noticeable results with my programs and he wasn't. I'd been telling my boss that he'd been taking constant shots at me, and my boss in essence didn't really do anything about it because he'd never seen the guy do any of that.

Finally this one day, we were *all* in a meeting together when the guy, with his outside consultants . . . well, he tried to push my button—you know, get me upset about an issue. I'd made a statement and he looked at me and said, "Well, Jack, you're acting just like a *white* manager would act."

I didn't respond. Finally I said, "Well, Robert, I'm sorry you feel that way."

Then he made another statement, and since I didn't react to that one either, he just *blew up!* He just—he looked like—in fact, he got almost irrational, and then he realized that he was getting irrational and I was sitting there calmly with my legs crossed. Then he looked around and stopped. But then it was too late; the others had seen it.

So, I've had white managers question the results that I got in terms of how important they are.

Why was my input important to Robert's piece of work? Because I'm a minority, I'd gone through a lot of learnings regarding black–white issues, and some of the principles involved are the same. Plus there were no other inside blacks on his committee. I wanted to be sure there was fair consideration for *all* the minorities.

During this time, I was busy tightening up my programs. And I was also attending a lot of outside management programs because what I discovered was, by going outside, I could get a lot of things I couldn't get from people inside.

I'd come back and use some of the techniques, and I could . . . I really had to be aware of the effect my own blackness had on the situation, because I'd roll some things out to people, like "time management," and talk about how I had my office structured and organized, and whites would look at that information and get very threatened by it.

Why? Because many of them had been around for years and hadn't tried a lot of stuff—but I did. New rookie on the block!! That's—that's how they looked at me, new rookie on the block. I didn't have their years of experience, and they figured I *must* be doing *something* wrong.

Oh sure! The same can happen and does to whites—but with the same degree of resentment? Tell me—whites can get help from other whites and that explains stuff, but how did that nigger get so smart? He's got to be doing something wrong.

Sure, they did have the same opportunity I had to learn and use the material. The difference is, I went out seeking information—they weren't seeking. Maybe they didn't feel the same need I had to get outstanding results or feel the same pressures to do a superior job so that the organization would notice me and see I was a good manager.

So, I guess what I'm saying is, as a black during this time, I had a strong need to ensure that whatever I did would be successful. I did not feel that failure was an option with me in anything I attempted—which meant I had to go out and get as much managerial knowledge as possible.

No way was this self-imposed pressure. Look at the situation in context. I was promoted and inserted into a white peer group—and with some of the new techniques I'd learned, because I needed them to help offset organizational racism, my white peers would look at that and get upset by it.

See, what all this would do is make them tighten up their game, because they knew they were going to be evaulated along with me and— initially, they'd look at me and make comments and behave in such a way as to say,"Well, I know I'm sharper than you, and I've got more experience; I'm white and you're black, and blah, blah, blah!"

But then I continued to get unique results that they were not getting, and they let me know in many subtle ways that they didn't like it *one bit!*

Most of the white managers did tighten up their game, and some of the managers started to use me as a resource instead of always the other way around. So . . . as you see, the more success I got, the more subtle people's negative behavior toward me became.

You know what? One of my peers went to my boss and said that I had a problem with another individual and that I needed his—my white peer's— help. So I sat down with my boss and I said, "Look, did you ask my white peer why he didn't come directly to me?"

My boss said, "No! But I'll go back and ask." So he did, and what he found out was that my white peer said he didn't come directly to me because he didn't think I would listen. He thought I would get upset.

To me that was racism. So my boss quite rightly told my peer, "Well, you go directly to Jack and work that out with him. Don't work it through me." And until this day, I still haven't heard from this guy.

So I went off and took care of the problem by myself. These kinds of things often happened.

Another thing . . . whites would go to my boss and say they had a problem with me. They'd say, uh, I was interacting with them in a way that they couldn't handle. In some cases, I had to confront my white peers as well as whites above and below me. But now I had to do it in a way so that they remained functional, and not be dysfunctional.

The key to me was to take their information and get them to look at it instead of handing out a lecture which they wouldn't have listened to anyway.

One afternoon, I was working with this white subordinate on goals and objectives and setting priorities when the subordinate got dysfunctional and in essence said that I didn't understand the situation and this wasn't the way he was going to do it and so forth and so on.

So I made an agreement with him. I said, "I tell you what, for the next two weeks you don't have to meet with me and I won't tell you anything. I won't give you any direction." At that point, I got a little angry and was *determined* not to interfere or direct him.

After one week, the subordinate came in with a blank sheet of paper, put his pencil down, looked at me, and said, "Jack, I'm ready to learn now."

That has happened a number of times. Once a subordinate came in and said, "I'm ready to let you help me now, Jack. I'm six feet under and sinking fast." [Laugh] His subordinates were about to march on his office.

It's a sad comment on the state of things for blacks in white industries, but every white subordinate I've ever had, I had at some point been forced to confront their behavior with me. Because what they'll do is try to read your experience and . . . and say, "Well, I don't know if I can learn anything from you." They're comparing your experience relative to theirs to see who is the smarter.

With blacks, its different. With black subordinates I had to be supportive because they were dealing with things like self-confidence and all the kinds of things I've talked about before. Sure I've had to kick blacks about their behavior, but in a supportive way.

For example, one black subordinate of mine had a task to do and he was going to get arrogant with it. He was going to go into a group of whites and just lay the stuff out—"Take it or deal with me!"

So before the meeting, I had him go to the board and put down his thought processes, outline them. Then we sat down and looked at it. I got him to look at what would motivate him to take that approach. When he looked at it, he realized he was meeting his own needs, not the needs of the people in the meeting.

I had to get him to understand he could meet his own needs through meeting the needs of the other individuals. That was a new way of thinking for him. You see, being a black, he had been positioned in a defensive position and had to learn to take an offensive posture.

That's right. Sometimes as a supervisor you have to, as we say, kick some butts . . . but it's different for blacks and whites. With blacks, you kick in a teaching supportive way; whereas with whites, I just had to use raw power at times because initially they wouldn't allow me to teach them anything. How can you allow somebody to teach you something if (a) you don't respect them and (b) you don't think they're as smart as you? And that's the difference!

Now, there *are* some blacks who cannot be reached through a supportive position. Some blacks are dealing with self-hate. That is, their blackness is a mean, shameful burden to them, and they would like to dismiss any connection with it.

In this case, you take the supportive role first. If they don't respect blackness, they won't hear your input. So if support doesn't work, you use raw power the same as with whites who have the same attitude.

With recalcitrant blacks, you let them know the same thing you'd reveal to resistant whites: "I've got my hand on your paycheck, and you need to understand that I am your boss and you can't just dismiss or disregard me. You have to respect me as your boss whether you like me or not. I'm not dealing with your likes."

What? Oh man! You couldn't begin to dream of some of the crazy stuff people did. I had one manager come in my office and say, "Well, I've got 23 years of experience; how many years experience have you got?"

What about my bosses? Well . . . for one thing, I'm careful to ask questions and make responses in a way that is not a put-down. In the work place, I think whites usually look for signs of whether or not a black subordinate is smarter than they are.

When a black subordinate gets arrogant with the boss in a public meeting, he, or she for that matter, is *asking* to be crushed. So what I deal with is not who is the smartest but are needs met and has the boss said what he really wanted to say.

And if I'm ever forced to take on my boss, I always do it in a room behind closed doors so he can keep his dignity. I'm also very careful to try to get some measure of closure in a conflict by putting things in terms of his self-interest—that is, in terms of what he can get out of the issue for himself.

I discovered that as a black I had to not only pay attention to the content of an interaction but also to the process of the interaction. I'd have to note the questions asked, how they were asked, and then ask people why they had asked me certain questions. I had to hear and watch people's interactions with me.

I became very sensitive to my environment. In other words, I had to learn to pay more attention to people's motives. OK? It became automatic. For example, in workshops sometimes people would get uncovered because they displayed negative racial behavior, and . . . after the workshop they would come looking for me. They'd want to fight with me and say the workshop was no good. I had to learn how to handle that.

What I had to do was get the person calmed down and get him or her to look at the data instead of fighting, because I discovered that so much was going on—until my energy was getting spread thin and I couldn't allow it to be spread out on a whole bunch of fights all over the place. So I was *forced* to—uh—be more sensitive to people and their motivations and—uh—be strategic so I could concentrate in order to use my energy on other things. I had to pinpoint hot issues and put my energy on trying to solve those for the organization.

My motivations? Did I get stroked a lot? No! I got fewer strokes than before. I think one reason for this was that I was now the peer of the group of people who gave me strokes. Since I was now their peer, they had no need to stroke me.

Promotion put me in competition with a different group of whites, and . . . and the higher up I went, the more pronounced the competition.

Oh, no. That doesn't bother me any longer. I discovered that I get strokes from my results—from the quality of the contributions I can make in my company. I got strokes from publicly taking care of hot issues.

Strokes came from my asking for more responsibility and having the organization give it. I could now see this as a stroke. Fewer people now verbalized strokes by saying, "Hey, that's a good job you've done."

There's less and less of that, but I don't need it any more. Successful blacks can see that the real strokes come from the organization giving you more control of resources—both monetary and people resources.

Yeah! I am more confident. I made a lot of presentations because I had to sell my programs. I had to become a skilled salesperson. And *that's* the real test.

If you can stand up in front of a group as a black and sell something that's, uh . . . people will tend to—their racism may come out. They'll potshot at you, and you've got to learn how to think on your feet and out-logic them or get them to look at their own data. I had to learn how to do that, and it can be very stressful at first—*very stressful!*

Also, as you move up in the hierarchy, you have to learn how to sell programs through other people. And that's a strange feeling too, because now I'm a level removed. Before, I did the hands-on work. I'd do the task myself. Now I have to direct other people to do the hands-on work.

No! That's not really any different from what a lot of white managers do. But man! I've seen a lot of white managers get destroyed when they moved up into the hierarchy and couldn't turn the hands-on work loose and learn to direct and delegate tasks.

But the whole company's made up of whites; there were only a few of us, and we couldn't afford to fail. We had no choice but to learn how to be good managers.

The thing that really got to me in particular was that I did not want to be insensitive to the needs of my people the way I felt people had been insensitive to me. So one immediate thing I did was to set up individualized training and development programs for each of the people who reported directly to me. You have to learn how to do this without shutting off other people's creativity. It has to be a balance between how you think it should be done and how the subordinate thinks it should be done.

So not only did I direct the tasks, but I offered development as well—opportunities to learn management skills. Man, that's funny! No, I didn't discriminate.

Yeah, yeah. Blacks do have to put in a lot of extra energy. That's why even today the average or mediocre black isn't gonna go far.

Ohhh, whew! There's so much! Let's see. I had to continue to refine my ability to tap the communications network because it was even more critical that I got the appropriate data from the organization. While I was training my own people, I had to be concerned about my own training and development and continue that, and uh . . . evidently I had to get with my boss and refine my yardstick so I'd know how I was to continue my development.

You know, there's something else I've thought a lot about that I haven't mentioned—uh—and—and it's about this power thing that keeps coming up in my conversation. There's something strange—let me see if I can explain what I'm thinking.

The power dynamic plays a big part in the relationship of a white boss to a white subordinate. It's like, whites are . . . accustomed to and accept having power used on them.

On the other hand, when a black subordinate has a white boss, the white boss will use the same approach as with his white subordinates, but something different happens. Blacks won't allow the power to be used on them in the same way, because blacks are trying to find out what part of the boss's behavior is racist and what isn't.

So, with blacks, there is an . . . an automatic resistance to the power, while—while at the same time acknowledging the white individual is the boss and that you are going to respond. It's like, before you respond, you'll seek clarity as to whether you're being put in a slave–master context with the person.

OK! Everybody responds to power, but whites don't have to worry about the less-than-human feelings from having power exercised over them.

So, when power is exercised over us by whites, resisting it until we understand the motivations and sense of it is like hanging on to our dignity and right to be equally human. See what I'm saying?

Wait, is that a car pulling up in front? Yeah, that's my wife. Good! She got here a little earlier than she thought.

You're gonna enjoy talking to her. Oh man! Does she have a lot to tell you about what it's like to be married to a black man moving up in an all-white organization. There are pressures and changes there, too. She can probably shed light on a lot of stuff I've told you about from a different perspective.

And . . . oh, shucks! That's a whole 'nother story.

ANALYSIS OF CRITICAL ISSUES

In the Success Phase, Jack's basic overall attitude was one of feeling good, confident, and positive about his ability to succeed. He had few illusions about his company or the people who worked with him. He knew that much of his success was dependent on how he approached his job and the skill with which he interacted with those around him. He was aware that he had learned many things, such as managing his anger. In addition, one of the biggest and most difficult things Jack had learned was to accept the added burden of being a *black* manager. This is very difficult for most blacks and is often another point at which the blacks who will continue to move and rise are separated from those who will remain at the lower levels of the hierarchy.

Jack was also very clear about the additional pressures placed on him when he was promoted because, unlike his white peers, he could not afford to make many mistakes or to fail. What he said to us was a below-average or average black probably would not become a supervising manager. Jack had now become fully aware of his blackness and its impact on the organization as well as how that dictated his behavior within the organization. Because Jack was a successful manager, he had to be concerned about his motives and the motives of others as he interacted in the organization. He also had to continue to resist the people who tried to pressure him into becoming totally socialized into the white corporation. Position power brings new problems to many blacks.

Blacks tend to feel strange when they are given power. Jack shared with us his feelings of strangeness and how he had to wrestle with himself over the use of that power. Most blacks feel ambivalent about the use of power. On one hand the person feels good because there is a greater ability to direct resources and get appropriate organizational results. On the other hand the person feels guilty because of the possibility of misusing the power. Jack asked himself if he would be guilty of doing to others what was done to him by the organization.

What blacks must understand is that they are now in control of their behavior and can decide whether or not they will mistreat others. The organization is not going to *force* blacks to mistreat anyone. So it is really up to the individual. What needs to be understood is that it is natural to feel this ambivalence and that it results from moving from one level to the other in the hierarchy.

This is again a new learning experience, because few blacks have had prior exposure to or experience with blacks being in a power position relative to whites. This should, however, be a positive learning experience. Blacks need to say to themselves, "I feel this way because this is something new and different and I have never been in this position before. I am stressful over it, but I will become less stressful as I learn how to handle my power appropriately. Power does not mean mistreatment, but rather it is a means of getting a job done more effectively and efficiently." Since over the centuries blacks have more often been on the receiving end and have felt the misuse of power, the ambivalence comes from the notion that possessing power means that you are expected to and will mistreat people. That assumption is *incorrect*.

Another burden or responsibility Jack felt was the necessity of managing blacks and whites differently. Treating *all* people the same is not really equal treatment. Truly equal treatment means that people should be treated according to their needs and cultural backgrounds. Before reacting to this statement, whites should attempt to understand the context in which Jack was speaking. This may be the first opportunity a white or a black reader has had to understand the differences in the dynamics that occur when a black is in a supervisory position. There is no point in getting upset over it, for what we need to do is understand why these differences occur; then both whites and blacks can understand that certain things need not happen if they are aware of the dynamics.

White subordinates may resent their black bosses, but those subordinates need to understand that the people above them selected the black managers and that by questioning the black managers they are really questioning the wisdom of the whites who made the selection. Instead, the white subordinate might say, "My organization picked my boss to hold this position. So rather than react to my boss, let me see what the reasons are that this person was chosen, because I might learn something." This is a healthy attitude to take.

Jack talked to us about the ease with which he could now handle himself in meetings. That speaks directly to high self-confidence in the Success Phase. The process for black managers is to start out with low self-confidence and build it rather rapidly as a successful track record is forged. At some point the need to have external praise or strokes will get turned into the need for internal, self-generated strokes. When that happens, blacks know they have reached the Success Phase. As Jack informed us, the results obtained become the strokes.

Initially, blacks unconsciously say, "I have been taught that whites are in a power position, and to feel good about myself, I must have whites give me strokes." As confidence builds, blacks begin to say, "I don't need that from whites to feel good about myself"; this is when blacks take more initiative and more risks. On the basis of these factors, an organization can manage blacks to be successful, or it can program them for failure by withholding strokes early so blacks never have an opportunity to gain self-confidence. Whites cannot say that to blacks in so many words, but they can certainly act it out.

Also, Jack was beginning to deal with black empowerment. Jack thought to himself, "Don't those white subordinates understand that I have my hands on their paychecks and that they must behave properly?" Blacks need to get to a point where they can say that publicly and feel OK with it; that is black empowerment. Whites will react to it, perhaps in a negative manner, but that is another burden blacks will have to bear at this time. Whites use power on other whites and are comfortable with empowerment.

Another feature of the Success Phase is the way people approach blacks because they have attained a power position. Certain kinds of outward displays of respect that are accepted as commonplace by whites in the same position can initially feel strange to blacks. The flip side to this is that prejudiced people approach the empowered black with more and more subtle racist behavior.

In the first two phases of the developmental model, blacks have great difficulty seeing themselves in a leadership position because they have been taught whites lead, blacks follow. Blacks often apologize in some way for taking leadership or initiative or for being put in a leadership position by the organization, even if it is temporary. They may have difficulty directing whites and will tend not to be as directive as they should be because of discomfort with black empowerment.

In the Success Phase, this will still be a problem, though not to the same extent as in other phases. It normally takes a great deal of time to overcome this particular problem. Sometimes blacks still dealing with the discomfort of empowerment will act as if they should not have the skills they are displaying. This comes across as being very modest. Sometimes blacks will disregard their skills or appear not to see them. They will use a sad look or tone of voice to dismiss what is obviously clever strategy. Consistent success can alter this, but progress is often retarded because whites inadvertently reinforce this kind of "modesty" from blacks.

When blacks gain a significant measure of comfort with having and using power, they behave differently—the walk is different, more commanding; voice tone takes on authority; and attitudes are different. Blacks no longer ask "Mother, may I?" Instead, they make the positive statement, "This is what we are going to do."

Jack told us racist behavior becomes more subtle during the Success Phase. He told us that blacks must continue to refine their styles so that subtle prejudiced behavior does not cause them, or white people, to become dysfunctional. In other words, the burden placed on the black supervising manager at this point becomes one of not responding to racist behavior. The black manager must also make the white person understand what is acceptable and what is not in such a way that both of them can retain some dignity in the situation.

Jack was faced with subtle racism in various meetings when he was asked questions by whites. He sometimes handled it directly by saying, in essence, "Can you help me understand what your core concern is, and may I speak directly to that?" Perhaps black managers are going to have to carry the burden of dealing with the negative prejudiced behavior of others for the next 20 or 30 years, because it may take yet another generation before enough blacks are represented in hierarchies to make significant changes from within institutions.

Attaining success can really be a letdown for blacks. They may ask themselves, "Is this it? Is this all there is to it?" This happens because the black manager has been charging hard and, all of a sudden, tasks that previously required a lot of energy now take significantly less energy.

Whites need to be sensitive to blacks in the Success Phase and keep challenging them to the best of the company's ability. If that does not happen, performance may drop off because the black managers are accustomed to running hard, and everyone will wonder why these previously sharp individuals are not producing the same output.

Jack discussed with us how blacks must operate at the next level before moving officially to that level. Some whites may think this is a logical way to make sure blacks do not fail since they are new to the corporate setting. However, blacks will not feel this is fair and may get very angry. Again, black managers are being asked to pay an additional price for the opportunity to succeed in corporations and institutions. Now, we as black managers can get angry and not pay the price, at which point we will not make the next level. Or we can say, "This is reality—I don't like it—I'm angry, but that is the price I have to pay to reach the next level. At least it is for now; in the long-term future, it may not be." White managers need to say, "We in the system need to change things so that blacks are given responsibility based more on potential in the same way that whites are." Now that leaves us with the core issue. What are the key characteristics that whites need to look at when evaluating blacks?

In summary, blacks have to demonstrate competence at the next level before they are promoted, whereas whites do not. Fairness will occur when blacks can be promoted or given more responsibility on the basis of potential as opposed to demonstrated competence.

At one point in the story, Jack mentioned he had whites talking to other whites about his success as a black manager. It is very interesting to note that even today whites will tend to listen more readily to other whites than to blacks, no matter how smart or logical the black may be. Jack was aware of this and used strategy to compensate for it. His approach was to be comfortable with allowing whites to speak on his behalf or to directly confront the situation. He let us know blacks need to be flexible and behave in a situationally appropriate manner.

Even when Jack obtained results, he still had to use strategy to ensure the results were properly seen by the right people in the organization. Again, this is a sad commentary but is something blacks must deal with because whites who do harbor negative prejudices against blacks will tend not to want to see the results blacks obtain. At the least, they tend not to put them in the correct perspective. Therefore, blacks must be prepared to handle this responsibility.

Even though they are generally not in policymaking positions in major white institutions in this country in the 1980s, blacks and other minorities are the ones who are learning and forming the precepts of multicultural management. Unfortunately, since these people tend not to be at the top of various organizations, the skills are being learned at the bottom. Somehow, this learning must be forced to the top because it is crucial for the future. American productivity is on a downward slide; we therefore need to make better use of *all* the resources that exist, and a lot of those resources happen to be blacks, women, and other minorities. If these resources are to be properly and efficiently utilized, then the managers in charge of the resources are going to have to learn multicultural management.

Teaching people to resist power is a very delicate issue, because what we are saying is the people at the bottom and in the middle must learn how to resist power from the people at the top. Viewed in a positive context, however, it will be good for the entire institution and the people involved. We can say this because, if the people at the top do not understand multicultural management and the people at the bottom and the middle do, then resisting the power of the people at the top can prevent them from making mistakes that will violate the precepts and concepts of multicultural management.

DEVELOPMENT OF HOW-TO SOLUTIONS

Problem I: How to respond to a direct challenge without threatening a person's dignity. Problem relates to critical issues 1, 2, 4, 5, 6, 7, 8, 9, 11, 12, 15, 16, 18

Solution 1: A direct challenge can come from a one-to-one meeting, from a group meeting, or from just standing in the hallway. The first move you should make is to relax. Do this even if you must force yourself. Sit back and cross your legs if you are sitting. Do not panic. The challenge may be laced with racism and you may have a strong visceral reaction, so this first step is very important. On the other hand, the challenge may be simply a deep concern on the other person's part about what is transpiring and may result in a better solution or proposal for all involved.

The second step is to be sure you understand the challenge and the motives behind it. Assume you have just suggested a proposal to a group and one person has challenged you. Ask questions of the challenger to make sure you understand what is being challenged. Let us imagine the challenger's concern was directed to the cost and schedule of the proposal. It may be a legitimate concern, or it could be motivated by the person's negative feelings toward you.

The third step is to repeat your understanding of what is being challenged and have the other person tell you whether you are correct. If the response is no, have the person repeat the concern until you reach an understanding of the issue.

Fourth, respond to the person's concern with whatever information you have. For example, "I understand why you would be concerned about the timetable for the execution of this proposal; however, let me give you more details as to why I think the timetable is workable." Then share your information with the person.

If the challenge continues and the person says something like, "I hear what you are saying, but I still don't think you can meet that deadline," then look at the person and say, "Since you are concerned with the cost and the schedule and I've explained why I think we can handle the schedule, will you share your core concern with me?" After the person has answered, repeat your understanding of the core concern. Now try to respond to that concern.

If the person is satisfied, then fine, move on. However, if the person is still concerned, then suggest a solution that will involve the challenger. For instance, you can say, "I would like for the two of us to meet with the person who put the schedule together." Later, have that meeting; you may have to compromise or provide still more data to help relieve the concerns. If the person is acting out of a prejudiced attitude—that is, just trying to upset you or make you look bad—then it is most likely the person will respond to your suggestion of a further meeting with, "Oh, I don't have to meet with you. Everything is OK." This is one way to flush out dysfunctional behavior.

Now let us recap the steps involved in this solution.

1. Lay out your data; if someone challenges you, relax and do not panic.
2. Ask questions to make sure you are clear about what is being challenged.
3. Repeat the concern to the person until you both agree that you understand what the person's concerns are.
4. Respond with more detailed information.
5. If the challenge continues, then ask for the person's basic, core concern. Repeat your understanding of this until you both agree on the core concern. Give more data.
6. If the person is still concerned, suggest a solution involving the challenger.

Solution 2: If you are pushed for time, a second solution is to say to the person who just challenged you, "That sounds like a legitimate question. However, could we work on that after this meeting?" Then after the meeting, get together with the person and work on the issue in private. This is a quick way to defuse a challenge, and if it turns out that the concern was not legitimate, it can be handled later in private where neither party will be subject to public embarrassment.

Problem II: How to operate at the next higher organizational level. Problem relates to critical issues 1, 2, 7, 9, 10, 11, 13, 14, 15, 16, 18

Solution: Determine what kinds of information you need to operate at the next level by identifying people who have a reputation for being successful and who are one hierarchical level above you. Closely observe what they do when they are being successful and take notes on their behavior. Look at what people they use as resources, what people they talk to, and how they talk to them. You need to do this with a minimum of two different people.

Hopefully, one of the people will be someone you trust and can have a conversation with. Meet with the person and have him or her describe the difference between how people operate at your level and at the next higher level. Ask how and why there is a difference. Take notes. An alternative to this is, if you have a close friend at the next level who is someone you trust and who trusts you, ask him or her to describe the difference between how people operate at the different levels. Ask the person to put this down on paper and give it to you. It can be marked confidential and may be handwritten. Please *be careful* how you use this information. *Do not* wave it all over the place.

Once you have the information, sift through it and pull out and document the common things successful people do. Now, implement the behavior *cautiously* and *only* if you are getting positive feedback in your present job position. It is inappropriate and dysfunctional to use this solution if you are in performance difficulty. It would not make sense to attempt to act at the next higher level if you have not yet learned how to operate successfully and smoothly at your present level.

Problem III: How to position the organization to see your results. Problem relates to critical issues 1, 2, 4, 5, 6, 7, 9, 10, 11, 13, 14, 15, 16, 18

Solution 1: It is best to set goals early. By doing this, it becomes easy to show results to an organization. Essentially, then, all you have to do is write a report or give a presentation on what you did and the results you achieved. If you did not write goals, then the following solutions will apply; if you do have goals, the suggestions can supplement the situation.

Write a short report on what you did to obtain your results. Use the following format:

Subject area
Key results
Statement of problem or issue resolved
Discussion of what was done
Use of the results

Send this write-up to your boss and others involved in helping to obtain the results. Ask them for comments and suggestions on additional uses of the results. Be sure to acknowledge the assistance of others in obtaining the results.

Solution 2: Arrange to give your boss and others an update and status presentation on what you did and the results you obtained. Use the following outline:

Subject area
Purpose (of meeting)
Key results obtained
Short discussion of what was done
Use of the results

You may choose to use a large newsprint pad, pass out 8½" × 11" sheets of paper with your agenda, or use an overhead projector. Visual aids offer an impressive addition to any presentation. Influential people give added meaning to seemingly small and insignificant events by dramatizing them. Now ask for comments and suggestions.

Problem IV: How to initiate management of a white subordinate. Problem relates to critical issues 1, 2, 3, 4, 5, 6, 7, 8, 9, 10, 11, 12, 13, 14, 15, 16, 17, 18

Solution: This is an important problem for discussion because a black boss–white subordinate relationship is antithetical to the business norm of society in this country. It is the reverse of what we normally see. We were reminded of this by a black boss who was told by a white subordinate, "Not only do I have to tell my family I work for a younger man, but I have to tell them you are also black." Occasionally, we see employees avoid introducing their families to the black boss or making any reference such as "This is my boss, Mr. Jones." Society inappropriately continues to teach that whites are the bosses and blacks are the subordinates. Therefore, in order for black boss–white subordinate relationships to be successful, the subject of race and its effects on the interaction must be opened up for discussion regardless of how uncomfortable it may be. You may need two to three hours for the initial meeting.

The two-part process involved in this solution is to get information from the white subordinate and to give information as the black boss. Both boss and subordinate need to think about their answers to the following questions against the backdrop of race and its effects on their interactions. (There will be a more in-depth discussion of this problem and solution in Part Three, Chapter 7, under "Management of Subordinates.")

PART I

First, ask what direction the subordinate wants to go in. That is, what does the subordinate want to do with the job? Then, what are the top three priority work items? In essence, the question is: "If I, the boss, give you, the subordinate, a job and you are going to do something with the job instead of just day-to-day tasks, in what direction would you like to take your job?" At this point, you may need to test the racial component by looking at the answers and asking, "If I were a white boss working with a white subordinate, would the answers be different?" If the answer is yes, then you and the subordinate need to look at and deal with the issues around the differences.

Now find out what major expectations the subordinate has of the job and of the boss. The white subordinate has expectations of the job that need to be shared with the boss. For instance, the subordinate may say, "I expect to be able to go and find out what the major problems are in the work area and solve them independently," or "with collaboration," or "with the boss," or "with the use of resources." These are the kinds of things you as the boss should look for. Regarding expectations of the boss, the subordinate may say, "I expect you to support me," or "I expect you to collaborate with me, to act as a coach." You need to know what your subordinate's thoughts are on these subjects.

It is not acceptable to have the white subordinate say, "I don't have any expectations." Everyone has expectations about their jobs and the people working with them. The black boss will have to take leadership in getting subordinates to discuss their expectations and also in pointing out the possible conflicts arising as a result of different cultural backgrounds. These issues need to be interwoven in the discussion of the answers to the job-related questions. For example, regarding the expectations of the subordinate, the black boss needs to ask, "Would the answers to these questions be different if I were a white boss?" Chances are the subordinate will say, "No." The boss then needs to slow the process and probe the issue. If a black boss does not ask for the white subordinate's expectations in the context of race, the racial element will get acted out anyway and maybe in a dysfunctional manner. Therefore, it is important to open the issue and ask.

There are instances when whites are put in awkward positions because of the racial attitudes of other whites. If race is introduced early as a legitimate area for discussion, whites will have an avenue to deal with problems that may arise. For instance, what does a white subordinate do when he or she sits at a lunch table and another white person makes a racist remark about the black boss, especially if it is designed to undermine the effectiveness of the boss? Does the white subordinate sit and say nothing? Does the subordinate defend the boss? These are the kinds of issues the subordinate may have to face.

Ask your subordinates how they like to work. Do they like to be given a task and left to work alone, collaborate with the boss, use resources, or not use resources? It is important for the boss to know how subordinates want to work because people will tend to produce at their fullest if they are working in the manner that is most comfortable to them. Again, race may play a part at this point since white subordinates may want to work alone without a lot of direction from the boss because of their attitude about blacks. This method of working may be counterproductive to how tasks are normally accomplished. If so, then the black boss may have to deal with that. This may not be the time or place to work on the issue, but at least the information will be shared up front. At some later time when it is more appropriate, the boss can prepare to negotiate a change in the working method of the subordinates.

Ask subordinates what their major concerns are about the boss and the job. For example, subordinates may be concerned that the boss does not have years of experience in their work area. This is a very common issue blacks face because of their newness to the white corporation. Also, whites tend to be concerned with whether or not they can learn from the black boss. The concerns will tend to be centered around power, control, trust, and intelligence. We can guarantee you these issues will arise.

It will be difficult for a white subordinate to come forth with these at the first meeting, so the black boss needs to take leadership in opening up these issues for discussion. At least in the subordinate's mind, there will be such questions as, "Will you offer me fair support even though I am white? Are you going to punish me for social ills I had nothing to do with? Are you going to help train me? Are you going to use reverse discrimination on me?" All of these are valid questions that at some time need to be dealt with by the black boss.

PART II

In Part II of the process, the boss should give information and take into account the information the subordinate gave. As the boss you should tell the subordinate in what direction you want the job taken and give three top-priority items for the subordinate's work area. This is a good time to discuss any differences that may exist in this area. You must be careful here not to apologize for being a boss. You need to say, "The company has put this responsibility in my hands, and I am accountable for it. I will take the leadership, and this is what I want the top three priorities to be." This is black empowerment.

The next step is to tell the subordinate what your major expectations are. For example, "I expect to be informed of problems encountered in accomplishing your tasks. I expect you to use me as a resource. I expect you to inform me of all major decisions you make."

You need to tell the subordinate how you like to work. "I like to be kept informed of the status of your various tasks. I want us to set regularly scheduled meetings. I like to collaborate. I prefer to see work in finished form." These are the kinds of working methods that the boss needs to discuss with the subordinate. You also need to talk about the kinds of problems you expect subordinates to bring to you.

You need to discuss your major concerns with the subordinate, and those concerns need to relate to the subordinate, the job, and other things, such as personal matters. If, for example, you also have black subordinates, you need to address that subject with the white subordinate, who may be concerned that you are not going to be fair in judgments and treatment. Discussion about these types of issues can help clear up many potential misunderstandings and leave the door open for working out such problems that arise in the future. This is an opportunity for the black boss to act as a resource for the white subordinate regarding any anticipated problems relative to cultural issues, because this is likely to be a new experience for many white employees.

The information from this meeting should be documented and shared with the black boss's boss. This can be done in one of two ways. The black boss can meet with his or her boss and go over the information, or the three individuals could have a meeting. What frequently works well is for the boss to first share the documented information with his or her boss, then have a subsequent meeting of the three individuals to discuss concerns. If there are a number of white subordinates in the work group, what works very well is to have the black boss's boss meet with the entire work group and discuss such things as direction setting and expectations.

Problem V: How to initiate management of a black subordinate. Problem relates to critical issues 1, 2, 4, 5, 6, 9, 11, 13, 14, 15, 16, 18.

Solution: The first important step in a black boss and black subordinate interaction is for the black boss to share his or her company history and personal work experience at the present place of employment with the black subordinate. This provides a connection between the boss and subordinate. That is, the black subordinate will be able to identify with the boss on the basis of common experience. This is important because many blacks have a problem seeing other blacks in leadership roles in a white organization, since, as we said earlier, it is antithetical to the normal role structure in our society.

Sharing this kind of information in the beginning of the relationship starts the process of support that is extremely important when both the boss and subordinate are black. Support is an essential ingredient because black subordinates must operate in an environment hostile to their achievement and need to know there is a reliable and organizationally empowered person who can be used as a resource. The role model aspect of the personal sharing along racial lines is also important. It lays the groundwork for the black boss and black subordinate to be connected for that necessary support. If black subordinates feel that the black boss is a part of the white establishment—that is, that the black boss is placing them in a less-than position—then the subordinates will relate to the boss as if he or she were white. The black subordinates may

use protective hesitation and sometimes may behave in a dysfunctional manner fueled by anger.

Three major issues are operative here that need to be mentioned
before moving to the solution. Keep these issues in mind as the
solution is implemented. The first issue is black self-hate. We will
not attempt to explain it fully here because it will be treated separately in Part Three, Chapter 6. Suffice it to say blacks tend to
project their group-identified shortcomings onto other blacks.
This is usually done unconsciously. Self-hate exists as a result of
the culturally assigned roles given to blacks over the centuries and
the fact that many blacks have unconsciously accepted those roles
and their status in the larger community. This also makes it easier
for many blacks to project their personal shortcomings onto other
people whom they see as being the same as or less than themselves.

Second, there are black-to-black power dynamics. White males
are still seen as more powerful, and the society continues to teach
and reinforce this precept. Some blacks have difficulty seeing
blacks in power positions and are reluctant to take direction from
other blacks. The thought is, "You're not supposed to be here
doing this because you're black like me and blacks are powerless."

The third issue centers around fear that black bosses have sold
out of the black brotherhood to the white organization. This can
cause a black subordinate to be angry and cast the black boss in
the same light as a white boss. There can be suspicion and doubt
that would cause the black subordinate to try to undermine the
authority of the black boss. In many cases, the feelings of a black
subordinate would be more intense toward a black boss than toward a white boss because of a feeling of betrayal by the black
boss.

This solution uses the same approach as the solution to Problem
IV. The same types of questions are asked; however, the dynamics
are different. The dynamics operating with the white subordinate
and black boss are intercultural; with the black subordinate and
black boss, they are intracultural. Black subordinates need the
additional reassurance that they will get support from the boss.
(Further discussion of this issue will be found in Part Three,
Chapter 7, under "Management of Subordinates.")

PART I

Ask subordinates what direction they want to go in. Now ask

the same question you asked the white subordinates: "If I were a white boss, would your answers be different?" Look at the significance of doing this by taking this example. Suppose a black subordinate wants to depart from normal procedures in accomplishing tasks. The black subordinate may be reluctant to try something new because he or she may feel the black boss does not have the organizational clout to support the change.

Find out the subordinate's major expectations of the job and boss. Again, ask the same series of questions as in the previous solution. Expectations exist whether people want to discuss them or not, so pull them out by taking leadership in opening up issues. This probing can set the stage for building a high level of trust and for the supportive boss–subordinate relationship.

Ask how the subordinate likes to accomplish work tasks. This discussion can give black subordinates the opportunity to free themselves up in relation to work procedures. Often black bosses can make an easier connection with some of the creative methods black subordinates have to use to offset resistant forces that white bosses have never had to consider or use. This offers further support to black subordinates in maximizing their task performance.

The boss should ask subordinates about their major concerns. Somehow, the black boss needs to talk enough so that black subordinates are comfortable in openly discussing their concerns with the boss. Perhaps black subordinates have some of the same concerns as white subordinates would have in terms of the boss's experience in the job and the boss's ability to train and coach. Black subordinates may be concerned over whether or not the boss has any real power or influence to get things done, whether they will get fair treatment or whether whites will be favored for the good jobs, and whether the boss has sold out. The boss may need to take leadership in drawing out these concerns.

PART II

In Part II of the process, the boss takes into account what the subordinates have said and discusses the direction that he or she would like to see the subordinates take in their job positions. If the black subordinate is working on some power issues with the black boss at this point, an argument could ensue. If it does, it will have to be worked through. One approach to this is for the boss to start where the subordinate is relative to personal and organizational growth, not where the boss is. The boss can help subordinates deal with their thinking processes and change their perceptions, instead of laying out heavy organizational power. Use power only if other options fail, because a black subordinate will react very negatively to this, especially from another black. Therefore, carefully work through the differences.

The boss should tell the subordinate his or her major expectations. Work these through also.

Then the boss should tell the subordinate how he or she likes to work. Be careful about the power dynamics.

The boss needs to discuss his or her major concerns with the subordinate. For example, if black perceptions about black bosses have not been discussed, this would be a point at which the black boss needs to take some responsibility and leadership in this area. The major concern is how the black subordinate and the organization will see the black boss–black subordinate relationship. We can guarantee this will be a concern whether it gets voiced or not. The subordinate will anticipate that the organization will expect the black boss to be unfair and give a disproportionate amount of support and attention to black subordinates. This anticipation of expectations will be correct, especially if the boss *and* subordinate have both personal and organizational power. The key question for all becomes, will the black boss be as fair with whites as with blacks?

At the same time, the boss can be assured that black subordinates will wonder whether they are getting a fair deal because the black boss is trying to prove to the organization that as a boss he or she can give white subordinates fair treatment. Unfortunately, it does happen in some cases that black bosses are so concerned about how the organization views their treatment of whites that they tend to give less help to black subordinates. Here is the opportunity to set the stage for a good working relationship so it does not become antagonistic or hostile. As with the previous solution, document the session and use the same options in sharing the information with the boss' boss.

Problem VI: How to develop a personal job strategy. Problem relates to critical issues 1, 4, 6, 7, 9, 10, 11, 13, 14, 16, 18

Solution: The development and implementation of a personal job strategy in the Success Phase is extremely important. Since success has been reached, using personal job strategy is a way to ensure success. This solution deals with the principles involved in developing that strategy.

There are four overview pieces in the solution: Be clear about what you want, be clear about how you operate, develop a plan and a strategy, and then implement the plan.

There are five steps involved in developing the job strategy:

1. Develop personal goals in the areas of job and home. Think in terms of one-year, two-year, and five-year goals. In the job area, there are three basic categories:

- Growth and development—learning how to do your job better and expanding your skills.
- Task accomplishment.
- Management of people and resources.

The goals for home will be centered around how you plan to integrate home with work; what you want for the future—new house, car, land; more education for self or family; and investments, financial planning.

2. Develop a vision of what you would like in the future. You need to actually see your goals brought to fruition.

3. Develop and be clear about your philosophy of operation. This means you must develop a set of personal beliefs and values about how you do things. You need this philosophy for both job and home. It should include the same categories as listed in number 1. For example, your philosophy on management of people might be that people will produce at their maximum if they are in a job that meets their needs so they have high interest and high energy. Another example might be, if you find out what people's needs are and match them to the right job task, then they will perform at their maximum.

4. Identify both power figures and resources. Develop a sponsorship-type relationship with one or two power figures. Be sure you make periodic use of resources relative to hot company issues.

5. Define your implementation strategy, which means your plan or technique for achieving some end. The substeps to this are:

- Define a plan for managing the working relationship between your boss and you. How will you ensure that you will get optimum results when you interact with your boss?

- Set priorities for your job and home. For example, under the category of home, you may have to decide whether you will save money first for a house, car, or investments.
- Develop action steps to meet your goals.
- Set dates for implementation of each action step.

BASIC CONCEPTS USED IN HOW-TO SOLUTIONS

Problem I: How to respond to a direct challenge without threatening a person's dignity.

Concept 1: The first concept from Problem I is Relaxing. Throughout this book, we have stated that when you are put in a challenging or confronting situation you need to relax. In this problem, we make a point of asking you to consciously relax. This is very important, because if you do not relax you cannot think clearly. If you do not relax, it is because you are stressful. If you are stressful, you will have difficulty thinking clearly or creatively. So, if you feel yourself becoming stressful in a situation, that should automatically tell you to force yourself to relax *before* you attempt to respond to the situation.

Concept 2: The second concept in this problem centers around the need to fully understand what the other person is saying before you respond. In this case, it was understanding a challenge being made. Understanding can be obtained by asking questions of the other person until you feel the information is clear. We have asked the reader to do this before; now we have put a label on it, and we call it Playback. The way this concept works is to listen to what is said, think about it, ask questions until you think you have full understanding, and then play back or repeat to the person what you understood him or her to say. This helps prevent misunderstandings, assumptions, jumping to conclusions, and overreacting.

Problem III: How to position the organization to see your results.

Concept 1: Write 'n' Tell is our catchy way of labeling this concept. It tells you to write a short report or to document significant meetings and other things you do in order to share them with your hierarchy at a later date. Write 'n' tell differs from jotting it down, which means taking notes for your own reference.

Write 'n' tell directs you to formalize information for sharing with others through a letter, a memo, or a report. This can be a very expedient way to disseminate information to a large group of people.

Concept 2: This concept is widely used in most institutions; we are giving it the name of our childhood activity Show 'n' Tell. Simply stated, you need to periodically prepare and give a presentation to others in order to share information. Writing reports may be all that is required of you, but it does not give you personal exposure. Often you can be remembered long after your information is forgotten, especially if you are able to present your most dynamic and impressive front.

Problem IV: How to initiate management of a white subordinate.

Problem V: How to initiate management of a black subordinate.

Concept: The basic concept found here is Open, Up-Front Discussion. Throughout the solutions to these two problems, the key approach was to confront issues in an open manner, seeking honest input on feelings and reactions. One possible drawback in using this concept is, once an issue is honestly addressed, you must work on it until there is closure. Discuss it enough right away to reach a resolution, or set some definite future date to complete the discussion so both parties can become comfortable with the issue. *Caution! Do not* probe in depth on personal values or private issues with the other person. Keep the discussion related to solvable problems that either facilitate or impede work tasks, especially in the racial context.

If you are not prepared to work an issue to closure or to some mutual understanding, then it is best not to open it up for discussion. If there appears to be a serious problem that can be a hindrance in the other person's relationships, you may consider engaging a professional third-party consultant to help deal with the pertinent issues. We repeat, *do not* open up a person to a painful experience when you do not have the skill or time to get closure on it.

Summary of Basic Concepts
1. *Relaxing* reminds the reader to consciously relax and remain calm so that you can think clearly in situations that have the potential to produce stress.

2. *Playback* refers to repeating what you understood a person to have said.

3. *Write 'n' Tell* means formalizing information for sharing with others through letters, memos, or reports.

4. *Show 'n' Tell* means giving periodic presentations to others to share information and to get personal exposure to the hierarchy.

5. *Open, Up-Front Discussion* is used to confront issues in an open manner and to seek honest input on feelings and reactions.

PART THREE
Critical Guidelines for Success

Part Three contains three chapters; each one focuses on critical guidelines for the successful black manager. As we promised in the Introduction, this part of the book will illuminate the concepts and key principles used to implement effective behavior to overcome difficulties. The guidelines are strategies involving the internal, external, and environmental systems in which blacks must operate.

The internal system deals with the intrapsychic understanding of yourself and how and why you think and operate as you do. The external system relates to the outside stimuli that impact upon you as an individual and on the interpersonal relationships in which you are involved. The environmental system deals with the setting in which individuals operate. We have identified concepts and principles in each system that are necessary to obtain success. We will discuss those problems and issues that have been most frequently identified by blacks as needing to be addressed and those that Jack portrayed in his narrative.

6

Internal Strategies

EFFECTIVE STYLE

For the purposes of our discussion, we define *effective style* as a person's manner of successfully expressing him- or herself in writing, speaking, behaving, and personal appearance. We will discuss two major areas of effective style: appearance and behavior. In the area of appearance, there are two subareas: dress and grooming. In the area of behavior, there are primary and backup patterns; both are displayed in verbal and nonverbal communication.

First, let us explore appearance. When you first see a person, you rapidly note such things as dress—colors, style, and fit of clothes—and grooming—whether the hair looks combed, the face is shaved or makeup is on, clothes are pressed, and shoes are cleaned and shined. Everyone is automatically perused with regard to outward appearances; in the case of blacks, however, the judgments attached to personal appearance are even more stringent. Members of corporations are very sensitive to the picture presented by blacks and the stereotypes these pictures feed into. Does the person wear a suit and look as if he or she is about to conduct serious business? Does the person wear a beard and unkempt Afro, slacks, and an ill-fitting shirt? Does the person have braids, no makeup, and overly flashy or too tight clothes? Would the person present a picture of a militant, or someone out for play, or a person with a careless attitude about him- or herself who would thus be less than serious about the job?

Personal appearance determines immediately whether or not you will be seen in a serious light and whether or not you feed into the negative stereotypes of the larger community. First impressions are hard to overcome; very often they are lasting. Showing up on the job dressed inappropriately gives some whites the impetus they may need to pull out their negative stereotypes to run a checklist against you. On the other hand, appropriate dress can add to the total charisma, particularly for blacks. It can help provide a mystique, a smoothness, and an attention-getting charm, and enhance your ability to draw people to you and make them comfortable. It helps to assure people that you are in control of yourself and the situation. Proper dress can work to help shift the balance in a racist interaction in a positive direction. This is especially true for blacks if the people in the organization dress in a bland manner and the black manager dresses appropriately with style. People will tend to be more attentive to that individual.

Some blacks have a problem with dressing appropriately because they feel it is yet another way whites try to socialize blacks into conforming for the purpose of further subjugation. As blacks move into all-white organizations, a certain amount of socialization will occur. A certain amount of conformity will also occur, and this is not necessarily bad. What many blacks fail to do initially is to connect an effective style to the goals that they have set for themselves. If there are no goals or interest in a career, then style is not a concern for blacks. But if blacks have high aspirations in their careers and personal lives, then effective style is extremely important in meeting those goals. Conformity *to a degree* then becomes a means to obtaining the goals rather than a sellout. Being well groomed does not necessarily mean a short haircut for a black male manager. Afros are fine if they are neat and taken care of, without a comb sticking out of them.

For example, we worked with a young black male from a small town. He was bright and sharp in his thinking and very creative in his ability to execute a task. However, he dressed like a farmer, and his hair always looked as if it needed combing. It became immediately obvious that he was dealing with issues related to his self-image. He did not present himself to others very well, and it was very difficult for them to listen to him. The picture he presented was: a black dressed for manual labor, unkempt, and apparently dull. It was reasonable then that the whites in his environment had questions in their minds as to whether he knew how to think and act appropriately in the corporation.

Another example is the college kid appearance some blacks hang on to after entering a corporation. These individuals continue to wear sweaters, open collars, slacks, and so on. They have become comfortable with this because it was the mode of dress in the college environment. Their stance is that the organization should accept them for who they are, not how they dress. These blacks have not stopped to consider that college is a learning institution where informal dress has become appropriate. Now they have moved to a different activity in society, that of wage earners, in a different environment, that of white-collar professionals, where the uniform that identifies their place in society has changed. Their continuing to dress as college students is interfering with their acceptance as competent workers and peers. They convey to the other members of the organization that they are trainees, not to be considered as serious full-fledged members of the work force.

In institutions where dress tends to be less formal and more relaxed, there are still rules to follow. In order to remove appearance from the checklist a racist may use to evaluate them, blacks need to stay away from the jeans and rumpled shirt look and to avoid being untidy or wearing ill-fitting clothes. There are many well-fitting, sporty garments to choose from, and there is never an excuse for being unkempt. A rule of thumb is to ask yourself, "What picture do I want to leave in the minds of the people who see me? What kind of first impression do I want to make?" There are two very good books written by John T. Molloy that discuss appropriate dress in more detail. We recommend these books because the author addresses some of the effects of race and gender on personal appearance and dress.*

The second important area of effective style is behavior. When we speak of a primary behavioral pattern, we mean each of us has a basic way of behaving under normal conditions. This includes how we talk, act, move our bodies, and so on—in verbal as well as

---

Dress for Success (New York: Warner Books, 1975), and *The Woman's Dress for Success Book* (New York: Warner Books, 1977).

nonverbal communication. When situations out of the ordinary occur, as in confrontation, we may use a backup pattern of behavior with a different display of verbal and nonverbal communication.

It is important for blacks to be clear about how their behavior is seen and impacts others. Just as we are immediately judged by others on our personal appearance, we are further judged on how we behave. If your primary behavioral pattern is offensive and dysfunctional to others, you will of course be negatively evaluated. This happens in any case no matter who you are, but if you are black interacting with a white person who has prejudged notions about you as a member of a less-than group, you will reinforce those negative attitudes and stereotypes of that person. Therefore, to do well in a predominantly white organization, it is critical that blacks develop a pragmatic verbal and nonverbal primary behavioral pattern that is appropriate to corporate settings.

Let us look at a couple of examples. A black manager may have a primary behavioral pattern of shaking a finger in the face of the person he or she is talking to. Or a black person may have a constant unconscious frown on his or her face. This would be irritating if done by a white manager, but a black will have additional negative connotations attached to the behavior. The black manager may be judged militant, hostile, and an individual who cannot get along with anyone.

Whites sometimes attach a lot of significance to habitual unconscious nonverbal or verbal primary behavioral patterns of blacks. This is why it is of paramount importance to first be aware of your behavioral patterns and, second, be willing to develop functional behaviors appropriate to the environment. Consider what you want people to think about you when they leave your presence. That will tell you the kind of behavioral pattern you need to establish.

Since environments are dynamic, behavioral patterns should also be dynamic. If the environment changes, as it normally does for most blacks entering all-white institutions, and your established primary behavioral pattern continuously gets you in trouble, the smart thing to do is to change the pattern to one that helps you meet your goals. We are not suggesting that a black person become an "oreo cookie" or act like a white person. Instead, we are talking about learning a different behavioral pattern that is more appropriate to the new environment and that is strategically organized and developed to get you what you want.

To sum up what we have thus far discussed, allow us to use an analogy. If you were going to participate in a formal wedding, you would not appear in blue jeans and a gaudy shirt nor would you shout loudly at the guests. Instead, you would dress meticulously in the appropriate garb and put on your best, most cordial behavior. This is all we are saying about the corporation. Hang on to your blackness, but do what is appropriate to the situation and environment. Conventionality gives order and purpose to our behavior and prevents us from performing in a chaotic manner.

In the area of effective behavioral styles, we would like to focus on 12 key principles for black managers.

1. *Be personable.* Few blacks are in a position to use raw power on others; therefore, control is most often available to blacks in the form of charismatic power. This is the ability to charm people. Charisma offers the black manager a viable means to assume leadership and give direction. Charismatic people draw others to them and make others want to follow and respond. When blacks are personable and charismatic, they inhibit the formation of racist or sexist attitudes in whites. If you are personable, it is very difficult for negatively prejudiced people to act out those prejudices against you and continue to see themselves in a positive light.

Being personable helps create a relaxed, trusting atmosphere that can break down the staunchest resistance of a racist. This works because even a racist has some white guilt about blacks and their position in society. Since whites deduce that you know they have negative feelings and you are still trying to get along with them, it triggers those guilt feelings and provides pressure to respond positively to you. The problem solutions in Part Two offered specific ways in which you might practice using a smooth personal style with people. We suggested conversing about people's special interests and commenting on some pleasing characteristic or manner during informal moments.

2. *Initiate conversation.* Show people you are interested in them. With whites who are uncomfortable with you because you are black, it is very important for you to take the initiative in the conversation, to set the stage for the subject under discussion, and to ensure the interaction begins in a relaxed manner. Most people are responsive to interest shown in them.

3. *Display humor.* Humor can often be a touchy matter with blacks because sometimes it can be interpreted as "skinning and grinning" in the white man's face or Uncle Tomming. A very common example of the reluctance to display humor is embodied in the situation of one young black woman discussing a project with two of her white male bosses. She presented the data matter-of-factly, with a stern businesslike affect. She never once took into account that her bosses were quite uncomfortable with having to interact with a black female in that business context. One boss looked at her and said completely off the subject, "Why don't you ever smile?" The other boss, jumping to her defense, said, "That's the problem with us whites; we always want blacks to smile and make us comfortable and feel good."

Some blacks get hostile and refuse to display humor, especially in the Entry and Adjusting Phases of their corporate development. However, bear in mind these are the guidelines for success, and the appropriate use of humor is very important to successful interactions with whites. Humor (not buffoonery) by a black can often calm a tense interracial interaction and cast the black in a favorable light. Humor can break a deadlock in a conflict and divert a potentially nasty situation to one that is less hostile. Humor can relax people and help keep a good perspective on issues. Some blacks may react and say, "I'm not going to try to relax other people! To heck with them! I'm going to do my job and let the chips fall where they may." That is certainly one approach to take, but it is less likely to contribute to success, whereas humor can be used strategically to enhance movement toward success because it is a key principle to effective style.

4. *Display confidence.* When blacks display confidence, it is a charismatic quality and will tend to cause people to follow. Confidence is displayed in verbal and nonverbal ways by supporting your body in an erect manner, holding your head high, and speaking in a self-assured tone. It is not important to actually feel confident at the time; affecting it will convince others that you are confident and often also works to help convince you that you are. Having a strong presence enables you to direct people.

If you are in a meeting and are working from a board or chart, form the habit of standing. It is a good practice to stand whenever you present lengthy data to a group. If you are asked a question, it is all right to pause to think about your answer. You will appear more confident if you do this than you would if you blurted out something inappropriate. Do not slouch down in your chair in a meeting or when conversing with others. As you talk, do not let your voice volume decrease at the end of a sentence, because it will convey a lack of confidence to others. As a result, they will not have confidence in you or follow your direction.

5. *Convey high self-esteem.* Show that you have a good opinion of yourself. This, however, does *not* mean you should be arrogant. If you display a good opinion of yourself when interacting with others and leading them, they will assume you have a high opinion of them since you are asking them to do something. On the other hand, if you attempt to lead people and you do not convey a good opinion of yourself and what you are doing, then people will be hesitant in listening to you, let alone following your direction. High self-esteem and confidence tend to be infectious and generate enthusiasm. Constantly practice displaying these characteristics until they are a part of your primary behavioral pattern. The nonverbal affectation of self-esteem is similar to that of confidence. People who have high self-esteem do not indulge in fruitless self-abasement for any reason but will acknowledge mistakes to themselves and move on.

6. *Display a relaxed affect.* This may be extremely difficult for some blacks, especially if they happen to be the only black in a meeting or organization. The comedian Don Knotts shows the extreme opposite of a relaxed affect—physical trembling, stuttering, and awkward, bumbling movements. We find his antics funny, but of course any degree of this uptight, stressful condition in blacks is not funny to us or to the people who must do business with us.

Again, regardless of whether you actually feel relaxed or not, it is important to affect a relaxed condition. Blacks who show their stress tend not to engender trust from others. A relaxed appearance will give others the idea that you have the situation under control, whether you do or not.

Sit back, cross your legs, and let your body relax, but without slouching. Play a game with yourself by visualizing yourself in a relaxed pleasurable situation that you have experienced in the past. You will be amazed at how quickly your body will respond and loosen up. Remove the worry and tension lines around your eyes and mouth. Unpurse your lips, if you tend to purse them, and relax your leg and arm muscles. Clear your mind and concentrate on what is happening around you. Now you will appear to be in command.

7. *Be flexible in your behavioral patterns.* Learn more than one style of behaving and know when to use each style appropriately. Learn how to be assertive* (confidently pushing back) as well as aggressive (vigorously attacking the situation). For example, depending on the situation and the end result you are seeking, it may be better to be assertive than aggressive in presenting a new project to your group. In some cases, however, you may want to pull out the stops and be aggressive, throw caution to the wind and not worry about being nice. You may want to be strong and get the task done, which is what it takes sometimes. If you are captain of a SWAT (Special Weapons and Tactics) team, you do not want to deal with assertive behavior; you want to be aggressive. In your normal day-to-day work environment, where you use your primary behavioral pattern, you will not want to be defensive as a rule. However, there are times when it is appropriate to be defensive; for example, you should defend your organization against inappropriate feedback. Offensive behavior may need to follow defensive behavior if some feedback is valid.

Being flexible means being willing to use backup behavior when your primary behavior is not getting you what you want, or when you end up in confrontation, argumentation, or other stressful situations. When your primary behavior is inappropriate for a particular situation, then it is time to be flexible and use a backup pattern. Flexible behavior gives you greater control over the events in your environment.

8. *Read the style of your audience.* An audience can be one person or a group of people. You should develop the ability to pick out the important pieces of another person's behavioral pattern. Form a psychological profile of your audience. Find out how

---

*We personally dislike the term *assertive* because we feel it came into popular use after blacks and women joined previously all-white male organizations. When organizations had only white males in professional roles, the word *aggressive* was a positive and acceptable term. However, when blacks and women joined the professional ranks, they were expected to be bold and active but in a *nice* way. Therefore the term *assertive* gained popular use. We are stuck with the word *assertive*, however, and the supposed difference between assertive and aggressive is the degree of hostility and combativeness attached.

a person receives data best—verbally, in writing, or with diagrams. Think about what you wish to convey and then use a behavior that the other person can understand, accept, and most easily respond to. Understand the needs of the other person and develop a behavioral pattern to use with that person so as to be effective in the interaction at that point in time. You will then satisfy the person's needs and ensure success in the interaction.

9. *Duplicate the style of other people.* This principle relates to the previous principle. Sometimes the most effective way to interact with a person is to do it in the style of the other person, especially if he or she is a power figure. In this case it is essential to have a good understanding of the person you are dealing with and what that person responds to. You must also be clear about what you are trying to accomplish. For example, the person you are interacting with may display a humorous style and you want a relaxed meeting with few hassles, so you use that person's behavioral pattern to help facilitate a smooth meeting. You may want to inhibit another's frustrating behavioral pattern when you interact with that person. You may, for instance, have a boss who asks a whole bunch of questions that disrupts your agenda. If you duplicate your boss's style and ask a whole bunch of questions, it is likely your boss will stop asking questions and you will be able to continue your agenda.

10. *Time your behavior.* You need to learn when to use primary behavioral patterns and when to use backup behavioral patterns. Some people seem to have a natural sense of timing. They know exactly when to be humorous, exactly when to be defensive, and exactly when to be aggressive. For those who do not have a natural sense of timing, the cue is when you realize the behavioral style you have selected is getting you no place—at that point, you should do something differently. Timing tells you when to argue, when to stop talking and listen, and how to behave as the situation dictates. Anytime a certain behavior does not feel right or causes additional problems or conflict, then you need to change your behavior, because the timing is not right for that particular behavior.

Most of us have a built-in timer, and it is a part of our viscera. Stop for a moment and remember the last time you felt a knot in your stomach. When you feel a knot, it means you need to examine the situation you are in. You need to figure out what negative feelings you are having and why you are having them and connect them with whether or not your behavior is appropriate for that situation. This exercise helps teach your timer to be more responsive and you to develop your sense of timing.

11. *Display high energy.* This principle is important for blacks to accept and use because of the stereotypes that persist. Too many whites still think blacks are lazy, for example. If you have high career goals, it is important that you show a high level of energy in your interactions with others. When you display high energy, you allow your enthusiasm for your job to come through and infect the people around you. It will affect your body movements, how fast you walk and do things.

To display high energy, walk faster down the halls than the average person, because it will appear that you are rushing to do something important, whether you are or not. Let your personal excitement come through in the tone of your voice. Talk with your hands, and let your face mirror what you feel. Talking faster can show people your excitement. One way you can get a group of white subordinates to follow your lead is to infect them with your high energy and enthusiasm. Use high energy with individuals and groups anytime you are excited about something. A display of high energy is one way to balance a racist view of blacks against reality.

12. *Be sensitive to others.* Be aware of other people's behavior and the reasons for it. Sensitivity today is extremely important for all managers, especially minority managers, because we now have blacks, Hispanics, Orientals, and women in organizations in positions that were previously held solely by white males. Insensitivity across cultural lines creates a breeding ground for misunderstandings, resentment, mistrust, and dysfunctional interactions. As a manager you must understand people, behave appropriately, and position things appropriately, for the success of the total organization.

MANAGEMENT OF RAGE

Little is ever said about black rage. Whites are afraid to discuss it openly, and many blacks deny it exists. Two of the few authors who dared expose and candidly discuss this volatile issue are Dr. William Grier and Dr. Price Cobbs in their book *Black Rage.* Admittedly, the subject is a difficult one to face and explore because of the strong implication of violence associated with the concept. However, we would be remiss in our task if we did not give this subject some attention and attempt to provide a positive perspective on a condition that we all know exists.

In very few places do we make all-inclusive statements, but here we say *all blacks are angry*—whether they act out that anger toward whites or not. Most black rage in American blacks is turned inward and sometimes comes out in self-destructive ways, as we will discuss later in this chapter. As we defined black rage in Part Two, Chapter 3, it is the furious anger born out of the person's blackness and all that means in our society. Black rage is the reaction of blacks to racism. The anger is the product of being and feeling powerless, less than whites, and systematically discriminated against.

Jack, in his narrative in the Adjusting Phase, gave a good example of how this black rage mounts and surfaces in blacks in the work environment. He also pointed out what kinds of prejudiced behavior triggers the anger. Jack told us how he was frustrated in his efforts to grow and learn. He talked to us about how this frustration and anger surfaced and how he became dysfunctional in his interactions with others. His behavior became more and more inappropriate, until he realized that he had just two options left—to learn to manage his emotions and channel that energy into something constructive or to leave the company.

This brings us to the management of rage—what is it, and how is it accomplished? We define the management of rage as the ability to control the vast amounts of anger that blacks feel and to cope with the other emotions that are associated with that anger. We will discuss seven key principles to be used in the management of rage.

1. *Rage is inevitable for blacks.* Given that blacks have for hundreds of years endured racial prejudice and discrimination, it would be ludicrous to believe that all is well and calm and that blacks are not angry. Rage is the natural reaction of a persecuted group to another group's ability to act out with power, authority, and desire its hostility and prejudice. Therefore, it is fruitless to deny that the rage exists and to think that denying it will make it disappear.

2. *Do not block your anger.* Since rage is inevitable, you should not block that internal anger. Particularly in white settings, blacks

tend to bottle up their anger. Evidence of this bottled-up anger is the prevalence of hypertension and heart attacks among blacks as a group.* We are not suggesting blacks should riot or punch their bosses in the nose or in any other way exhibit inappropriate behavior. We are saying recognize your rage, understand what it is and why it exists. You need not feel strange about getting emotionally upset. Your black rage can be a source of strength if you allow yourself to freely experience it.

This brings us to the next principle.

3. *Rage can be cathartic.* Rage can have a cleansing effect because it is a built-in pressure relief valve that when used appropriately prevents the individual from exploding from within. Much of the harm we do to ourselves and others is a result of pent-up anger, frustration, and resentment. What is most common is that the rage we feel and yet deny leaves us feeling crazy, as though we are losing our minds. Again, Jack brought this phenomenon to our attention in his narrative. This is a frightening experience. The feeling of going mad can end when we accept our honest feelings of anger, realize they are justified, and know there are ways to deal with the emotions constructively.

Initial release can come in many ways. Some blacks discuss their feelings with their mates or close, trusted friends. Sometimes strenuous activity, such as exercise or sports, may help. We personally enjoy our hobby of building furniture to vent initial rage and to think through and gain perspective on situations that triggered rage. Sawing and hammering can bring great relief in letting out hostile feelings and pent-up emotions.

4. *Rage can be managed.* Anger can be controlled and the strong emotions coped with if you are clear about what they result from and that you should not block them but rather allow them to be cathartic. Rage can be managed when you feel OK with your emotions and know you are not going to misuse your feelings by hurting someone or yourself.

In essence, the strength and energy in the rage can be harnessed and used strategically to confront and resolve major issues. It can physically drive you to confront those issues and correct an intolerable situation you may be experiencing.

5. *Use rage as a strategic constructive tool.* As we said before,

*William H. Grier and Price M. Cobbs, *The Jesus Bag* (New York: McGraw-Hill, 1971), p. 183.

rage can be a source of strength for blacks. When you feel rage internally and you are managing it because you understand why you have it, where it is coming from, and what it is, then you can let it surface in a controlled fashion. Believe us, it will get the attention you seek. You can do this without turning people off, frightening them, or jeopardizing your career.

As an example, let us take the case of a young black manager who administratively reported to one boss but in addition performed tasks for another functional "boss." In essence, the black manager was responding to the directions and needs of two different people. He had two full-time jobs in this situation and was constantly being asked to do more. The two white bosses normally did not talk to each other about what the black subordinate was doing for each of them. Both bosses wondered why the black subordinate could not do more tasks. The black manager tried to explain he was doing work for two people. The two bosses never seemed to get together, and the black subordinate was never able to get them together either. Finally, one day out of utter frustration, the black manager became so angry at the pressure and so filled with anxiety and emotion that he could not take it any longer. He literally pounded the table of one of the bosses. He shouted, "Dammit! It's not fair! I can't and won't take this any more!"

In this example the black manager used his rage, without attacking the other person, to get one manager's attention. As a result he got his boss to understand that something must be seriously wrong because he did not normally behave this way. The boss figured he had best stop and really listen to find out what the problem was. Once the black manager had his boss's serious attention long enough, he was able to explain the situation. The white boss said, "Oh, I guess you and I had better go talk to the other guy. I didn't know we were putting that much pressure on you." The black subordinate had tried to tell the boss before, but the boss would not listen. On the basis of the information we have already covered, we can speculate on why the boss failed to listen. The black manager finally allowed his rage to surface so that he could force his boss to face the issue of what he was doing. He was able to use his anger strategically and constructively to get the boss's attention so the white manager would slow down, listen, and help change the untenable position he had helped to place the subordinate in.

6. *Do not personalize your anger.* Do not direct your anger toward a specific individual but rather toward an issue. You gain nothing by berating a John Doe but may gain a lot by attacking John Doe's dysfunctional or inappropriate behavior. A person may have done something hurtful and unnecessary or may have exercised bad judgment in a situation involving you, but you need to direct your rage toward the person's judgment, not toward the person's character and dignity.

7. *Rage can lead to creativity.* When blacks become very angry about an issue or situation, they will often refuse to let it defeat them. Blacks often develop very creative and innovative ways to get around the barriers set up to stop them. In the management of rage, blacks focus on alternative ways of reacting to something negative that has happened to them. Being forced to look at options also forces creativity.

Jack, in his narrative in the Adjusting Phase, presented us with examples of his creative thinking after he became enraged over the situation in the personnel office. Despite his company's statements about its inability to find qualified blacks, Jack realized the company did not attempt to look in places where blacks were; when Jack recruited, he found more qualified blacks than the company could use in all the various fields. Jack also became enraged over the insensitive manner in which the company responded to its black employees; he reorganized the office and found creative ways to improve the situation. He was ultimately able to make an impact on an unjust and anger-producing situation.

GETTING THE NEW JOB TOGETHER

It is of the utmost importance for blacks starting a new job to begin in the right mode and direction. As a black, you cannot afford the luxury of waiting for the informal communications network to help you get started or for your peers or your boss to know what to tell you to do. They may not be skilled in multicultural management. The principles we will discuss in this section also apply when you move from one job area to another within the same company. It is important to have a documented plan to give yourself a purpose and direction before you dive into your job tasks. There are four basic principles.

1. *Obtain preliminary information.* Before moving into the new job, ask your boss the following questions. When you have several

FIGURE 6.   Joining-up checklist.

Area	Discussion Topic	Action
Job content	• Core mission of your organization • Major tasks • Hot job issues and concerns • Your organizational role • Status of present work in job area	(Use this column to list your action steps.)
Management of job	• Boss's expectations • Success factors for the job • Setting goals and objectives • Setting priorities • Identification of resources • Relationship with other organizations	
Management of people (self and others)	• Identification of and meeting key people • Development of evaluation criteria • Identification of adversaries and supporters	
Training and development	• Personal training and development needs • Training and development resources • Documentation of your plan	

pending job options, or when a transfer is imminent and there is more than one job area possibility for you, you may want to ask these questions of each potential boss. It is important in order to get a clear understanding of what kinds of things you are looking for, what the job is all about, and what direction you desire for the future. Your new job needs to be a step to reaching your overall goal. There are seven questions to ask the boss:

- What are the major tasks to be accomplished?
- What are the hot issues and concerns in the job area?
- What is your timetable for my accomplishing the major job tasks?

FIGURE 7. Job plan.

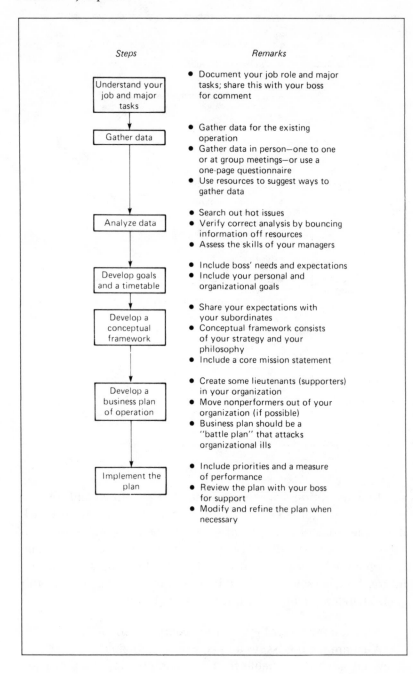

- What do you personally want me to do with the job?
- What skills and positive characteristics does one need to be successful in this job position?
- What skills and characteristics do you see me bringing to this job position?
- What will the things I learn in this assignment permit me to do in my next assignment?

These questions are key to beginning your new job because they will provide you with all kinds of preliminary information that can be used to develop a "joining-up checklist."

2. *Develop a joining-up checklist.* Use Figure 6 to lay out the steps you should use in setting up your job. For those of you who are more experienced and view Figure 6 as being too elementary, we suggest you use Figure 7. Perhaps a combination of the two charts would be appropriate for some of you.

3. *Develop a job implementation action plan.* Consider all the preliminary information you gathered and, after making the joining-up checklist and checking off the items on that list, develop a job implementation action plan. In other words, take all your information, organize it, and develop a strategy in order to implement some action to start performing the job tasks, whatever the job is. Part of the action plan has to be some way of expanding or refining your existing job so when you leave the job it will not be the same as it was when you started it. We leave the action plan up to you, since it must be specific to your needs; however, remember to include a timetable. It should be a step-by-step plan with dates that will show how you are going to start to perform in the new job. For example, step one might be to identify the tasks you need to perform in the next two weeks. Step two might be to plan and organize in order to perform the tasks by the end of the third week, and so on.

4. *Seek a sponsor.* If you already have a sponsor and you have merely moved from one job area to another, you can continue your relationship with the existing sponsor or develop a new sponsor. If you have moved into a new job area and you do not have a sponsor, it is to your advantage to develop one as we have stated in previous chapters. (To review the specifics of developing a sponsor, we refer you to the problem solutions in Part Two, Chapter 4.)

RESISTING POWER

In the context of our discussion, resisting power means that a black manager will push back on someone who is in a position of power when the situation is viewed as one that places the black in a one-down position in power, intelligence, self-esteem, and so on. Resisting power is a touchy issue for blacks because the boss has the ability to punish subordinates by giving them bad evaluations and dead-end assignments. In resisting power, it is performance that counts, not knowledge of how to do it.

With this definition and explanation in mind, let us look at why resisting power is important for blacks. Again, we must look to the historical plight of blacks in this country and to their position in society. We know blacks have been considered to be second-class citizens, and as a result of the long-standing propaganda and consequent discrimination, most blacks have at some time bought into some pieces of this negative stereotype. Blacks have to push back to challenge white managers' negative stereotypes. When this is done in the work place, the bottom line is of course greater productivity and efficiency. Pushing back eliminates a lot of dysfunctional behavior between managers of different cultures that would cause a loss in productivity. What we are saying is, if white managers hang on to their negative stereotypes about blacks, it will cause them to give blacks smaller jobs, have lower expectations of blacks, and deny blacks opportunities to use their expertise and creativity. Therefore, there will be black managers who are not working at their maximum potential. That affects the productivity and efficiency of the total organization.

There are five key principles associated with resisting power.

1. *Effective leaders at one time or another resist power.* They use the concept as a strategy in accomplishing tasks and resolving issues. If you desire to be an effective leader, you must learn to appropriately resist power. Effective leaders do not give in totally to people who use intimidation as their primary style of interacting.

2. *There are two kinds of resistance to power.* When individuals push back, they use either *immediate* resistance or *delayed* resistance. Immediate resisting of power occurs at the time when a stimulus in an interaction causes a reaction. Delayed resisting of

power occurs during an interaction subsequent to the one in which the initial stimulus occurred.

Everybody, no matter what the level in the organization, will be told on many occasions in essence to "shut up and draw." That means do only what the boss tells you to do, no more or no less. In the case of a black manager, this kind of order will cause automatic resistance, often immediate resistance. It will occur because it is tied into the self-concept of the black, which plays a big part in his or her primary and backup behavioral pattern. Take Jack as an example. When his boss said, "Go over there and do this job just as I told you to do," or "Shut up and draw," Jack did not have to use any of the expertise he had developed in school or through his years of experience, he reacted automatically.

If you're a black, you are going to try to protect your self-concept. You will say to yourself, "I *am* somebody, and if I *am* somebody, I can think on my own and I need the boss to tell me what end he is trying to reach and let me use my own expertise and creativity to figure out how to get to that end point." Depending on where the black manager is in the four phases of development, he or she may externally resist power by saying, "Wait a minute. Can't we discuss the end point that you're trying to reach by taking that approach?" This would be immediate resistance to power.

With some managers, their primary behavioral pattern is one of intimidation to get people to respond to them. When a very strong upper-level white manager uses intimidation on a black manager, it is often done rapidly or it may be done in a situation where other people are involved. The black manager will tend to react internally but will not externally display resistance to power. The black will take in the message, go away and think about it, analyze the situation, and decide not to do what he or she has been told but to go back and open the issue again. Blacks have to resist power when they do not understand why they were told to "shut up and draw."

If the intimidating white manager is one level up, then it is relatively easy to come back in a one-to-one setting and engage that person in conversation. If the manager is two or more levels up, the black should use a data base to develop an alternative way of accomplishing the task. In this case, resistance should be based on data analysis. The black manager should first gather data, analyze the situation, and then come back to resist the power of the upper-level white manager. It can be done very smoothly by saying, "I understand you want me to do X, Y, and Z; however, have you considered the risks involved, and do you really want me to do this in this way? If you do, I will. But recognize I'm not in agreement with it even though I will do it."

Those blacks who do not resist power will become intimidated and not fight back. This will have a detrimental effect—a continued low self-concept and reduced productivity.

3. *Use the concept of resisting power only when logic and explanation fail.* This is a good rule of thumb to remember. We must be truthful with you; resisting power can have negative consequences for blacks. When you sense you need to resist power, first try using logic to explain your position on an issue or problem. Introduce facts and figures. Only if this fails should you use the concept of resisting power.

4. *Depersonalize the resistance to power.* Focus your resistance on the task or issue and not on the person involved in the interaction. You need not exclaim, "Are you crazy?" It is inappropriate to get angry and scream, "Have you lost your mind? Do you think I'm incapable of knowing how to do my job?" or any other personal attack on the individual. You should not strip people of their dignity.

5. *Resisting power is triggered by external events.* You will resist power when you feel rage. You will resist power when you feel in a less-than position. When you cannot separate the boss's directions from his or her racism or sexism, you will react and resist power. When you have been positioned so that you cannot use your expertise or creativity to do your job, you will feel it necessary to resist the power of others. There are times when you may be asked to take some inappropriate action that protective hesitation tells you not to do; then you will resist the power of the person who has attempted to intimidate you. You will resist power when all options in a situation have not been considered and when you strongly feel you are right or when you substantially disagree with someone in a power position. Resist power when you could potentially be labeled a follower or weak leader. You may also have to resist power in order to push or sell an idea of yours.

SELF-EVALUATION

Self-evaluation is especially important *against the backdrop of race or sex.* Its purpose is to help you (1) find out where you are relative to your goals; (2) evaluate yourself against some preset organizational standard of performance; and (3) assess your personal growth and development, which includes the impact the organization has made on you as a black as well as the impact you as a black have made on the organization. This information will position you to determine your future direction. Self-evaluation can also be helpful to you when used as a yardstick to measure your distance to go to meet goals. The results of self-evaluation can help build self-confidence as a black and increase self-esteem.

You should evaluate yourself because you are black with a different cultural reference viewpoint from that of the dominant culture in a typical organization. Self-evaluation is a legitimate system of performance counseling that is not used very often. It is helpful to perform self-evaluation because the odds are you know a great deal more about yourself than anyone else does. You know what your needs are, what you want for yourself, what your skills and abilities are, and what motivates you. The system of self-evaluation should, however, be integrated with the official formal organizational evaluation that your boss will give you.*

Self-evaluation should occur at least every six months. It should be done at transfer time and before a formal assessment by your boss. Anytime you feel you want to test yourself to see where you are in terms of your personal development, stop to evaluate yourself. Also, do it anytime you need to answer the following questions:

- Where am I rated in terms of my job performance?
- Where am I located in the four-phase black development model?
- Where am I with myself, or am I comfortable with my blackness or femaleness?
- Am I on a fast or normal track of movement for increased responsibility within the organization?

*Lois Borland Hart, *Moving Up! Women and Leadership* (New York: AMACOM, 1980), p. 119.

There are five key principles to remember in self-evaluation.

1. *Obtain internal information on your job performance.* Make your own judgments on how well you are performing your job. Ask yourself what your areas of strength are as you see them. What are the areas needing development? This is all based on how you feel about yourself. Do not deal with what is right or wrong. Jot down notes that will answer the questions strictly from your perspective and from your perceptions of yourself in your working environment. Include your perceptions of how you operate as a black in a white setting. Then relate these to relationships with bosses, peers, subordinates, if any, and your own control over your environment in terms of how you get your needs met to do your most efficient and productive work.

2. *Obtain external information on your job performance.* Ask yourself, "What is the gist of the latest information I have received from others in the organization? Is it positive, negative, or neutral?" What specific things have others asked you to improve on? What suggestions have they made to you? Others can be peers, bosses, and subordinates. Try to weed out the racist and sexist pieces. You will need to ascertain what is legitimate feedback and what is inappropriate.

3. *Test where you are against your personal job goals.* By this time, if you do not have personal training and development goals, we are sure you will at least have thought about some. We suggest you stop now and jot down at least five of these. If you do not have goals, you cannot do a good job of self-evaluation. Assuming you have already developed some personal job goals, find out where you stand relative to the accomplishment of those goals. Remember, you want to be able to test where you are relative to where you want to go.

4. *Test where you are against your organizational goals.* If you are confused about the difference between personal job goals and organizational goals, let us look at an example of the difference. A personal job goal might be: "Within three months, I will develop an effective personal interactional style. I will know I have accomplished the goal when I do not receive any negative input on my style for a three-week period."

An organizational job goal might be: "Within three months, I will develop a new set of procedures to accomplish one of my major job tasks. This will be evidenced by more efficient and productive completion of the job."

5. *Document your evaluation.* Jot down all the information you have gathered using the first four key principles. Consolidate this and put it in some order. Run the information past a trusted friend, spouse, or peer. You may also use your boss or sponsor. However, if you do use your boss, you must have a good relationship so there will be no misunderstanding or misdirection from the boss. If the boss is racist or sexist, you should not run this information past that person. You may decide to share your information with your sponsor. Remember, you cannot use every sponsor for every need. You may have to develop different sponsors to meet your different needs. Sponsors, too, can be racist and sexist. Be sensitive and use good judgment when sharing information about yourself with others.

SETTING YOUR SIGHTS HIGHER

Complacency is a form of living death for blacks and other minorities that affects not only the individual but the group as well. It certainly satisfies the racists who insist that blacks are happy with their status and that the "agitators" who would like to cause friction should leave blacks alone. It also satisfies sexists who feel women belong in the home, caring for children. Minorities need to thoughtfully and continuously set their sights higher throughout their work lives to be successful.

Set your sights higher when you find yourself stuck in any of the development phases. Even the Success Phase demands more success. Set your sights higher when you find yourself accepting less than what you desire or less than what you feel you are capable of achieving. If you are the type of person who feels a strong group alliance and a need to be a role model for other minorities struggling to achieve success, and you are angered by the plight of minorities in business institutions, then you have an additional reason to set your sights higher. Mayor J. Kenneth Blackwell of Cincinnati, Ohio, speaking at the Second Annual Salute to Black Achievers on April 17, 1980, summed up the above by stating, "The human condition is *not* a spectator sport; either act or be acted upon."

Many great people have encouraged us to first have a dream. This makes sense because how can you experience desire without a dream? Setting your sights higher is the beginning of fulfillment of a dream. Not only must you have a dream, but you must have a strong desire to make the dream come true. You must *want* to be successful. You should set goals, develop a plan of attack, and implement the plan. Setting goals is important because without this step you cannot be clear about what you are reaching for.

When you develop a *strong* desire for success or when you sense that your self-concept is lower than your skills level (see Figure 4), set your sights higher. In setting your sights higher, there are five key principles to remember.

1. *You must have a very strong desire to succeed.* If the desire to succeed is not present, or if complacency has set in, blacks will find advancement nearly impossible. Success and advancement are seldom automatic; they require effort. All blacks are not going to succeed any more than all whites are. Some people decide they do not want the hassle of being a leader or manager. If that is where a person is, that is fine. But if you are a person with a burning desire to succeed, you will seek to set your sights higher. You need to periodically fuel your dream in order to begin your plans. Sit down and fantasize as you did when you were a kid. Think about what you will be doing when you have reached your goal. Detail everything in your mind so there is a complete picture of yourself in the situation. Paint a picture of the person you are talking to, what you are wearing, whether you are sitting or standing, and so forth. You must feel, touch, and taste the dream. Now savor the positive emotions you feel. If you do this often, it will increase your desire to succeed and build up your energy level. You will surely depress yourself and lower your energy if you allow yourself to believe you must not dream, because then everything is set against your being successful. This is self-fulfilling because you will not be able to set your sights higher and will ensure that you will not be successful. If your dream is a part of your day-to-day reality, it is more likely you will make it happen.

2. *You must have the proper attitude.* Mayor Blackwell of Cincinnati also stated at the previously mentioned meeting that his grandmother always told him, "Your attitude determines your altitude." In other words, your attitude will determine how high you rise in any endeavor. If you are black with a negative attitude working in any predominantly white institution, you will ensure that you will not succeed.

For example, we have an acquaintance who is a black assistant principal working at a predominantly white high school. He is bright, energetic, and next in line to become principal in the school district. In talking and working with him on some projects, we found him to have a very negative attitude about himself, the system, and his ability to get things done. He sees injustice, but rather than positively attack it head on, he complains about it, tends to be angry much of the time, acts disgusted, and frequently strips people of their dignity. His co-workers will not help him solve problems. He is working to achieve failure by refusing to believe in his dreams and can therefore not set his sights higher. He wants to be principal, but his negative attitude is ensuring he will be passed over. We can assure you that developing a proper attitude will have a profound and positive impact on setting your sights higher and achieving success.

3. *You must take risks.* If you are not willing to take some degree of risk, then it is difficult to set your sights higher and achieve success. You will not push to resolve some of the key hot issues that may be facing you, whatever institution you are in. Different people are willing to take different degrees of risk. If you are serious about setting your sights higher and you are a low risk taker, you need to use role modeling techniques to draw the essence of how other people take risks and role play that.

4. *You must have a major goal to achieve.* You need to define a major goal because it gives you something to race toward in order to achieve success. You do not want to be all over the place, racing in many directions, depleting your energies, and diverting your attention.

5. *You must have an action plan that can be implemented.* It is obviously a waste of time to develop an action plan that you cannot implement. Be realistic about what you can and cannot do. Here you must be careful because you want to be sure you are taking a risk and not choosing goals that are too easy to achieve. Goals that are too easy are not going to *really* achieve anything because they will not challenge you or give you an opportunity to grow. One way to test a goal is to ask if it stretches you; does it create some anxiety, and does it have growth potential for you? Think about your hardest but most enjoyable course in school; it does not matter what educational level or type of course it was. Recall the feeling of anxiety that you had in the pit of your stomach after about the second week in the course. That is how you should feel about your goal. If you do not, then it is not difficult enough. That means you are not setting your sights high enough.

We would like to close this section with the sage words of John W. Newbern: "People can be divided into three groups: those who make things happen, those who watch things happen, and those who wonder what happened." Seriously consider these words, and set your sights higher.

RESISTING BLACK SELF-HATE

In this section, we will introduce the issue of resisting black self-hate. We will not attempt to explore the issue fully here; that would require volumes. Several fine books that can help further enlighten you on the subject and related areas are listed at the end of this chapter. The key principles we give for resisting black self-hate represent some of the things that blacks can do to offset the destructive forces of racism on one's self-respect, and a building of a positive self-identity.

When a black person wants to be identified with the white majority and accepted by its members as one of its members, then the black person has succumbed to a condition called black self-hate. How much a person is affected by this condition varies with the intensity of feeling and the subsequent behavior associated with rejection of the person's own group. A person experiencing black self-hate will actively seek relationships and friendships with white individuals while avoiding, when possible, ties with other blacks. For example, the person might choose to live in an all-white community, limiting contact with other blacks. This may include joining an all-white church, participating in functions and activities that other blacks seldom become involved in, and making friendships with whites who have limited experience and exposure to other blacks.

Total acceptance by whites is impossible because blacks cannot hide the color of their skin. Whites cannot truly dismiss this difference nor can they help projecting social prejudices, many of which they may be honestly unaware of. After all, no matter how much a black person conforms to white cultural practices and values, the individual is *not* white by cultural upbringing. The differences may be subtle for some blacks, but they are nonetheless there.

There are two sides to the difficulty for blacks who experience black self-hate. Other blacks greatly resent blacks who reject their in-group. For many blacks this rejection is seen as the ultimate affront. They, in turn, will discriminate against blacks who deny their blackness. On the other hand, all blacks grow up in this society rejected by the majority, having their dignity, character, and self-worth attacked. Blacks suffer ridicule, deprecation, contempt, and discrimination at the hands of whites. Those who come to hate themselves for their blackness must learn to deny what society has trained them from birth to believe.

Some blacks are so hurt and have suffered so inside that they buy into the stereotypes whites have about blacks and in a desperate attempt to salvage self-respect will try, as we said earlier, to separate themselves from the hated group and identify with whites. These blacks show contempt for themselves and other blacks and often betray their in-group in order to get closer to the majority group. The self-love that should be everyone's right gradually turns to self-hate. These blacks mimic what they think is white and behave as they think whites wish them to. They *believe* the dominant group is right and accept the state of things. They feel deeply and inwardly ashamed of being black. They possess qualities they despise and feel self-repugnance as well as repugnance for other blacks who surely also possess these qualities. Blacks who have black self-hate believe that the lower the economic status, the more of these hated qualities must be present. They feel "those lower-class people just make it hard for everyone else."

Now let us look briefly at a few of the reasons black self-hate occurs. Until very recent history, most American blacks were inadvertently or purposely raised to feel handicapped by their blackness. The intent was not vicious, but rather it was done as a way of passing on knowledge of how to survive and gain some measure of success in a hostile environment.

Blacks continue to find themselves having to overcome the handicap of language, when in fact English is not spoken well by most Americans, black or white, who are influenced greatly by regional dialects. Physical appearance is a handicap because the American standard is white skin, blue eyes, and blond hair with thin regular features. Normal self-pride, assertiveness, initiative, and aggression become handicaps for blacks if they surface, because whites prefer blacks to be passive. Blacks are forced to sublimate and camouflage their natural feelings and personal aspirations.

These are only a very few of the handicaps blacks face through no real fault of their own. Is it any wonder then that many blacks fall victim to black self-hate and seek to strongly identify with those who are seen as so much more perfect? It is very much like a crippled person who feels a need to hang on to someone who is whole.

Blacks who have been born with lighter skin and straighter hair have had better opportunities to identify with whites because whites often reward those blacks for their similarities to the dominant group and will further reward them for their attempt at assimilation. These are the blacks most frequently accepted socially, for educational opportunities, and for promotions. The delusion is that fair-skinned blacks and assimilated blacks feel they will always be rewarded, but there is a stopping point, a ceiling. The person is still black and will never be white.

Black self-hate is a complicated issue, deeply rooted in our history. It is not easily overcome, nor is it a simple matter to handle or resolve. Some people are too deeply hurt for this book to help and may need personal professional assistance. However, for those who may merely need insight into the problem, we offer three key principles that can help a person begin the process of resisting black self-hate.

1. *You must be able to recognize the condition of black self-hate in yourself.* One way to check this issue is to ask yourself the following questions and be *honest* with yourself in answering:

- Am I at ease, that is, accepting of myself and my identified cultural group?
- Do I often feel ashamed and embarrassed by other blacks when they violate some rule and value I hold, especially if whites are witness to that behavior?
- Do I then want to ensure whites who witness the other person's behavior that I am different and seek to illustrate that?
- Am I comfortable in thinking about and discussing race?
- How do I relate to members of my own race?
- Do I feel more comfortable relating to members of another race?
- What race are the individuals I feel most comfortable with? Those I trust most? Those I want to get most of my input from?
- Do I use my cultural experience, or do I discount it?
- Do I tend to identify myself more with whites?

- Do I deny racial issues exist, or do I admit that they do exist but do not apply to me?
- Am I *very* concerned that whites feel comfortable with me?

To recognize the symptoms of black self-hate, you need to think logically about your attitude and behavior. Are you behaving the way *you* want to, with self-pride and self-dignity, or the way you feel white managers want you to behave? You also need to look seriously at where your present attitude and behavior will take you. Ask yourself whether it has gotten you what you want. Will it in the future? Are you really getting the kind of results you need and want without a severe sacrifice to your self-esteem?

Blacks experiencing self-hate tend to have blind faith in white organizations as well as in white individuals because they insist on believing most whites have blacks' best interests at heart. These blacks will accept the white viewpoint unquestioningly because they have bought into white stereotypes about blacks. They do not seek black input and will refuse to accept or listen to it when given. They do not want the unvalued information and will also tend to separate themselves from the black group. Often they become arrogant in the presence of both blacks and whites. These blacks tend to see themselves in intense competition with whites, because they need to *prove* themselves superior to gain acceptance.

There is danger in this method of seeking acceptance, because black self-hate has two stages. In the first stage, blacks will feel they are better than other blacks and will behave in that manner. If a person is successful in this, the second stage is to move to becoming and feeling smarter and better than most whites. This is dangerous, because once whites sense this, the black is in danger of getting shoved aside in the organization. The kind of competitiveness that is an accepted part of the white cultural norm continues to be somewhat alien to most blacks, and they still tend to have little knowledge or experience with this form of politicking.

2. *Understand what black self-hate is and why it exists.* Acting white when you are black is a contradiction and puts you in an ambiguous situation. Whites do not seem to really appreciate that kind of behavior from blacks or to identify with it as much as blacks who behave that way believe whites do. Whites very subtly

punish blacks for the transgression into their group, even though whites cause blacks to behave like whites by appearing to reward the behavior. Whites expect blacks to behave like blacks whatever that means to them in their context. Whites may try to mold a black's behavior so that the behavior is comfortable to whites. However, this does not mean that whites are going to accept the black totally in the same way another white would be accepted. There are cultural and physical differences that cannot be ignored. Therefore, whites often put blacks in an ambiguous state. This is a situation that is confusing to the person experiencing black self-hate. If you understand black self-hate and its pressures, then you can understand what is happening when a white manager tries to operate with you in this way. You will be able to see that what may appear to be rewards in reality are not and be able to deal with this.

Sometimes white managers will tell blacks that they are different from other blacks in order to manage their behavior and become more comfortable. In this manner, a white is able to control a black so that the white person can feel at ease and not feel threatened in any way. Nearly all blacks have at some time experienced this type of interaction with whites. For some blacks, this experience triggers black self-hate and its characteristic behavior. These blacks want to be different from those held in such low esteem.

3. *Recognize and actively use a black support structure.* Have a person from the black support structure help you explore reasons why you bought into black self-hate. This may be touchy for some people, but you do need to do this with someone you trust and respect. You need to keep informed about what is occurring with other blacks in the organization. Of course, you do need to establish a reputation with powerful whites, but do not get totally wrapped up in establishing your reputation and do not do it to the exclusion of keeping in touch with other blacks. Interact with other blacks so you can keep a realistic picture of who you are and where you are going in the organization. Find some brothers and sisters in the organization with whom you can have day-to-day contact. These should be individuals preferably at your level with at least two more years of experience than you have so they can share their experiences with you on how to survive and succeed. A person such as this will be helpful in some instances because

the memories and experiences should be fresh and more relevant to your immediate needs.

You need to develop a framework in which to view yourself as a black so you will not be dependent on a white viewpoint of you. You need enough information to define yourself as a black and be comfortable with your definition.

Develop different behaviors in your organization. Develop some way to behave other than buying into self-hatred. Do not act white; that is, do not mimic your perceptions of whites and try to make your behavior indistinguishable from theirs. You do not need to attempt to prove you are smarter than whites as well as other blacks. When you do this, are you not saying you are the smartest person in your organization? That in itself is an unrealistic view to have; you also leave yourself open for attack from all areas. And nobody is so smart that they do not need help from anyone.

In the 1980s most organizations will operate on the principle of teamwork, because businesses and technologies are so complex that one person cannot run the whole show the way Henry Ford did when he developed his Model A automobile. Black self-hate is an insidious crippler. Because of it, too many blacks will never develop their creative potential, and too many will ultimately lose their souls trying to be accepted by the dominant culture, which will never recognize the price these people paid.

Recommended Reading

These titles are all included in the bibliography, but they are worth singling out here for their special value in dealing with black self-hate:

The Nature of Prejudice, by Gordon W. Allport
The Jesus Bag, by William H. Grier and Price M. Cobbs
Black Rage, also by Grier and Cobbs
Black Experience Analysis and Synthesis, by Carlene Young, editor

7

External Strategies

MANAGEMENT OF RACIAL ATTITUDES

In Chapter 1, we defined and briefly discussed the management of racial attitudes as a part of the learnings of black managers in the Planned Growth Phase. We feel it is appropriate to again define that skill. The management of racism consists of a group of behaviors uniquely developed by blacks to counteract and neutralize demeaning, prejudicial, and discriminatory behavior directed toward them by persons of another race or ethnic group. We would like the reader to keep in mind the word *unique* in this situation because, as we have stated continually, there are some learnings blacks must gain that are a result of their second-class citizenship in our society. A great deal of a black manager's energy is often devoted to offsetting, defusing, and neutralizing racial barriers that are inherent in every facet of life.

Although whites do not have to develop the management of racial attitudes as a part of their job skills because they are not objects of racial discrimination, we believe they must be aware of this as a need for blacks. Whites will be managing blacks more and more in the future and therefore cannot continue to deny that certain prejudicial acts occur. In order to ensure maximum productivity, efficiency, and teamwork for *all* employees, white managers need to begin to understand they have a responsibility to help blacks learn how to manage the racism of others. Whites also need to learn how to manage the racism of other whites. For blacks, the management of racism is intimately tied to both their survival and success in a white corporation. Some aspect of this skill is used every day in the various interactions of the black manager.

There are four key principles blacks need to consider in managing racism.

Be able to recognize racism in action and its consequences. You cannot manage negative racial attitudes of others if you cannot recognize racism operating on you. Denial of racism for the sake of comfort ensures that you will not grow internally or advance in the organization. Notice how whites respond and interact with you and other blacks, and also how whites respond and interact with other whites. See what behaviors are the same toward both blacks and whites and what behaviors are different. Look at the dynamics of the various situations in which you interact with whites, and pay attention to your *visceral reactions* of discomfort. When you have repeated negative visceral reactions to a white you interact with, you need to consider the subtle dynamics in the interaction.

Be willing to take a risk in confronting dysfunctional behavior. Push back appropriately when a person's negative racial attitudes have negative consequences for you. Throughout this book, we have mentioned many negative consequences discriminatory behavior has on the progress of blacks. If you are in a meeting and you have important data to input and it is not being heard, it is certainly appropriate to risk a confrontation in order to be heard. Call attention to the behavior you see and share your perspective on it.

Pick your fights appropriately. Remember to be sensitive to whom you fight with, how you fight, and when you fight. Making an upper-level boss lose face in front of subordinates will not win you any points. Also understand that everything is not worth fighting for. Make sure your battle is an important one so you do not get the reputation of fighting everything all the time.

Increase your knowledge base about the black–white dynamics that occur between individuals and in groups. Whites can have negative attitudes about blacks, and blacks can have negative attitudes about whites. When blacks and whites interact in a group, the negative attitudes of the majority toward the minority are apt to surface.

There are some behavioral differences between blacks and whites. If conflict arises as a result of these differences, it can have a negative impact when you are trying to accomplish a task. In essence, whites' negative racial attitudes can get translated into negative behavior, and blacks, as a result of their negative prejudices, can overreact in the situation. This will then create barriers from both sides to the accomplishment of work tasks and will reduce the productivity of the work group.

Learn the management of racial attitudes. Below are five basic principles used in managing racial attitudes. Each principle has some specific behaviors that have been used by black managers in becoming successful in the white corporation.

1. Racism is managed by strategy.
   - Recognize racist behavior and implement a plan to neutralize it. One of the best ways to counteract racist behavior is to be proactive rather than reactive; this renders the negative behavior as harmless as possible. Neutralizing racist behavior also tends to have positive consequences for all involved.
   - Use anger as a strategy. Anger needs to be under your control, used as a tool, and displayed publicly only when it can provide a means to positive problem solving.
   - Sell "immaculate" ideas that are carefully thought out beforehand. Try to develop foresight in preparing your ideas and also prepare contingencies for possible difficulties that may arise.
   - Use tact as a strategy. Building a keen sensitivity to others is invaluable to job success. Learn how to approach people in a way that avoids unnecessary conflict. That old cliché "You can catch more flies with honey than vinegar" still holds true.
   - When whites are illogically resistant, lay out data and let them think they came up with the idea. Often you will find the most important task is to sell a good idea rather than worry about whether or not you get credit for it. If your idea is accepted, chances are you will eventually get credit since the idea will have to be developed and implemented.

After all, because it is your idea, you will be the one with the knowledge of how to make it work.

- When appropriate, confront whites directly with their racist behavior or imply you feel that may be a part of the issue. In this way, you can slow down the dysfunctional interaction and force the other person to look at his or her behavior.
- Make ideas known to many people in writing. Public knowledge of your ideas both protects you and gives you needed exposure in your hierarchy.
- Present your ideas in terms of white's self-interest. Most of us are more willing to listen to and consider input when we feel we have a stake in it.
- Give something back to whites when using them as resources. Do not hesitate to give the person a stroke. Everyone likes to feel appreciated, even people who appear not to care. Share information that you know the person needs even if he or she did not ask for it.
- Be amicable with whites. Often whites react negatively to blacks who display distant, hostile, or unfriendly behavior. On the other hand, whites tend to react positively to blacks who are friendly and willing to be sociable with them. You will have to decide what type of response you wish to receive from whites in your interactions.
- Confront whites in such a way that they can keep their dignity. When you strip a person of dignity or self-worth, you will likely make a vengeful enemy. Allow others to save face. You lose nothing and may gain much.

2. Racism is managed by controlling the behavior of others.
- Manage through others. Sometimes whites listen better to other whites or may single out blacks they are more comfortable with to listen to. If this is the case, it can be helpful if you manage through others to facilitate accomplishing a task.
- Tell whites how you expect them to behave. In many instances inappropriate behavior is a result of a lack of knowledge. Share information on what you feel is appropriate behavior. Tell whites how you would like or expect them to behave in a given situation to prevent inappropriate behavior from occurring as a result of insensitivity.

- Manage a racist with personal style and charisma. A racist tends to calm down and stop displaying racist behavior when a black displays a smooth personal interactional style and a quiet power.
- Be careful in using organizational resources, so they do not evaluate you. When using whites as resources, couch your need in organizational terms rather than in personal terms. Never approach a white resource by openly discussing your personal deficiencies.

3. Racism is managed by controlling yourself.
   - Listen to whites interact, watch them, and duplicate their behavioral approach. Learn white organizational norms by observing how whites interact with each other and how power and control are appropriately and most effectively exercised. Now you can decide whether it is more appropriate to follow a given cultural norm or to strategically disregard it to accomplish organizational tasks more efficiently, especially in face of racist behavior.
   - Be selective about what key organizational issues you discuss with whites. Never walk up to your white boss and say, "I want your job." Be careful how you phrase your needs relative to hot issues.
   - Pay attention, sort out the important data and issues, and make your stand known. Particularly in a critical situation or interaction, be sure you have the relevant information before making your position on a subject known. When you do not have the pertinent facts or when you sit on the fence, it is easy for a racist to control you.
   - Do not depend on organizational rewards; generate your own strokes. Whites tend not to expect public strokes and rewards; nor do they tend to give many. Blacks must not expect to be publicly stroked or rewarded for every major organizational accomplishment. Many times the reward is inherent in the accomplishment.

4. Racism is managed by using organizational norms and values.
   - Ask for more work. You will help shatter negative stereotypes about blacks while casting yourself in a favorable light.
   - Put information in writing. This fits with most organiza-

tional practices. Putting things in writing allows you to share experience and expertise with others. It also shows others what you know and as a result can help defuse any negative input about you.

- Ask key questions indirectly. Learn when it is appropriate to ask questions indirectly so that racist individuals will not have a reason to react negatively to questions that they could perceive as threatening or irrelevant.

5. Racism is managed by using the communications network.

- Develop productive relationships with powerful people in the hierarchy. These people may or may not be sponsors. These relationships will help ensure that you and your expertise are known by the right people in your organization.

- Eat lunch with whites to obtain information from their formal and informal communications networks. This offers you an opportunity to obtain information and make personal contact. Personal contact will offer future opportunities for you to obtain additional information from the communications network.

- Eat lunch with blacks to share information and to keep in touch with the grapevine. This offers you an opportunity to relax and obtain psychic energy.

EFFECTIVE BOSS–SUBORDINATE RELATIONSHIPS

Although there are black boss–white subordinate relationships, this section focuses on white boss–black subordinate relationships. An effective boss–subordinate relationship is one in which both boss and subordinate can use their full measure of expertise for optimum completion of their work tasks. Blacks should separate whites' interactional style from their knowledge. Even racist individuals have data and expertise to share. Blacks tend to respond well to stylish and open people, bosses as well as peers. Some people are neither stylish nor open, and blacks tend not to respond as well to them. This normally leads to unfortunate consequences for both boss and subordinate, preventing optimum use of each others' talents.

Bosses fulfill many roles; they are resources, counselors, teachers, coaches, and leaders. If you as the subordinate do not have a good supportive relationship with your boss, then he or she cannot effectively fulfill these various roles. Your boss may also have negative feelings about you for not recognizing or utilizing his or her expertise. The two of you, therefore, will not exhibit optimum productivity. An effective boss–subordinate relationship can be a big plus to a subordinate's performance evaluation. Remember, the key ingredients in an effective boss–subordinate relationship are productivity and output. There are eight key principles to the effective boss–subordinate relationship.

1. *Understand your boss's goals, organizational needs, expectations, and criteria for success as they relate to the job.* A boss in an interracial relationship should help the black subordinate obtain this information. On the other hand, as we have previously stated, the subordinate should share the same information with his or her boss. In essence, subordinates should aim their actions and energies toward solving the boss's problems. This is how the black manager gets that extra edge on the competition.

2. *You and your boss must be willing to learn multicultural management techniques.* Because you and your boss are working within the context of an interracial relationship, you both must understand the cultural differences between you and make them work for you rather than against you. Very often people of a different culture can bring unique and creative solutions to problems that people of the dominant culture might not consider. In addition, the white boss will find multicultural management techniques help the black manager grow and develop at a rapid pace, which allows the needs of both the boss and the organization to be met sooner.

3. *It must be permissible for you to resist the power of the boss in the relationship.* Bosses and subordinates must develop relationships wherein it is OK for a subordinate to appropriately challenge a boss's suggestions, directions, and analysis of work tasks. The subordinate must be comfortable in resisting the power of the boss, and the boss must be comfortable in being challenged by the subordinate. However, bear in mind, as we have stated before, you must not strip your boss of his or her dignity, especially in a public meeting. In other words, leave the boss a way out. Not doing this is one of the easiest and surest ways to cause a racist to become dysfunctional with you.

4. *Allow your thoughts and actions to be appropriately shaped*

by the boss. This is important since bosses become bosses because they have a certain amount of experience and expertise. They may not be the sharpest people in the organization, but they will always have something they can share. So seek the counsel and support of your boss before tackling a major task.

5. *Feel comfortable in managing your boss.* In any boss–subordinate relationship, it is appropriate for a subordinate to manage the boss so that the boss is not always overmanaging the subordinate. Manage the boss's needs by being aware of what those needs are and understanding how to go about meeting them. It is a given in an organization that an outstanding manager will manage up the hierarchy as well as laterally and down the hierarchy. Average managers manage only in a downward and lateral fashion. Subordinates can manage their bosses by structuring and organizing the boss's time so the boss is not bogged down in a lot of unnecessary discussions and details.

6. *Develop a profile of the boss.* Know the boss's needs, style of operating, and decision-making processes. If you are aware of the boss's style of operating, then you can effectively respond to it. If the boss needs things structured and organized, then you will know to present things to the boss in such a manner. Peter F. Drucker discusses in his book *The Effective Executive** these next seven items that are important for a subordinate to know about the boss.

- Know whether the boss is a reader or a listener.
- Know what the boss's strengths are and how they can be used.
- Know whether the boss is political or nonpolitical in the organization.
- Know whether the boss is a team player or an individually oriented worker.
- Know whether the boss needs to see figures and calculations or just results.
- Know what the boss does well.
- Know whether the boss is people or task oriented.

If a subordinate knows all these things about the boss, then he or she knows exactly how to go about relating to and interfacing with the boss.

7. *Remember bosses are human and can make mistakes.* Blacks

*New York: Harper and Row, 1966, pp. 93–99.

tend to assume bosses became bosses because they are sharp. This may not necessarily be true. A boss does deserve respect, however, because of his or her position, but the person, whether sharp or not, is nonetheless human and will make mistakes in tasks as well as in relationships.

8. *Bosses should make step-level counseling available to their subordinates.* Step-level counseling, as explained earlier, is an opportunity to obtain counseling by a member of the hierarchy at least one level above the subordinate's immediate boss, an opportunity to get the benefit of the boss' boss' experience. It is also an opportunity for the boss' boss to find out from you how you are doing in the boss–subordinate relationship and how you are doing in your job. In the context of multicultural management, step-level counseling helps prevent a racist boss from taking advantage of a black subordinate.

MANAGEMENT OF SUBORDINATES

The management of subordinates deals with planning and organizing in addition to motivating and controlling subordinates. In this section, we will focus on the black boss and white subordinate. Black bosses initially tend to feel anxiety and stress about the use of managerial power because, as a cultural group, blacks have been on the receiving end of the power spectrum. There are a number of issues that may concern black bosses: (1) desire to be fair to all subordinates, both black and white; (2) concern about mistreating people as they themselves have been mistreated; (3) discomfort because of the newness of being in control of whites; and (4) concern over whether or not whites will take direction from black bosses.

A key to managerial effectiveness particularly for the black boss is the development of personal goals, organizational goals, and a business or game plan. Having goals and a plan allows the manager to assume the role of a teacher and get rewards from seeing subordinates become successful through his or her help. In addition it makes the boss look good to the organization by being known as a developer of people.

Here are 15 key principles for the black manager to focus on in managing subordinates. Most of these are self-explanatory, and some are critical to the black boss in effectively managing white subordinates.

1. *Understand that effective black managers are those who:*

- Bring things to conclusion, work jobs to completion.
- Act appropriately independent.
- Are creative.
- Have good interpersonal skills and get along well with people.
- Possess the ability to use resources.
- Free up their bosses by doing part of their jobs.
- Make good decisions.
- Have the courage to take appropriate risks.
- Have the capacity to do many jobs and do them all well.
- Are able to manage their bosses.
- Manage their area in the most effective manner from a corporate or institutional standpoint.
- Possess a good sense of timing in managerial situations.
- Provide constructive dissension in the organization.
- Accept defeat and bounce back without a loss of productivity.
- Actively seek opportunities to contribute.
- Read the direction of the organization and provide leadership.
- Manage the racism of others.
- Resist power appropriately.
- Resist black self-hate.
- Possess the ability to make a quick assessment of people.
- Manage organizational conflict well.

2. *Tell your subordinates how you work best and how you would like them to work.*

3. *Share with your subordinates your goals, organizational needs, expectations, and criteria for success as they relate to the job.*

4. *Be sure that subordinates are clear about their job roles and tasks.*

5. *Develop a list of priorities and criteria for setting priorities.*

6. *Develop profiles of subordinates.* Insight is fundamental to the management of subordinates. Profiles should be able to provide this necessary insight. Below are some of the things you should learn about your subordinates.*

---

*Items c–g are based on Peter F. Drucker, The Effective Executive, pp. 93–99.

a. The subordinate's needs, interpersonal style, and mode of operation.
b. How the subordinate's decision making processes work.
c. Whether the subordinate is a reader or a listener.
d. What the subordinate's strengths and weaknesses are; how these may be used, strengthened, or corrected.
e. Whether the subordinate is political or nonpolitical in the organization.
f. Whether the subordinate is a team player or individual worker.
g. Whether the subordinate is people or task oriented.
h. What the subordinate does well, how the subordinate learns best, and what motivates him or her.
i. The subordinate's job interests.
j. How the subordinate defines rewards and punishments.

7. *Create a motivating and supportive atmosphere for subordinates.*

8. *Do not get into competition with subordinates.*

9. *Delegate appropriately by considering your subordinates' interests, willingness, abilities, and experiences.*

10. *Coach and counsel your subordinates.* Coaching is used to supply skills and knowledge. Counseling helps provide subordinates with direction and is also used to determine why subordinates do not use the skills and abilities they possess.

11. *Give continuous performance feedback to subordinates.*

12. *Understand different racial boss–subordinate dynamics.* Black subordinates tend to need support and will seek to verify for themselves if the black boss will be supportive. White subordinates tend to initially challenge and test the black boss's intelligence, experience, and abilities to handle the job. If white subordinates are properly managed, they will stop this type of behavior.

13. *Encourage subordinates to give input or feedback on job procedures, work problems, morale, and personnel needs.**

14. *Discuss what level of authority subordinates will be allowed to have in carrying out job assignments.* It is difficult to be more specific here since a subordinate's level of authority will

---

*Judy Simmons, "Managing Organizations: Listen, Learn and Lead," *Black Enterprise* (November 1978), p. 56.

vary depending on the type of job held and the institution. However, some levels might be (1) full authority to decide and act; (2) authority to decide, act, and report; and (3) authority to decide and recommend.

15. *Know how to control a recalcitrant subordinate.* Occasionally a boss must do something more drastic to manage a subordinate who has become recalcitrant. Subordinates can be controlled by giving them special projects to prevent them from being disruptive and dysfunctional to the group. The special project should be one that reduces the subordinate's use of discretionary time and energy. Direct the subordinate to obtain more information about a task or project. You may also withdraw such resources as money, people, and data from the recalcitrant subordinate. Withdrawing your support is yet another way of managing and controlling the subordinate.

USING RESOURCES

One of the characteristics of a good manager is the ability to recognize and use resources. This ability is very highly prized by organizations. Positive job results occur when the correct resources are used. The use of resources can be a growth experience, because it enables you to learn new information that might have been closed to you if you did not search it out. The use of resources is not automatic with many people. For blacks, it may have negative racial implications based on past experiences. There are two key issues with blacks relative to the use of resources:

1. How can white peers, supervisors, and others be used as resources if they exhibit racist behavior or if they are reluctant to share their expertise?
2. How can whites be used without a loss of self-esteem, dignity, and pride?

As we have already seen illustrated by Jack, protective hesitation is a coping behavior that often prevents blacks from using resources. At some point a black manager has to say to him- or herself, "I don't care how I am viewed by a resource. That person has what I need, and I will interact with that person to get it regardless of what he or she thinks of me."

FIGURE 8. Vertical and lateral integration of knowledge from resources.

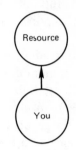

Vertical Integration

Building on existing knowledge

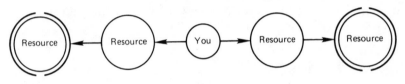

Lateral Integration

Obtaining new knowledge

We have established that no one can be successful in an organization without seeking and using the expertise of others. A person's career progress is tied directly to the use of resources, which allows new information to be integrated both vertically and laterally. Vertical integration means that you add to your present knowledge base; lateral integration means that you take new knowledge from many sources about things that you do not know. This concept is shown diagrammatically in Figure 8.

Once you have decided to use resources, decide whether you need vertical or lateral resources. When a lateral resource is needed, you should seek input from a minimum of two people; often more are needed. When a vertical resource is needed, then the use of one outstanding resource is sufficient because you are building on your existing knowledge base.

A good thing to know is that you can get strokes and praise from your boss and organization for using resources, because they know you grow in the process and become more productive. Also, ideas are easier to sell if you show evidence of having used resources. Blacks sometimes mistakenly think if they use resources it means they are incompetent in that particular area.

The process for using resources is outlined below. Additional helpful information on how to overcome reluctance and hesitancy in asking questions of whites can be found in the solution to Problem I in Chapter 2.

1. Be clear about why you are using resources and the area in which you want help. Be as specific as possible about the information you need from the resource.

2. Locate a good resource. If you do not have personal knowledge of someone, ask a trusted friend or acquaintance to suggest a resource.

3. If you are concerned about the reaction of the resource to your request for information, then find out how the person responds to blacks. If such information is not available, then predict the person's reaction on the basis of whatever information you have and weigh the personal risk for you against how badly you need the information.

4. Decide on an approach to use and proceed to get the information. Refuse to quit until you obtain what you want. A little preplanning and strategy can take you far. Remember, if the resource becomes nasty with you, you can always back off and try someone else. Do not become discouraged and give up.

5. If you are a black boss, send a white subordinate to do the resourcing and report back to you.

6. Have your boss or the resource's boss request the resource to work with you, thus making the resource accountable to the boss for the quality of the resourcing.

READING CUES

We are constantly receiving cues about something each day. Nature provides us with cues about what is going on around us as well as what is likely to happen. People also provide indications of events to come. Some of these messages are explicit; we do not have to guess at the events. However, many are implicit, leaving us to speculate as to what the messages mean. When we must interpret a variety of information to make sense of some message, then we must read the cues.

Most of us are accustomed to reading the many cues nature provides. A weather forecaster might say that rain is not forecast for today, but you see heavy clouds in the sky, the air feels heavy with moisture, and tiny flying bugs have collected in clumps as if expecting something to happen. The sky did not roar, "No matter what those weather instruments say, I'm going to rain!" Nature implied an event was about to occur. You take your umbrella with you as a precaution because, even though the explicit statement was that rain was not in the area, the implicit messages were to the contrary. Nature was giving signals that you interpreted on the basis of some additional messages and through logic, past experience, and emotional reaction to all the information. As a result, you put two and two together to predict what was really likely to happen. Perhaps it did not rain, or the radar missed the clouds and it did rain after all. In any case, you read the cues and were prepared for the possible event.

This same process applies to reading cues from people. We define reading cues as the integration of explicit, implicit, verbal, and nonverbal information about an event or impending event or about things that occur during an event that tell us what may be hidden beneath the more obvious information. This is accomplished by using affective and cognitive modes, that is, using emotions as well as logic. It is what we call reading between the lines of verbal and nonverbal information in an exchange. We look for what is not obviously stated and for discrepancies in body movement and gestures.

When it comes to reading messages from people and particularly organizational messages, our ability to collect implied information and interpret it breaks down. Many of us shroud the reading of organizational cues in mystery. The reading of cues, however, is essential for being able to effectively tap into the informal communications network of an organization. It is unrealistic to believe people always have the latitude to openly discuss with us exactly what we want to know in explicit terms. There are secrets in all organizations, and it is inappropriate to discuss them openly. However, organizations do have ways of legitimately sharing data with those people who are astute enough to pick up the information. Cues serve this purpose by allowing people to give enough information without violating any confidences to let others make a guess at the event. Being able to pick up cues is also an additional way outstanding managers separate themselves from average managers. Later in our discussion, we will see why this is true.

Blacks have survived from slavery to the present by highly developing the ability to read cues. Curiously, however, blacks seem to fail to integrate and apply this cultural ability when placed in the context of the organization. It is as though they throw away this knowledge because they do not understand what it is, how to apply the skill in an organizational setting, and the importance of being aware of it and using it. If black managers fail to integrate and apply what is usually a normal part of their cultural background, it can serve as yet one more barrier to achieving success.

There are a number of reasons why the reading of cues is so important. Just as we must be aware of nature's cues because weather forecasters cannot always predict the weather correctly, we must be aware of organizational cues because people in the hierarchy cannot for many reasons openly tell of coming events before they have crystallized or become a reality. Good managers will realize and respect this and be open to seeking information that may be suggestive of what they want to know. Often people will attempt to prepare us for some change or impending decision that may affect us by hinting at it. If we are able to put the many pieces of information together, then we can speculate about the coming event and be prepared to deal with it when and if it happens.

If you cannot read cues, you will miss a large part of the information that moves through the informal communications network. It is this network that often allows you to get early information about what is happening in the organization. The sooner you know what is going on, the sooner you can act in your own behalf or at least be in a position to react appropriately when the information is formally shared with the entire organization. Reading cues helps in your decision-making process. It may at some time be critical to your career advancement to be able to read cues. It can give you an edge on your competition.

The ease with which you read cues makes you stand out from your peers because it shows you can understand the implied messages of the organization. For instance, it is impressive if in a meeting with high-level people you are able to read the cues about when it is the most appropriate time to speak up or be quiet.

Upper-level managers like subordinates who can read power figures and their needs and respond to them without being directly asked to do so. Also, being able to read cues makes you appear to be an intuitive manager, that is, to possess the ability to make the right decisions on the basis of what others think and say is insufficient data.

As we stated earlier, blacks have a culturally developed ability to read cues. A remark that is often heard in explanation of this skill is "I just felt in my gut that it was the right thing to do." It is important to trust your gut feelings. This is the emotional, or affective, mode of reading cues. When listening to people, also look for the contradictions between what is said and their body positions. This is the logical mode of reading cues. When powerful people seem to be interacting with you in an out-of-the-ordinary manner, they are usually giving you cues. Be sensitive to reading them. Outstanding managers will constantly be reading such cues and will work to develop this skill to a high degree. Below are some tips on reading cues.

1. In meetings, be especially attentive if you sense something different is occurring. You must be alert to reading information that seems to be leading to some conclusion. Continue to look and listen until you see a pattern by using your gut emotions and logic. Put all the cues together until you can draw some logical conclusion about what is going on.

2. When you hear indirect information being shared that tells you there is a hidden message, listen to and watch closely what follows so that you can be prepared to draw some conclusions based on both verbal and nonverbal actions.

3. When information is not explicit, you cannot interpret the underlying meaning of the information until you have collected *all* the implied information. This may occur over a long period of time from several meetings, from comments made at lunch or in the halls, from memos, and so on.

4. When reading cues from someone, *never* ask the person for verbal confirmation. The person will not want to give it. That is why you got the information in the form of a cue in the first place. Asking for confirmation causes the person giving you the cue to become disgusted and to question your capabilities for subtle comprehension. Instead, ask a series of indirect questions using cues to verify the information; but do this *only* if needed.

5. Be sensitive to the many ways cues are given; some are given

within one situation, while others occur over a period of time. One secret to reading cues is to integrate seemingly isolated events, comments, and observations over a period of time to gain needed information.

6. Very important information is usually given with cues over a period of time, not all at once.

SUCCESSFUL CONFRONTATION

Successful confrontation is facing an issue, usually one about which there is conflict, in a way that mutual agreement can be obtained and action steps developed and implemented. Our discussion deals specifically with successful confrontation within the context of multicultural management. We are primarily concerned with confrontation as it applies to blacks facing and resolving conflict with *whites*. However, we do not mean that this section is *only* for blacks; white managers can certainly increase their confrontational skills, especially when in conflict with blacks.

People generally know how to do their jobs, but they may not know how to manage or deal with the conflict associated with fulfilling their various job roles. This inhibits the accomplishment of their job tasks. Using successful confrontation allows people to manage the conflict so they can perform their job functions. When conflict arises among white managers in performing tasks, it is not an uncommon part of the organizational culture to gloss over it and do nothing. In time, the power structure will settle the issue, and most people are content to follow its decision. With the entrance of blacks into the dominant organizational culture, normal organizational reactions to conflict fail to work well because blacks respond differently to conflict, cognitively as well as emotionally. We have already ascertained that blacks will resist power when their self-esteem is in question.

In organizations, blacks tend to operate in a more personal manner, while whites tend to operate in a more depersonalized organizational manner. As a result, blacks tend to take disagreements more personally, which may lead to dysfunctional behavior such as overresponding. Whites, on the other hand, not understanding how blacks operate, often approach blacks in ways that seem cold and insensitive. This triggers anger in blacks because they feel as though they are not being taken seriously or that the white person is trying to put the black person in his or her place. A black individual may feel as though he or she has been "kicked" by a white person for some reason and become angry. (We are *not*, of course, referring to a physical act. *Kicking* is a colloquial term denoting verbal chastising.) The white person will see or sense the anger in the black person and will tend to become more insensitive and arrogant and feel forced to use his or her organizational power. This sets up a situation wherein the black will feel placed in a slave–master position, and the conflict will escalate.

Blacks cannot afford the luxury of walking away from conflict in an organization. When they do, regardless of who is to blame or who initiated the conflict, whites will tend to project all kinds of negative things on the black individual. If blacks do not work to help resolve the conflict, they will find whites consider them a principal cause of the conflict. Another reason blacks need to learn successful confrontation is that whites in an organization tend to punish blacks by confronting them with negative feedback that is often not well thought through and may be inappropriate. This is especially true if the white person is in a power position. While whites do not tend to be very confrontational with each other, they tend to be so with blacks for the purpose of control and punishment. If the black individual is beyond the Entry Phase, this behavior from whites will almost always lead to conflict.

Let us now introduce you to a five-stage confrontation model to help you deal more successfully with conflict.*

Stage I. Approach

In this stage, you *approach* the individual and bring up the subject that is in disagreement. The subject should be brought up in a functional manner so that the other person is willing to listen and to discuss the issues. The black individual should avoid a display of emotionalism because it will divert attention away from the issues under discussion.

Stage II. Impact

At this point, the black individual should *impact* the other person with his or her interpretations of the issues. Confront the

*The five-stage confrontation model was developed by Dr. Duke Ellis, Assistant Dean of Student Affairs, School of Professional Psychology, Wright State University, Dayton, Ohio.

other person by sharing your feelings, attitudes, and opinions about the issues. Be sure to give the other person an opportunity to respond with his or her feelings, attitudes, and opinions.

Stage III. Penetrate

In this stage, each person should *penetrate* the other's feelings, attitudes, and opinions. This can be accomplished by asking questions and repeating the answers to ensure understanding of the facts. This stage is used primarily to narrow the focus of the conflict so that only the facts involved in this particular incident are being discussed.

Stage IV. Follow through

Follow through in this stage by being as cognitive as possible. Be less emotional, and select the appropriate pieces of the narrowed conflict by making logical sense out of the facts revealed in the penetration stage. At this point, allow logic to lead you to the next stage. You should now have a picture of how and why the conflict arose.

Stage V. Closure

In the *closure* stage, mutuality is sought. Areas of agreement are discussed and mutually acceptable action plans or thoughts are agreed upon. If at this point you cannot reach mutuality, stop the process and leave each other's presence. Perhaps both parties need more time to think through the situation. Meet again at another time, and repeat the entire five-stage process. At some point, one or both of the parties will compromise.

Below are some additional pointers that are helpful in a conflictual situation.

1. It is always appropriate to attack a person's process, but never the person, in a meeting where others are present. Process as used here refers to the sequence of events used by a person in an interaction. Look at *how* something was done. You can look for deficiencies in a process and examine them by pointing out problem areas or stating your negative reaction to how something was done. Examining a person's process of interacting is a key to good management.

2. You can confront superiors in one-to-one meetings behind closed doors but not in a meeting in front of others.

3. When inappropriate pressure is placed on you and you can

ascertain that a person is attempting to intimidate you, place the pressure back on the other person by asking questions. Then let that person deal with your questions.

4. When you are in a meeting with others and are verbally attacked, ask for clarification of a point made by others to give yourself time to think about a response to the attack.

5. When someone writes or states something that you do not agree with, say, "That is your perspective. However, I have some concerns about it." Then point out some specifics and give your perspective on the information.

6. Say that someone has made an error in judgment instead of saying, "You are wrong."

7. Sometimes it is essential to acknowledge that a person's negative feelings and thoughts are correct. After the acknowledgment is made, say to the person, "Now where does that take us?" or "What's next?" Do not *always* deny the negative feelings and thoughts of others.

8. Approach an issue by asking questions and giving answers that narrow the focus to points of immediate disagreement that can be resolved. Eliminate any other issues that do not have a direct bearing on the problem at hand.

9. When you read criticism directed personally at you, react emotionally to yourself and trusted friends and peers. Then go back and look at the written information from an organizational rather than personal perspective. This allows you to see more of the strategy of others. This applies especially to written performance appraisals of you that are completed without your input or knowledge.

10. When a white person reacts negatively to your attempt to help, sometimes it is productive to say, "I tried to help you and you reacted negatively. I don't feel good about it. I've got more data in the area under discussion, but I can't seem to get it across. Can you help me understand what went wrong? Can we work things out so that we can both benefit from this interaction?"

11. Peers and those below your peer level can be "kicked" in private and in meetings. However, with superiors, blacks should sublimate their anger and use that energy to manage the conflict by outthinking or outmaneuvering them.

12. When appropriate, people can be "kicked" with theory, information, and probing questions.

13. To help prevent confrontation when presenting a proposal to managers, have alternatives available to allow for the managers' input. This provides them with some degree of latitude and ownership.

14. If you find yourself disagreeing with someone in a meeting and you know a fight will ensue and that you cannot win, let the other person do all the talking. Gather data about the issues that concern you, say "Thank you," and leave. Then write a report about those concerns. Use the report to say some things you would have said in the meeting.

15. When you have to "kick" a person in verbal confrontation, be sure to stroke the person when you win and offer some assistance.

16. When people in your organization are having difficulty with a manager in another organization, do the following:

- Meet with the manager and state that the manager's approach is hurting the efficiency of your organization. Then ask, "What can we do to solve this problem?"
- Focus your efforts on the process and not the content.
- Negotiate or establish a different process to accomplish the work.

17. Look for contradictions. Point them out and discuss them.

18. Use Dr. Carl Rogers' mirror technique by repeating a person's statements, thereby forcing the person to deal with them.*

---

*For basic information on the mirror technique, see Chapter 28 of *Psychology Today: An Introduction* by Communications Research Machines, Inc. (New York: Random House, 1979).

8

Environmental Strategies

USING STRATEGIC MANAGEMENT

Strategic management is a process that causes change and results through others. It is used by blacks who are not in power-wielding or controlling positions. Blacks who are in controlling positions also use strategic management in order to get more results than are normal in an organization. Strategic management is an organized way of thinking and planning, of using special techniques for achieving some end.

Our research and experience indicate that the use of strategy is seen as an essential skill by black managers in surviving and negotiating the white corporate system. Many black managers take great personal pride in the development of in-depth strategy skills. Blacks who are ambitious and have high levels of skill and ability have to use strategy against institutional as well as personal racism in order to impact the system. They must plan in order to affect the outcome of any given situation. Everything becomes important—dress, style, and timing. To implement a strategy, blacks must have high levels of interpersonal and behavioral skills—higher than whites, because whites do not have to overcome racial barriers to attain success. Overall, strategy is a very important component in enabling black managers to use their job skills.

There are numerous other reasons why strategic management is essential to black managers in successfully negotiating a white institution. It helps to balance power by compensating for a lack of power among blacks. It helps blacks accomplish work tasks with less expenditure of energy. Strategic management is an essential part of managing the racial attitudes of others. Its use is fundamental to blacks in white institutions in order to be heard, responded to, and given available job opportunities, because external forces work on blacks to reduce their impact on the system.

Blacks need to use strategic management whenever their survival in the organization is in jeopardy. It is certainly essential when programming successful career moves. Strategic management is necessary when attempting to change a long-standing work practice or procedure, the direction of an organization, or organizational culture; when reorganizing a work area; or when expecting a conflict to occur with someone possessing greater organizational power. When attempting to resolve a critical organizational issue, the use of strategic management is paramount.

Here are 12 key principles to understand in using strategic management.

1. You must be able to identify people with power.
2. You must be clear about what you want and when you want it—that is, in terms of change or bottom-line results.
3. You must be able to predict the reaction of the people involved.
4. You must assess the personal risks involved in reaching your goal.
5. You must be clear about how much risk you are willing to take.
6. You must be prepared to deal with conflict.
7. You must have a face-saving contingency plan to withdraw in case it becomes necessary.
8. You must know how to make the power of the people involved work for you and not against you.
9. You must be able to use the power of the boss.
10. You must be able to identify critical issues and problems in the organization.
11. You must have an effective interpersonal behavioral style with whites.
12. You must stay on the offense by asking more questions than you answer.

Below are some simplified steps for using strategic management.

1. Identify what you want to happen and when you want it to happen. This, then, becomes your goal. (Our assumption here is that your goal is a legitimate organizational goal that will benefit your line of business.)

2. Weigh the probability of obtaining your goal; if the probability is low, then use strategic management.

3. Develop a rough tentative plan of action by conceptualizing your ideas. Look at your ideas in a broad sense, but do not work out the details yet. Test them for logic, and see if they meet both organizational and personal job needs.

4. Identify your adversaries, supporters, and resources in the situation.

5. Connect your goal to the needs of your supporters.

6. Consider the needs of your adversaries and incorporate them in the plans to meet your goal.

7. Bounce major ideas and concepts off your resources.

8. Predict the reactions of your supporters and adversaries to your attempt to reach your goal. Make the prediction from your knowledge of those individuals. That is, consider what they like, how they behave, what they are good at doing, what their strengths and limitations are, whether they are readers or listeners, what they need in order to use their strengths for you, and so on.

9. Incorporate the above information into your tentative plan of action to meet your goal.

10. If the goal is a high-risk one or very important to your success, then informally run your tentative plan past one or two resources, friends, or trusted peers.

11. Lay out your tentative plan either on paper or in your mind's eye. Test each step of your plan by predicting the reactions of the people involved. If a negative reaction is predicted, then consider asking a supporter to help you neutralize the reaction. If this is not possible, then change your plan.

12. Develop a contingency plan in case you cannot reach your original goal.

13. Implement your plan and make "in-flight corrections" as appropriate.

USING THE GRAPEVINE

As we discussed earlier, organizations have basically two communications systems from which people may secure information: the formal communications network and the informal communications network. The formal communications network is the official verbal or written means of issuing directives, orders, and so forth through the hierarchy. The informal communications network consists of people at various organizational levels who pass information among themselves through social means and often in the form of organizational cues. The information includes organizational issues and concerns, gossip, the latest professional discoveries and innovations, outside professional development opportunities, and the like. Whether or not the information is factual, the addition of editorial comments, perspectives, and opinions by individuals also plays an important part in the passing of the information.

If the organization has three or more black members, there is a third communications system called the grapevine. The grapevine satisfies the needs of the black employees to pass and receive information because of their exclusion and insufficient support from the regular informal communications system. It is very much like the regular network but with some differences and additional functions. The informal communications network serves the common needs of the white members of the organization. In the same way, the grapevine meets the common needs of the black members as they add their own editorial comments, perspectives, and opinions based on their common experiences, attitudes, and feelings.

The grapevine is also a support system for blacks that goes beyond the type of support system needed by whites. That is to say, the grapevine passes messages of encouragement, warnings, and sometimes chastisement. The grapevine is often the system used by more experienced blacks to instruct and coach other blacks on organizational norms, culture, and politics. There are additional vital functions the grapevine serves for blacks other than the passing of information. They are:

1. Helping blacks learn how to use their anger and behavior in more beneficial ways.
2. Helping to make contact and establish relationships with other blacks for mutual survival and psychic support.

3. Helping each other sort out mixed messages received from the organization.
4. Providing corrective measures to negative feedback.
5. Helping blacks identify the skills they bring to the organization.
6. Being a relief valve when organizational stress and strain reach the saturation point.
7. Providing blacks with the needed strokes and encouragement, especially when things get rough.

The grapevine is the cornerstone of black development. (Black development relates to the growth activity of black managers and will be discussed in the last section of this chapter.) The grapevine exists in predominantly white organizations (businesses, service organizations, and educational institutions) as a means of communication for survival and success. Like the regular informal communications network, the grapevine is based on social interactions that occur at lunch, during breaks, in the hallways, in offices, and after work hours.

Although the grapevine is vital to the survival and success of the black manager, too many blacks fail to use the grapevine effectively or do not use it at all. In his narrative, Jack conveyed a loneliness and a sense of being the only person struggling with a system not fully understood. In reading about the phases Jack went through, we saw that Jack did not initially avail himself of the grapevine. In fact, Jack did not see the importance of developing a black support system until he was "knee deep in alligators."

By this time, the reader will be aware of many of the reasons some blacks fail to link with the grapevine. However, let us again point out a couple of the most prevalent reasons. The most common reason is black self-hate. In essence, the hidden self-message reads: "Since I don't think much of myself as a member of this outgroup, I can't respect the intellect of other blacks or accept their input as having any value or relevance. If I am unvalued, then how can I value other blacks whom I perceive to be just like me?"

Another reason many blacks do not link with the grapevine is one that is related to self-hate and is called the "dumb-nigger syndrome." The individual thinks, "I cannot allow whites to see I do not know or do not understand. Neither can I allow other blacks to see this. They will see me as dumb. These other blacks are doing OK, and they will ostracize me if I appear dumb, and I could not take that." Such individuals are primarily concerned about their self-images. In their need to appear superior and supercompetent, they devalue the common experience and information sharing provided by the grapevine. In both of the above cases, the piece that is missing for these blacks is the *value* of the information and support that is received by keeping a continuous link with the grapevine. Another important factor is that they do not understand the critical importance such a system within the broader informal communications system has for their survival and success.

USING POWER

Blacks tend to think of power in terms of the "Peace in the Valley" concept.* That is, many blacks think when they reach a certain point in the hierarchy of the organization their power will be seen by all and their struggles will be over. Is this a familiar refrain? "When I get to that position, I won't have to put up with this crap any more." Nothing could be further from the truth. Maintaining *power* requires constant effort, and blacks in particular have to stay on top of things and continue to struggle.

When blacks face the use of power, there are three key issues: (1) how they feel about using power on others; (2) black empowerment, that is, the *right* to use power; and (3) how to use power effectively. Let us look at the first issue. Nearly all black managers are at some point faced with having to examine their feelings about using power on others. There are, of course, a variety of feelings and reactions based on each person's life circumstances, but there are a couple of common responses blacks have to using power. Many blacks do not feel good about using power on others or at least feel uncomfortable about it, as though they should not have it. This is a normal response to having always been in a one-down position to the dominant society. Since we have previously discussed this issue, let it suffice to reiterate that many blacks tend to think of power as a means of victimizing rather than as a tool to get things done.

When blacks examine their feelings about power, they must

---

*This is a term coined by Dr. Ronald B. Brown, Organizational Consultant and Managing Partner for Marketing, Pacific Management Systems, San Francisco, California.

also ask themselves "Do I want to be liked; do I want to be respected; or do I want both?" When the answer is "I want to be liked," blacks will inhibit their acceptance of power and the ability to use it effectively and appropriately. In many instances, people may not want to do what the black individual in the power position wants them to do and may try to personalize the power held over them and turn it into something negative. Blacks reacting to a negative response to their use of power will be hesitant to use it for fear of angering people.

When the answer is "I want to be respected," then blacks are most likely to accept and use power effectively and appropriately, knowing that power over others is not always a popular position to hold. The person who wants to be respected as well as liked has a very difficult, but not impossible, task. Because some decisions and directives from blacks will be unpopular, being liked must be a secondary consideration. The method of using power will then play an important part in whether or not others accept the power of the black manager without a lot of negative reactions. Blacks can reduce such reactions to their use of power if they recognize that people tend to respond favorably when the person in the power position is able to meet their organizational needs.

The second issue a black person must face in the use of power is black empowerment. Their right to use power in the organization is a confusing issue for blacks and it is definitely a racial issue. Blacks are placed in the untenable position of being caught between the proverbial "rock and a hard place," and whites tend to reinforce that position. Organizations sometimes promote blacks and give them organizational power or place blacks in positions of authority and then move to diffuse their power.

Black empowerment becomes operative when an organization authorizes and enables black managers to accomplish various tasks for the good of the organization. That part is easy. The difficulty and confusion arise when black managers attempt to use the empowerment. Whites tend to react and subtly pressure black managers into not using their organizational power charter. This ambiguity causes stress and anxiety in black managers. More specifically, when black managers give directives, whites tend to react negatively, insist upon certain behavior and results, make demands, or get visibly angry. Blacks can certainly see for themselves that whites do not react this way to white power figures. In addition, white subordinates will be alert to, and frequently be testing for, indications that the organization will not support a black manager's empowerment.

Once black managers resolve the first two issues, the next issue is how they can use power effectively. The central theme here is they do not want to use too much power or too little power to accomplish the job task. In other words, there needs to be a proper balance between using too much power on others to get the job done versus using too little power and encouraging people to ignore their power.

We have been discussing some perceptions blacks have concerning power, especially as it relates to them. What is power? Power is the ability to cause people to perceive that you can give rewards when they behave properly and give punishment when they do not respond to you. Power is responsibility. Having power in an organization can mean more money, more prestige, more opportunity to run things your way, more satisfaction doing your job, more success, more personal leverage with others, a private office, better assignments, a better boss, and the ability to be one up on someone else. Authority is given, but power must be earned.

One of the basic goals in organizations is to attain power. Every individual strives to sell him- or herself and to influence organizational leaders to get power. This is new to most blacks in this context and may seem alien. Blacks have only recently been freed of the mentality of a working person—that is, wait to be assigned work, do it, and have it checked. As a group, we are more accustomed to being managed than being managers. We as blacks must deal openly with ourselves about our concerns with power and learn to feel comfortable with its use, because power can help us realize our creative ideas. Power need not be equated with victimization or dysfunctional behavior, but rather it is a way to make beneficial things happen for you and the organization.

There are many books on the subject of power, and as you explore them you will find there are many different kinds and many different uses of power. We choose to focus primarily on the four kinds of power presented below because these are ones used most often by blacks in the attainment of success.

1. *Organizational or position power* is power you earn, bestowed upon you by the organization because of your position in

the organization. Authority to use power is given as a result of the organizational role you hold. The higher the position in the hierarchy, the greater the authority to use power. For instance, vice presidents in a company are listened to more than others at a lower level and are responded to faster when they issue orders or give directives.

2. *Expert power* is gained as a result of technical expertise and a reputation for competence in your field. This is based on achieved organizational results.

3. *Power of influence or interpersonal power* is your ability to influence other people. This is usually done by indirect means, such as with the use of aggressiveness, assertiveness, tenacity, and your ability to reason.

4. *Charismatic power* is the power that causes people to stop talking and look up when you enter a room. It is an attention-getting presence based on personality, likability, and social skills. Charismatic power is greatly influenced by your dress—having a pleasing appearance, hair neat and shoes shined. People with such power seem to exude internal strength and tend to dramatize what they do. They are perceived to be winners.

Below are some key principles that relate to the use of power and are important to blacks. Keep in mind these are a selection of principles, and we would like to refer you to the book *Power!* by Michael Korda for further information. This is a good book to examine to increase your understanding of power. However, since there are no books on power expressly written for blacks to our knowledge, we do suggest that as you read the material you keep in mind that you are black and that this will affect your use of power. In other words, you may have to translate some of the material to fit the reality of how you most successfully relate to the dominant culture.

1. If you are a black in a power position, people will automatically challenge you. When this happens, relax and think about the challenger and why you are being challenged. If you decide to engage the challenger, use the following rules of thumb:

- If the challenger is a subordinate, use organizational, charismatic, or interpersonal power, whichever one is appropriate to the situation.
- If the challenger is a peer, use charismatic power, expert power, or the power of influence as appropriate.

- If the challenger is your boss or another superior, use charismatic power and the power of influence. On some occasions you may be successful in using expert power, but this will work only if the superior invites you to use expert power.

2. If you are in a power position, you can personalize information in an interaction with subordinates. However, as a subordinate you should not personalize information when talking to a superior (including your boss). In essence, you can personalize information with people below you in the hierarchy, but not with those above you.

3. Power can be assumed by challenging organizational norms at the appropriate time. If you have an idea that violates an organizational norm and if the implementation of your idea will meet organizational goals, then you should push and fight for your idea. Use the power of influence, expert power, and charismatic power.

4. Power is *always* involved when you meet with upper-level managers. You cannot change this. You must respect their power by at least listening to them. There is no way to remove the power factor from the interaction. In this case, you should use charismatic power and/or the power of influence. You may also be able to maneuver yourself into being invited to use your expert power.

5. Timing is important when you talk to a power figure:

- Subordinates can interrupt for clarification and amplification.
- Subordinates should not interrupt for negation or confrontation but should wait until the power figure finishes his or her point.
- Subordinates should not interrupt to defend themselves.

If you are the boss or superior in the situation, you can interrupt people at any point. If you are a subordinate, you can accrue power from your self-control by following the above rules. Now, if you are angry enough and feel black rage, you may choose to interrupt a power figure to confront that person. If you decide on this course of action because you deem it important to you, be sure to follow sound rules of confrontation (see Chapter 7) and to stick to factual and logical data. Rely on the use of the power of influence.

6. Black managers can increase their charismatic power by developing a smooth style of operation and dressing in a stylish corporate manner.

7. Use the power of your insight to move to the heart of a problem when you are a member of a problem solving group. Influence and charisma are helpful here.

8. Competing with your subordinates is a misuse of your power as the boss. You are the boss, and there is no need to continuously prove it; you already have position and expert power.

9. Additional organizational power may be gained by developing a style and behavioral pattern that is a combination of your style and behavioral pattern plus the successful power style and behavioral pattern of your boss.

10. One key to the use of power is to be flexible and use the different kinds of power appropriately.

11. Blacks can use charismatic power to compensate for a lack of organizational power. Charisma can be their best source of power until they gain other kinds of power.

USING BLACK DEVELOPMENT

We have periodically made reference to black development throughout the book without explaining what it is. Quite simply, black development is the process and act of learning those skills and techniques that are unique to the survival, adjustment, planned growth, and success of blacks. It is learned predominantly from other blacks who are successful in white institutions. The end product of black development is another black person who can be successful in a white institution.

Black development provides blacks with an opportunity to come to grips with their need for different or additional relevant training and development. It provides an opportunity to learn to harness the potential energy of rage and convert it into a useful corporate behavior. Black development provides blacks with an opportunity to learn how to interact effectively with others who possess suppressed racism as well as those who display overt racism. It provides insight into how to recognize corporate norms of behavior and identify the differential consequences that some of these norms may have for blacks. Black development provides insight into how to seek help with technical and managerial matters without feeling a loss of dignity. It provides an opportunity to develop skills that will allow blacks to identify and change those aspects of the black–white interface for which they are responsible. In essence, black development is needed to reach the Success Phase.

How do you begin your development program as a black manager?

1. You must begin to understand yourself, which in turn allows you to understand how you relate to others and to your environment. To understand yourself, you must know how you learn best. Learning here relates to learning technical skills as well as such nontechnical skills as giving presentations and managing others. Ask, do you learn best from reading, listening to others, reflecting on interactions with others, experiencing activities or experimenting with new behavior, or taking a different approach to doing your job? You must admit to *yourself* what you do not know. Denial is unproductive and keeps you from taking in the new learnings you need.

Be clear about your strengths. Everybody does *something* well. Be clear about your black development needs. If you have been honest with yourself about your strengths and shortcomings, you can develop a clear picture of what you need to gain to do a more effective job. Be clear about your *personal* barriers and key issues. For example, a key issue with you may be that you get angry in interactions with whites and stop interacting with them. Along this same line, a personal barrier could be that once you are angry you do not know how to make your anger work for you but rather you become dysfunctional.

2. You must trust the black intellect of other blacks and of yourself. Do not allow black self-hate to prevent you from trusting the wisdom and experience of other blacks or to allow you to deny your gut feelings and experiences.

3. You must understand the effect of being black in a white institution.

In addition to knowing what is involved in beginning your black development, you also need to know what is going to be important for you to learn. The key components of black development are an understanding of:

1. The four phases of black development that managers move through.
2. Your blackness and its meaning relative to the existing conditions in the organization.
3. The double bind of needing information from your boss and

being seen as ignorant by your boss because you asked for information the boss thinks you should know.

4. The use of resources to increase your expertise, add to what you know, and provide new knowledge.
5. Effective style, which conveys energy, personal organization, confidence, and the ability to read cues, manage emotions, and use strategy.
6. The management of the racial attitudes of others.
7. Your support system, which is knowing your advocates and your adversaries.
8. Your boss's expectations.
9. Your job role.
10. Ways to obtain performance feedback from your boss.
11. The four basic types of power and how and when to use each.
12. Goal setting.

Lastly, there are several techniques the black manager may employ for meeting black development needs.

1. Identify and use black and white advocates. Pick these to fill your learning gaps. They can be peers or superiors.
2. Observe white and black power figures in action. Watch how they interact with others and how you interact with them. Observe how they influence others. Watch them use power. Listen to their thought processes. Observe how they handle conflict. Take the time to discuss these things with the power figures and duplicate some of their behavior. Fit their successful processes into your style.
3. Attend meetings with your boss or other high-level managers and observe them as they interact.
4. Read cues in interactions and learn how the people you work with interact with each other.
5. Pick role models for certain behavior and duplicate the behavior, fitting it into your behavioral style.
6. Attend relevant outside seminars. Sometimes it is helpful to get away and compare what you know to what others know.
7. Learn to think like a racist. Try to see things as a racist would by using the concept of "Behold! The other side of the coin."

8. Attend relevant inside seminars. Be willing to translate material for yourself when it does not allow differential consequences.

9. Develop a personal reading program. As a minimum, we suggest you read the following books to help provide you with some insight as well as some basic knowledge. Remember to allow for differential consequences and the impact of your blackness and/or gender when applying some of the concepts presented in the books.

   Black Rage, William H. Grier and Price M. Cobbs.

   The Effective Executive, Peter F. Drucker.

   Manager Today, Executive Tomorrow, Charles C. Vance.

   The Gamesman: The New Corporate Leaders, Michael Maccoby.

   Power! How to Get It, How to Use It, Michael Korda.

   Moving Ahead: Black Managers in American Business, Richard F. America and Bernard E. Anderson.

   Dress for Success or *The Woman's Dress for Success Book*, John T. Molloy.

10. Seize opportunities to make *significant* contributions to your organization.

PART FOUR
Planning for Success

The theme of this last section is developing a battle plan for success. Here we would like to offer black readers a way to combine the information of the preceding chapters into a general plan for success. We feel strongly that you need *data* before you can develop a viable battle plan for your career in an organization. Furthermore, you need to document and test your plan before attempting to implement it. Now that you are armed with some data and maps of the area you wish to attack, you need to take a global look to see what this all means to you and how it fits in terms of developing strategies to prevent failure.

Let us begin by saying no matter what the phase of development (Entry, Adjusting, Planned Growth, or Success) or the length of time in an organization, blacks should plan for success. Ideally, black managers should begin planning for success upon entering the work force. As we stated in the beginning of this book, whites tend to begin their jobs with the idea of having a career. As a group, blacks in the past have been happy to secure a good job and could not afford the luxury of thinking in terms of a career; they were too busy just surviving. Today things have changed to such a degree that blacks can no longer enter the work place and be satisfied with just having secured a good job. The demands for success placed on black managers require them to begin their jobs thinking in terms of building a career just as their white peers do.

The next two chapters will help you focus on the larger issues of personal planning (getting what you need and want from the organization) and corporate and institutional planning (being able to meet the needs and desires of your organization).

9

Personal Planning

DATA GATHERING TOUR—WHAT IS NEEDED?

This section deals with the data gathering tour, which will help you understand what is needed to plan for success in your particular organization. A data gathering tour is a number of one-to-one meetings with people in or outside your organization arranged to obtain data needed to plan for your success in an organization. During the meetings, you should ask appropriate questions to obtain the desired information.

The data gathering tour is not an absolute necessity for attaining success in an organization, nor is planning for success an absolute necessity. However, if a black manager goes on a data gathering tour and subsequently develops a career plan, the odds for success will be greatly increased and the time required to gain success will be greatly reduced. If properly executed, a data gathering tour can become an opportunity to learn through both the technical and nontechnical experience of others. This approach can shave months off the time it takes a person to move through the development phases. For example, if young black managers start with an organization by going on a data gathering tour, they can find out in two weeks what it takes to make a contribution to the organization instead of discovering this through on-the-job experience. The discovery process could take months, even years.

A person who is new to a company or institution should go on a data gathering tour between 4 and 12 months after starting a job. The specific time should be determined by the person, allowing sufficient opportunity to first meet and get to know people in the organization. The person should also give others enough time to get to know him or her. Four to 12 months should be sufficient time to determine who the outstanding and average performers are. A person who is not new to the work force and has previously worked for another company or institution, or who has been transferred within the same company, should go on a data gathering tour after 2–6 months.

At this point, the next obvious question is: How do you organize a data gathering tour? The first step is to select people to talk to in one-to-one meetings. Select at least four people who fit the following criteria:

1. A black and a white who serve in a position comparable to yours in your organization or another organization in your company or institution.
2. People who have been members of your organization for 2, 5, and 10 years.
3. A man and a woman (if possible) for different perspectives.
4. A person who is seen as a sharp and outstanding performer.
5. A person who is seen as an average performer, so that you can clearly identify for yourself the boundaries and indicators of the company's acceptable performance range.
6. People who work in and outside your field of endeavor, so that you can broaden your information base of task disciplines in order to position yourself to be a manager.

Prepare an agenda to use in the meetings. You may want to send the agenda to people before you meet with them so they can be better prepared for the discussion. The agenda should be structured as follows:

I. Purpose of meeting.
II. Discussion of personal background (such as where you grew up, the school you attended, previous jobs, experience, and other ice-breaking information. Be friendly and personable, not distant and businesslike.)
III. Discussion of information.

(list questions here)

The following questions should be asked. You may wish to expand the list to suit your additional needs.

1. What are the key ingredients for success in this organization in general and specific to my field of work?
2. What advice would you give someone in my position about how to make a maximum contribution to this organization?
3. What are the characteristics and behaviors of successful people in this organization?
4. What things, both technical and nontechnical, do you think I should learn in the next year?
5. What are the most important organizational norms I should be aware of?
6. What results are successful people in this organization expected to produce in general and specifically in my field?
7. How do you get additional responsibility in this organization?

Record the data you are given. After meeting with several people, reduce and consolidate your information into a list that answers the question, "What is needed for success in this organization?" Your information should reflect the views of a cross-section of members of the organization.

CAREER PLANNING PROCESS— WHAT DO YOU WANT?

Career planning is a personal experience because, although we may all have similar goals and needs, these are a product of our own personal value systems and our own sense of what is important to us. Many people have somewhat different ideas of what career planning means to them. Generally, we define career planning as the setting of a direction and the listing of kinds of opportunities to be seized; chance is involved as well as being in the right place at the right time. Being prepared is a must.

In one career planning seminar, bosses and their subordinates defined career planning in these ways. The bosses said career planning is (1) preparing a road map to growth, to developing the capacity to make a larger contribution; (2) positioning yourself to get what you want from an organization; (3) doing what satisfies individual needs and expectations; (4) appropriately meshing individual and organizational needs. The subordinates added that career planning is (1) getting work you enjoy doing; (2) not letting the boss plan your career without your input; (3) giving specific information on what a career will look like; (4) developing a way to get beyond an entry-level position.

It is vital that blacks learn to think in terms of career planning as early as possible after acquiring a job position. It is important for you to begin planning your career early to avoid being trapped in a position that will become just another job. Let us at this point examine the differences between a job and a career. A job is one that has a nine-to-five time orientation. It is more structured and controlled and has little responsibility. There is little opportunity to impact the business of the organization. A job is task related and ends at some point. It has less mobility, is impersonal, and is not highly satisfying. A career is oriented toward discharging a responsibility. It is less structured and has more flexibility; its boundaries are not clearly defined. A career has more potential for receiving a bigger reward. There is room for change in a career, and the person can exercise initiative. A career is ongoing and has the potential for being more satisfying, because it can be designed to meet personal as well as job needs.

Another reason it is very important for blacks and other minorities to plan their careers early is because it helps to either eliminate, reduce, or compensate for the effects of the following barriers in the work scene. It compensates for a *lack of black role models*. Career planning helps to reduce the effects of *racism* that prevent blacks from being able to take advantage of available opportunities. It can cause the *white fear* of blacks to be managed. Career planning helps to reduce the effects of *sexism* that prevent women from being able to take advantage of available opportunities. It can control *subjectivity* in evaluations and increase objectivity. It can help reduce or eliminate *low trust among the racial groups* by removing doubt so trust is not an issue. Career planning helps reduce the *low awareness of the effects of being black* on relevant individuals. Career planning helps eliminate *racial stereotypes*. It also helps whites to not be concerned about *reverse discrimination*, because career plans are usually worked up and down the hierarchy with agreement from key people.

Subordinates in general should always be sure that they have a career plan that is reviewed and updated at least every 12 months.

For blacks at the lower levels of management in organizations, this is a must. New employees should initiate a career discussion with their bosses after being employed 6–12 months. This gives the subordinate sufficient time to survive a probationary period and to become acclimated to the work environment.

There are a minimum number of things required of a boss and subordinate before they can use our career planning process. A boss must have the skills to do the following:

1. Look at a situation through the eyes of others in the situation.
2. Listen nonevaluatively.
3. Integrate knowledge of the organization and options available into the career plan.
4. Evaluate a person's potential objectively.
5. Integrate different pieces of information, needs, and options.
6. Develop and sell an action plan.
7. Analyze data.
8. Counsel and give feedback to a subordinate in an appropriate manner.
9. Receive feedback from a subordinate without becoming defensive.

A subordinate must have the skills to do the following:

1. Exercise initiative.
2. Use resources.
3. Manage racism.
4. Push back and resist power.
5. Articulate input.
6. Listen nonevaluatively.

Before we discuss the details of the career planning process, let us look at a simplified career development philosophy. Career development basically is nothing more than the appropriate matching of an individual's skills and interests with the business needs of an organization.

Each of us has a personal list of needs, desires, likes, dislikes, goals, skills, interests, and so on. The organization has a similar list. Figure 9 shows the two as separate entities. If you were working in an organization whose characteristics coincided perfectly with yours, then the two separate lists would coincide. However, people and organizations are rarely, if ever, perfectly matched.

FIGURE 9. Career development model.

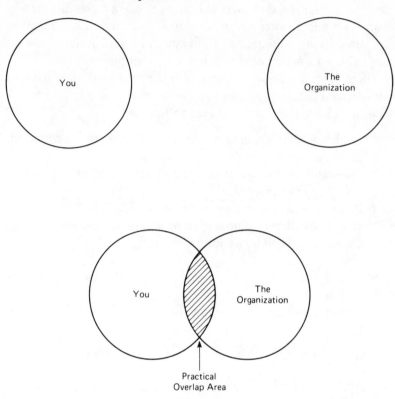

Practical
Overlap Area

Therefore, it is not practical to expect that the two lists can coincide. Realistically, there is an acceptable area of overlap, shown in Figure 9. The main objective of career development, then, becomes to maximize the size of the overlap area. If the overlap area is maximized, employees will produce at their maximum potential levels and will continue to grow and develop. Employees produce at their maximum when they are interested in their work, have their job needs met, and are having fun.

Career planning is a ten-step process.

Step 1. The manager should share his or her managerial philosophy on career planning—that is, fundamental beliefs, concepts, and attitudes toward career planning.

Step 2. The subordinate should share his or her philosophy on career planning.

Step 3. Identify three to five areas in which the subordinate does well and three to five areas in which the subordinate needs improvement. Discuss these in depth so that each of you understands and agrees on what the areas are and why improvement is needed.

Step 4. A. The subordinate should fantasize and describe work scenes in which he or she is most motivated and produces at the highest rate.* At this point we are asking subordinates to imagine as they did in childhood when they used to fantasize about being adults. The boss can set the scene by asking the subordinate to fantasize operating in his or her work world, while the boss, figuratively speaking, watches through a one-way mirror. The boss can see the subordinate, but the subordinate cannot see the boss. The boss can start by asking the subordinate to paint a verbal picture of the scene. Subordinates should paint the picture by telling the boss what they are wearing; who they are talking or listening to; the location of the scene (is it in the office, in the field, a plant, a laboratory?); whether they are standing or sitting; who else is there; what action is taking place; the purpose of the action in the scene. The supervisor should ask additional questions if and when the need for clarification arises. Repeat this for at least two scenes, with subordinates fantasizing where they would like to be in two years, to cross-check data from the first scene.

The supervisor should listen, ask questions, and jot down the key aspects of the work scenes. The supervisor should pay particular attention to needs, dislikes, desires, things that motivate, likes, skills used, and tasks or jobs that give happiness and pleasure.

B. Do the above, with subordinates fantasizing five years into the future.

C. Consolidate the information from A and B.

Step 5. The supervisor should discuss his or her perceptions of the subordinate's fantasized work scenes as they relate to the items in Step 4. In this discussion, look for those things that motivate and those things that inhibit work output as well as the common threads that run through all the work scenes, such as leadership, control, and use of power.

---

*Dr. Ronald B. Brown, Organizational Consultant and Managing Partner for Marketing, Pacific Management Systems, San Francisco, California, shared this concept and process with us.

Step 6. From the discussion in Step 5, the supervisor and subordinate should extract key objectives, needs, desires, interests, and likes to be met in the next assignment.

Step 7. Summarize the above information in clear and concise terms in the following format:

- Three to five areas in which the subordinate does well.
- Three to five areas needing improvement.
- Key objectives, needs, desires, interests, likes, and dislikes.
- Key motivators.
- Description of desired job without naming a specific role.

Step 8. The supervisor should test the plan by discussing the summary with his or her manager to seek input and agreement and obtain information on the needs of the organization as they relate to the subordinate's needs.

Step 9. The supervisor should arrange a step-level counseling session with the supervisor's boss. The purpose of this meeting is (1) to give the subordinate an opportunity to use the experience of the supervisor's boss and (2) to allow the supervisor's boss to formulate his or her own opinions and perceptions about the subordinate's career direction.

Step 10. The supervisor and his or her boss should search various organizations including their own to find a job position that matches the subordinate's desires, interests, and skill level. The subordinate and supervisor should then review the career options that are open.

There are roles for people at various levels of the hierarchy. Each level has a responsibility to secure the effectiveness of the career planning process.

Third-level boss:
- Probe, monitor, and test career plans.
- Provide resource and organizational input to the process.

Second-level boss:
- Probe, monitor, and test career plans.
- Provide organizational information needed in career plans.
- Work out the career plans with the next level of the hierarchy.

First-level boss or supervisor:
- Initiate and develop the career plan along with the subordinate.
- Work out the career plan with his or her boss.

Subordinate:
  • Work with the supervisor to develop the career plan.

Here are some key points to remember about planning your career.

1. Be proactive and push the direction of your career.
2. The fantasizing process is innovative and novel, and it works to quickly collect your thoughts, feelings, and ideas into an organized whole.
3. The boss's interpersonal skills must be well developed in order to contribute to career planning most effectively.
4. Barriers that look difficult to overcome should not stop career planning.
5. Career planning is a logical follow-up to a performance improvement plan.
6. Understand that career planning for minorities is different from that for white males because race and/or gender are involved and must be considered.
7. Keep the overlap area in mind when you do career planning.
8. The boss should communicate the subordinate's needs up the ladder.

IMPLEMENTING YOUR PLAN

Subordinates should be given time to make selections for their future assignments from the career options made available. A time range or specific month and year should be selected for a move to the next job assignment.

The subordinate's selection should be reviewed by the supervisor with his or her boss. This will establish a contract for the subordinate's future. In some cases it will be appropriate for the subordinate to change assignments immediately. If so, this should be done. The subordinate's supervisor should review the contract or career plan for implementation at least two months before the time of the job change (if one is scheduled to occur).

It is the subordinate's responsibility to ensure that proper time and attention continue to be focused on his or her career plan. The subordinate should be given a copy of the contract or plan.

10

Corporate and Institutional Planning

LIVING IN THE CONTEXT OF YOUR WORK ENVIRONMENT

Blacks must learn to live successfully in the context of their work environment or get out, but under no circumstances should they give up and stay. Giving up is much like suicide; there is no productivity from the dead. Unfortunately, some corporate and institutional environments drain the psychic energy and creativity from their employees, and many employees seem to become willing victims. These may seem to be harsh words, but reality is often harsh.

In unchartered environments and little-trodden pathways, it takes strong and determined men and women to clear the paths for others. As is true of all new roads, the road to learning and coping in the corporate world is rocky and full of barriers, but it can be traversed successfully. Blacks and other minorities are the new pioneers of the corporate world; they bring with them the concept of multicultural management to a world that is growing smaller because of improved communications and transportation. We will speak more about multicultural management and its application to a smaller world concept later in this chapter.

Most new graduates, black or white, starting new jobs enter institutions expecting to work and solve textbook kinds of prob-

300

lems that include making decisions devoid of emotional considerations. The new members enter with new technological ideas, no matter what field of study they are in. They cannot wait to get into an institution to change things, having been led to believe the world awaits their expertise. The rude awakening is that institutions tend to resist change and hold on to existing ways of doing things. Some institutions initially influence new employees to learn how to be good followers and loyal members of the organization. In many instances, companies also think they know what career direction is best for their employees, and employees are expected to fall in line.

Upon entering a white institution for the first time, black professionals face a dilemma somewhat different from that of their white peers. How does a black person work, meet organizational goals, and prosper in a system that is biased against blacks and that places additional barriers to the black individual's attainment of success. Blacks forget to consider that the organization is a small replica of the society as a whole, having the same social system, values, morals, power structure, and so on. Blacks, therefore, start their careers at a disadvantage because of external circumstances. They have to face and deal with the same dilemmas as new white employees, but in addition they must deal with racism. The bottom line for blacks is to either (1) learn to live in their work environment by surviving, coping, learning, growing, and being successful; (2) give up and exist, thereby relinquishing their personal hopes and aspirations and thus providing minimal productivity; or (3) get out. That is the harsh reality for blacks. White managers with the best of intentions attempt to use traditional management techniques to manage blacks. Therefore, *both* blacks and whites must bear the responsibility for changing management techniques for the future.

Blacks made their greatest gains by applying external pressure on institutions in the 1960s and 1970s. The flight for equal rights shifted from the streets and lunch counters, from the buses and stores of the 1960s, to all the established white institutions of America in the 1970s. These included the universities, armed services, profit-making industrial complexes, government agencies responsible for making policies, and even church and family. While inroads have been made, in nearly all areas parity for black professionals does not exist. We have a *long* way to go before we reach parity. We have not seen any information that indicates that we are even close to parity in areas of policymaking.

The real challenge for blacks and white institutions in the 1980s is to unlock productivity in blacks for mutual benefit. Corporate barriers to further progress must be removed. Corporations and other institutions have an excuse that explains why blacks are not in the top echelons of their hierarchies. They say that blacks have not been in the institutions long enough. This may be true, but let us remind the reader that there is a process called "fast track" development that can be used for blacks in the same way it is used for whites.* Fast track development refers to an official program of moving a person ahead faster than normal by providing support, opportunities for learning, and the right assignments. Blacks are anxious to succeed and are positioned to improve productivity. White organizations need to remove or help remove barriers so blacks can improve corporate productivity.

In the 1960s and 1970s, blacks in various corporations and institutional systems challenged the social norms. In the 1980s, blacks must remove the barriers to the full utilization of their creativity and productivity. This can be accomplished by challenging the corporate and institutional technical and managerial norms of the 1960s and 1970s. One way to live in the context of your work environment is to challenge norms and initiate change by exerting pressure from the bottom to attract attention to the need for change. This pressure will build up until it reaches the top of the organization and come back down in the form of policy change.

For example, in the middle 1960s when equal opportunity legislation became law, many companies complained about not being able to find black professionals. A few blacks in various companies and institutions exerted pressure on personnel managers to include blacks in the recruitment process. Pressure was exerted until it reached the top of the companies and institutions, at which point policies were changed to allow blacks at low organizational levels to actively participate in the recruiting process. As a result, black professionals were identified, interviewed, and brought into the companies and institutions. This same proc-

---

*Richard F. America and Bernard E. Anderson, *Moving Ahead: Black Managers in American Business* (New York: McGraw-Hill, 1978), p. 14.

ess can apply to get blacks into such areas as marketing, sales, advertising, cost management, and school system supervisory slots. In essence, policy change within an organization comes from the top in response to needs at the bottom. Managers in the middle are then held responsible for developing, instituting, and insisting on behavior change that will give equal opportunity to *all* employees.

Upper-level black managers can improve productivity and continue to be successful by challenging existing norms in corporations and institutions. Blacks in top slots sometimes are reluctant to press hard for other blacks. Whether top-level blacks like it or not, blacks at lower levels insist that those blacks in upper-level jobs push to remove the organizationally biased barriers to black success.

Blacks have developed a high tolerance for stress and uncertainty (one price paid for this is a high rate of representation in hypertension statistics) and they are risk takers when it comes to survival. Blacks as a group have existed with this stress and anxiety for many generations. When sharp, energetic blacks with high survival skills are placed in all-white organizations, the productivity of whites improves. We can look to the field of professional sports for a possible answer to why this happens.

Can an all-white professional team beat an equally skilled integrated team? Probably not. When a sharp, energetic black is introduced into an all-white group, productive competition increases. Racism will tend to cause the whites to work harder and become more productive in an effort to outproduce the black. This occurs because one basic tenet of racism is that whites are smarter and more competent than blacks. Many whites will work hard to make this a true statement. If we can keep the competition healthy, *everyone* gains. We believe the sports world has the answer for increasing team productivity and reenergizing many whites.

Since the 1960s, when white institutions opened their employment doors to blacks, the following four phases of black professional employment can be seen.

Phase 1. Because of the civil rights equal opportunity laws of the 1960s, many white institutions developed affirmative action programs. These programs focused on the recruitment of blacks and other minorities. In other words, the corporate and institutional doors of white America were cracked for black professionals. Blacks entered but not in large numbers, because only a few individuals were available.

Phase 2. In this phase, white institutions in America provided for a small measure of socialization, assimilation, growth, and development of blacks. As a result of this, blacks were promoted into low- to middle-level jobs but in insufficient numbers to achieve equity or even make significant difference to the organization.

Phase 3. In Phase 3, opportunities were made available for the further growth and development of black managers. Consequently, a very small number of blacks moved from middle-level positions to upper-level positions, such as department heads to division heads.

Phase 4. Phase 4 is the challenge for the 1980s. This phase represents the new ceiling for blacks. This is the phase in which a small number of blacks will get promoted to the vice president level and still fewer to the corporate executive level. This may include positions on the board of directors.

MULTICULTURAL MANAGEMENT: A NEW FIELD

In the Introduction to this book, we defined multicultural management as the act, art, and practice of leading and directing people other than white males in the attaining of organizational goals. We further stated that with an increased number of minorities, including women, joining the work force, there is a need to manage different people differently and appropriately.

In this section we will explore the value of multicultural management. There are two points that will be discussed:

1. Institutions must learn to utilize more of the productive potential of minority resources (employees) in the 1980s.
2. American industries must position themselves to take advantage of profitable opportunities in international markets.

In the first case, we need to make better use of our human resources because we are faced with inflation that is shrinking our dollar and driving up the cost of goods and services. To deal with these issues, we need *all* creative minds and perspectives, not just the white male middle-class ones. In the second case, we must

learn multicultural management techniques to be really successful in international markets. America's arrogant posture of the
past no longer intimidates minorities at home or people abroad.

The field of multicultural management must be further defined
and expanded in order to be used effectively. Industry and other
institutions are hiring more minorities. We must learn to remove
the barriers that prevent the full utilization of this new work force.
We have tried to assure you that equal opportunity does *not* mean
treating everyone the same. In fact, treating everyone the same
perpetuates racism and sexism. Some whites feel they have been
fair because they have treated blacks the same as whites; but this
forces blacks into a mold they cannot possibly fit and dismisses or
minimizes the different difficulties blacks are faced with every
day. This is why equal opportunity is really seldom equal if it
means "the same." Equal opportunity should mean treating different people appropriately and not always the same under all circumstances. When whites are confronted with this realization,
they tend to feel hurt and become angry and defensive. Attempts
are made to dismiss the very differences that may be added assets
to the corporation. Multicultural management techniques are
tools to obtain increased productivity by utilizing these differences.

Let us look at an example of what we mean. As many of you
know, drug companies develop their markets by having salespeople visit doctors' offices with drug samples. In many instances,
these salespeople must wait their turn to see the doctor just as the
patients must do. This means drug salespeople can spend a lot of
time just sitting around waiting to see the doctor to give free drug
samples and discuss new drug products.

A drug company in the East decided to try a new technique. The
company took one sales area, as an experiment, which consisted
of all-white neighborhoods serviced by all-white doctors. They
pulled their white salespeople out of this area and replaced them
with black salespeople. They did this because they figured that
the doctors in these neighborhoods would not have black patients.
Evidently, they had guessed correctly, because when the black
salespeople showed up they were immediately ushered in to see
the doctors. They did not have to wait. That meant the productivity of these drug salespeople increased dramatically because they
were able to see more doctors in less time, and profits and sales

increased dramatically for the company. This is an example of how astute white managers can take advantage of racism using multicultural management techniques. Such techniques can affect the bottom line (that means an increase in profits).

Now let us take a look at the second area we mentioned, that of international markets. The world is shrinking because we can get from point A to point B in increasingly short periods of time; countries have a greater need for each other's resources, and sophisticated computer tchnology has made world communications faster and more efficient. Companies are going into international markets at a rapid rate. We need to learn multicultural management techniques so that we can not only cope with but become successful in the overseas markets. One tragedy is that a lot of companies do not recognize the resources they have within their ranks, resources that could help lead the way in the international markets. These resources are minorities who hold the key to multicultural management.

Multicultural management teaches respect for other people's cultures and intelligence, as well as respect for the way other people do things. Minorities have already had to learn how to operate in different cultures. The problem is that minorities are often not allowed to display their competence in these areas. In other words, minorities are *underutilized*. Multicultural management can teach us that interdependence will ensure our own survival and success. If we waste human resources in our own country, it is unlikely that we will be able to take advantage of the world's resources. If we refuse to understand how we can use our human resources effectively, how can we hope to make effective use of the world's human resources, which often come from cultures far more alien to us?

Oil-rich Arab countries now have funds, as a result of selling us petroleum, to construct cities and to demand different and higher-quality goods that the United States would like to supply. How will we successfully interface with them? More third world countries, such as emerging African countries, can afford our consumer goods. How should we behave toward them? China has again opened its doors. How can we quickly understand Chinese culture and respond appropriately in business meetings?

As an example, let us look at Japanese culture. When the Japanese say "yes," in many cases it means "Yes, I understand, but I do not necessarily agree." We may take their "yes" at face value as "Yes, I understand and agree" without checking further. Also, Japanese culture is based on a collaboration and consensus model, even in their various industries, whereas American culture is based on a confrontation model. That is one reason there are more lawyers in the United States per capita than in Japan.

If we can learn to understand other cultures, and use multicultural management techniques, then we will know not to enter into hard negotiations with the Chinese at the first meeting. We will understand that we may personally disagree with the Nigerians' polygamous social system but not use that to evaluate them negatively. We can respect their cultural differences and not allow those differences to interfere with our ability to successfully interact with peoples of different cultures to our mutual benefit.

As difficult as it may be for some white corporations to admit, blacks and women may be in a better position to open up overseas markets because their social training has generally allowed for greater development of abilities to tolerate differences, to be sensitive to another's needs, and to understand the concept of survival. Unfortunately, these minorities are seldom in decision-making or power positions that would permit them to act or or take advantage of their special talents that society has *forced* them to develop in order to survive. Corporations will continue to lose money each year as the price of perpetuating an outdated status quo of minority underutilization and lack of creative use of human resources.

ROLE MODELS ARE IMPORTANT

There are several messages we would like to convey to the reader in this section:

1. Black and white role models are important.
2. Whites need to act as role models for blacks and should be rewarded for doing so.
3. Blacks must sometimes use white role models.
4. Blacks need to be role models.
5. Corporations and institutions need to fast track blacks.

Now let us discuss each of these messages separately.

Black role models are important in corporations and institutions. Blacks who have gained some measure of success need to have that success become public knowledge. Their very existence can help to counteract racist opinions that blacks cannot succeed. Companies often experience white backlash because the competence of blacks is not public knowledge. Whites, therefore, may see rewards received by blacks as being unfair and without justification. Public knowledge of outstanding contribution can help dampen the furor.

Recognition of black role models can open doors and make opportunities available for other blacks, thereby allowing fuller utilization of existing talent. Younger blacks have a need to see that they *can* make it in the organization, and they can do this by looking up the hierarchy and seeing that there are successful blacks in the organization. Organizations sometimes underestimate the importance of role models to blacks and other minorities. Corporations and other institutions need to plan for outstanding blacks to hold visible legitimate leadership positions if other blacks are going to be brought into the organization. These dynamic and energetic black role models need to be visible to both blacks and whites. Black role models can make other blacks feel as though they can succeed, and this in turn makes these blacks more productive.

White role models are important to blacks. If we look at a newly integrated organization, all the experience and expertise will be vested in the white employees of the company. By becoming role models, whites agree to share their experience and expertise with blacks. Whites who act as advocates and push the organization on behalf of blacks to offer opportunities for success become role models for other whites. Of course, this is sometimes risky for whites in that some organizations will attempt to punish whites for this role rather than offer encouragement or reward.

Whites need to be rewarded for behaving as positive role models for blacks. No one is going to continue to carry out a function that is not rewarded in some way. Whites must be rewarded for their efforts, otherwise they will cease being role models and the organization will likely lose their investment in getting the quality and the creative output blacks may be capable of with the white role models' assistance.

Blacks must use white role models and should actively encourage whites to become role models. Blacks need to learn to feel OK about doing this. Remember, when we say use role models we mean for task process duplication, not for personality or even behavior mimicking. In some organizations, there may be no other choice but to use whites as role models in the absence of black success symbols in that organization.

Blacks need to think in terms of being role models. Successful black managers cannot isolate themselves from the group of blacks in the organization. They cannot just work and live for themselves at this point in history. Successful blacks must be beacons for other blacks with potential. They must offer encouragement to blacks to take risks so they too can become successful and realize they can affect the bottom line of the organization, which is increased service or increased profits.

We personally feel that successful blacks owe something to other blacks who are less successful. It is not an individual struggle, but a group struggle. What successful blacks owe is the privilege to be used as role models and to encourage and share skills they have learned. We also need to fight the double standard that exists as a result of racism: That is, if one black fails it represents the failure of all blacks; however, when one black person is highly successful, then that person was just different from the rest of the group. We need blacks as role models to turn that around so the standard becomes: If one black fails, the group does not fail, just an individual has failed; if one black person succeeds, then the group is capable of succeeding.

Corporations and institutions need to put some blacks on a fast track so that black role models are produced. Corporations need to consciously develop plans to fast track sharp blacks in the same way as they fast track sharp whites. In the late 1960s, some companies played it safe in that they sought out a super black and put him or her in a role; when that person became successful in that role, the person was moved. The organization then put another black in that role and followed the same procedure with black person after black person. In this way, the organization created black job positions. That was a way of safely integrating the organization. This was done for two reasons—for self-protection against putting a black in a job where the black might fail and the organization could be accused of some racist act and to protect the black person from failure by reducing the odds of failing.

This is, however, also one way to stifle creativity in blacks.

Companies also cheat themselves out of the utilization of effective black managers, who should be given the opportunity to find their own most productive niches in the same way that white managers are. The only thing companies are sure to gain by creating black job positions is numbers for government reports, and they must eventually ask themselves if the price in lost productivity was worth it. At this point in time, corporations need to stop talking about what will be done in terms of moving blacks and show good faith. What we need is a writ of habeas corpus—produce the body in his or her new deserved role!

CURRENT AND FUTURE NEEDS OF INSTITUTIONS

As corporate and institutional upper-level managers become increasingly concerned with inflation, a decrease in American productivity, reduced buying power due to higher taxes, and a drop in profits, they must not forget that *all* Americans have a vested interest in solving these problems. Blacks and other minorities are underutilized valuable resources to tap for additional or new approaches to solving these national issues. As Americans with today's high technology and rapid development, we will either *all* gain or *all* lose.

The potential for greatness in our country lies not in how effectively we can annihilate ourselves but in how we can put to full use the creative efforts of all our people in a collaborative manner for the benefit of all. We wish to continue to impress upon the reader that the world is getting smaller and more of our resources and products are the results of transnational manufacturing and trade efforts.* As blacks and women enter the work force in more professional capacities, they bring with them fresh creative approaches to old problems. They have often displayed a greater sensitivity that allows them to understand and effectively cope with cultural differences that are an increasing part of our transnational business environment.

At this point, let us enumerate the current and future needs of institutions and organizations with respect to blacks. Organizations and corporations need to do the following:

---

*For a full discussion of this topic, see Peter F. Drucker, *Managing in Turbulent Times* (New York: Harper and Row, 1980).

1. Recruit more blacks in profit-making companies and allow them to progress to positions of responsibility and decision making. Remove ceilings and constraints from levels blacks can reach and job roles they can fill.

2. Offer blacks opportunities to learn how to survive and to prosper in white companies. Organizations need to prepare themselves as well as blacks for Phase 4, the new ceiling for blacks.

3. Develop managers to use multicultural management techniques. White managers need to be appropriately rewarded for training blacks and for learning and using multicultural management.

4. Remove the barriers that prevent organizations from making bigger profits or providing better services; that is, eliminate those practices that inhibit creative productivity of interfacing cultures. Modify organizational culture so blacks can be accepted as rightfully belonging to the organization.

5. Recognize, understand, and use the unique skills blacks bring to the corporation. Companies need to fully utilize the potential of blacks, increase productivity by using their unique skills, and stop seeing them as a drain on the organization. Some of the unique or highly developed skills and abilities of blacks that we have discussed are:

- Sensitivity to human needs (important at this time when management and labor are moving farther apart).
- Ability to surface, manage, and resolve conflict.
- Ability to manage racial attitudes.
- Highly developed interpersonal relations skills.
- Highly developed use of influential behavior.
- Highly developed use of strategy.
- Ability to recognize conditions or situations in which behavior should be closely observed.

6. Learn to work effectively with people of other cultures, not solely because our country comprises people of many different cultures, but because more of our products are the result of transnational manufacturing efforts. For example, an electronic device may be made in one country, shipped to another country to be added to a larger device, and sold in a third country.

It is not our intent to discuss detailed solutions to the problems presented above. However, we would like to offer three solutions for your consideration. When large organizations decide to integrate their work force on a large scale or promote a number of blacks and other minorities into management jobs, proactive thinking dictates that a cadre of people in the helping fields should join the organizations. The helping fields we are suggesting include psychology, social work, counseling, organizational behavior, and sociology. This cadre of professionals can identify needs and set up the appropriate programs to change organizations so that blacks and women can realize their potential. We are not suggesting this as a new social experiment, but instead because the bottom line will be effectiveness—that is, more productive output can be realized per dollar spent by an organization.

As a result of white institutions opening their employment doors to blacks, on-the-job black–white problems occur. Professionals in the helping fields are needed to help blacks and whites resolve these issues. White managers still attempt to use traditional management techniques to manage blacks. This causes blacks who should be working as a team to work instead as individuals or to actively pull against the team. When this occurs, social workers, for example, trained in clinical techniques can step in to lead racial awareness workshops. Social workers can act as third-party consultants to resolve issues between black and white bosses and subordinates. Social workers can act as consultants to teams to ensure that dysfunctional racial interpersonal relations do not interfere with team effectiveness. More specifically, social workers can lead team building sessions to enhance team productivity. Some industrial organizations have hired professionals in the helping fields on a full-time basis to help resolve racist and sexist issues that detract from efforts to increase or maintain profits for the organization.

A second important solution is human resources development. As blacks and other minorities enter organizations in large numbers, development programs should be designed to teach multicultural management techniques. The development programs should include a design for a systematic change effort. In addition to teaching multicultural management techniques, these programs must speak to (1) the relationship between culture and organizational style; (2) the effects of racism and cultural paranoia; (3) the effects of insufficient black role models; and (4) the importance of the black self-image. In summary, the human resources development program must surface and resolve issues associated with the minorities coming into the organization, the present managers in the organization, as well as the environment (culture and norms) of the organization.

A third important solution is fast track development for minorities. Organizations should feel comfortable with placing sharp, innovative, and creative blacks on a fast track in the same way as they do whites under similar circumstances. As a result of using fast track development, blacks will be positioned to help influence an organization's operations and, therefore, can affect the profits or service input to a larger extent.

BUSINESS PLAN OUTLINE

The following business plan outline can be used to develop a plan to integrate an organization, improve and change the status of minorities (women, blacks, Hispanics, Orientals, and others) in the organization, and promote minorities into higher-level job positions. It is offered in the hope that as a result of reading this book, individuals in some organizations will be moved to make changes. This outline may also be used by an organization that wants to move its business ahead and increase profits in areas other than human resource development.

Business Plan Outline

I Business Needs
II Core Mission
III Key Issues
IV Vision of the Future
V Operational Philosophy
VI Goals
VII Strategy
VIII Key Potential Risks
IX Major Action Plans
X Evaluation Process

The outline is called a business plan because bringing minorities into or moving them up in an organization will positively affect the bottom-line profits of a business. This outline should be used by individuals who are high up in the hierarchy of various companies and institutions.

I. *Business Needs.* List the legitimate business needs for bringing in minorities or for moving them up in the organization.

II. *Core Mission.* In this context, *core mission* refers to a statement that explains why you are bringing in or moving minorities up in your organization.

III. *Key Issues.* Key issues refer to the hot issues that can reduce productivity if they are not resolved. For example, one hot issue that could result from integrating an organization is white backlash.

IV. *Vision of the Future.* The manager responsible for putting this business plan together should either have or develop a vision of what will exist when the goals of the plan have been reached. The vision should be described here. For example, one part of the vision could be to see whites working for black male and female bosses and blacks working for both white male and female bosses.

V. *Operational Philosophy.* The basic philosophy relative to having minority individuals in your organization should be stated here. An example of operational philosophy is: Minority members of the organization should be given an equal opportunity to work in all job positions in the organization because it is morally right and because profits or service can be increased.

VI. *Goals.* It is important to write achievable goals, both short and long term, that key managers will support. Short-term goals could cover a period of up to two years, while long-term goals could cover a period from three to ten years. An example of a long-term goal is: Our organization will have at least two minorities in each of our hierarchical levels in the next five years.

VII. *Strategy.* Strategy as used here refers to a directional plan or technique for achieving the above goals. One strategy could be to have the top manager of an organization send a one-page letter to the other members of the organization that shares some of the goals and lays out a plan for achieving them.

VIII. *Key Potential Risks.* This portion of the plan should contain a list of potential risks that might result from an attempt to meet the goals listed in Part VI of this plan by implementing the strategy in Part VII.

IX. *Major Action Plans.* The major action plans to meet the goals should be listed with a date for completion of each step. The action plans may fall into two categories: interim and final. Sometimes the implementation of interim plans can effectively position an organization before final action plans are implemented.

X. *Evaluation Process.* An evaluation process is necessary because it can be used to confirm the achievement of the goals. Also, if you do not evaluate whether you are achieving your goals, others may do so in an inappropriate way.

The development of the business plan outline is an iterative process, so key managers in an organization should be involved. During its development phase, the business plan should be reviewed and commented on until the key managers agree on and support it. Accountability for its implementation should be established, and it should be updated appropriately.

Postscript

The most difficult step in writing a book is closing the last chapter and shutting down the writing process. At this point we feel we have only scratched the surface and have a lot more to say. However, it is time to close.

We started by saying we had conducted research that led to a four-phase structured model of development for black managers in white corporations. It is our hope that this book contains an appropriate amount of information that can help both *minority* and *white* managers grow and develop in their interactions with each other.

Needless to say, our table of contents changed many times before we completed the manuscript. The last change was to add the business plan outline to Chapter 10. We did this because we felt some people reading the book will be moved to implement action to correct past injustices and to prevent future injustices. At this juncture, our spirits are high with the hope that we have made an impact on the field of management.

Because the affirmative action pendulum is swinging in a negative direction, black managers and *all* black Americans must continue the struggle for dignity and the right to use their creativity and competencies. As blacks, we must demand our rightful place in history based on our abilities to perform and the results obtained. Black managers must be willing to pay whatever price of pain it takes to correct the inequities of white corporate America. We cannot allow our spirits and energies to burn out. White corporate America must remove the barriers that prevent blacks from properly performing their duties and from contributing to the greatness of our total society.

Appendix
The Research Method

WHAT WAS DONE

An exploratory search was conducted to pinpoint behavioral, attitudinal, emotional, and job skill factors that a small sample of black managers employed over a span of 3–13 years in surviving and becoming successful in a predominantly white male corporation. The above factors were ones that the black managers had to use in order to survive and be successful that were perceived to be different, or different by degree, from those white male managers used. Survival was defined as remaining employed and being successful as gaining at least one promotion in a major white corporation.

We already know that the managerial profession presents all types of problems for individuals and that blacks in managerial positions in an all-white environment present special problems for both blacks and whites because of the additional racial feature. A body of knowledge exists about white coping mechanisms in organizations; however, very little is known about blacks and their coping patterns in white organizations. These patterns are not only important for blacks adjusting in the work situation but have implications for black–white interactions in the society at large.

HOW IT WAS DONE

The research project was an exploratory descriptive study. Fifteen black male subjects were used—all college graduates, all managers having gained at least one promotion. They consented to participate in the project, which consisted of two phases: the completion of a detailed 17-page questionnaire and an interview that ranged from one to two hours in length. The questionnaire was designed to provide general data on whether a black manager approaches management issues in the same manner as he perceives a white manager would approach them. The questionnaire identified how the manager behaved in management situations as compared with how he saw his white peers behave. It also looked at his attitude and feelings toward his job, his company, and his role as a manager as well as toward his white peers, subordinates, and supervisors and their roles. Finally, it reported his perception of his job skills compared to those of his white peers.

The second phase was a taped interview that further pinpointed those behaviors and attitudes used by the black manager in negotiating in the white corporation. The interview questions followed up on the answers given in the written questionnaire and provided more specific information supplementing questionnaire data collected on each subject. The data were analyzed to find common patterns of behavior, attitudes, emotional set, and specific job skills developed by these black managers to cope with racial discrimination in the white corporation that could be seen as useful to survival and success.

The ethnomethodological research approach was used in the study. Ethnomethodology deals with research done in a framework of common understanding of the givens of everyday life shared by the researcher and the respondents. Traditional research uses tests and statistics to analyze data, while ethnomethodology relies heavily on common cultural understanding of observed phenomena. Ethnomethodology gives researchers additional methods of analyzing data on commonplace real-world occurrences that are qualifiable for study, and it is used in analyzing these data because it is responsive to the respondent's cultural framework. Therefore, the small sample data from ethnomethodology is highly qualifiable as opposed to more traditional quantified data. Ethnomethodology provides a basis to study practical activities of commonsense knowledge and of practical organizational reasoning.

GENERAL FINDINGS

The research showed a common pattern of developmental movement under each category—attitudes, emotions, behaviors, and job skills. This development pattern was broken into four distinguishable phases of adjustment and learning called Entry, Adjusting, Planned Growth, and Success. Each phase has its own set of characteristics from which some general findings unique to the position of blacks in the white corporation can be drawn. In the attitudinal category, it was found that black managers (1) must be aware of their own blackness and how that blackness impacts the existing conditions in the white corporation; (2) must develop a protective hesitation and a cultural paranoia; and (3) must also learn and accept that for them making mistakes or failing is not an option.

Under the category of emotions, the black manager must be able to sublimate his emotions, that is, convert many of his energies into acceptable social manifestations that are based on dominant cultural norms.

In the category of behavior, the black manager must (1) tap into the informal communications network to seek out company norms and values, even though that network may not be receptive to his needs; (2) learn how to use resources that are obviously discriminatory; (3) use more physical and psychic energy to accomplish tasks than white peers do; and (4) be able to resist power.

In the fourth category, job skills, findings were that the black manager must (1) learn how to manage racism; (2) use strategy more than whites do to compensate for the deficit model he is cast in; (3) learn how to manage conflict; and (4) possess higher interpersonal–behavioral skills.

Bibliography

HISTORICAL

Bennett, Lerone, Jr. *Before the Mayflower*. Baltimore: Penguin Books, 1970.

Blauner, Robert. *Racial Oppression in America*. New York: Harper & Row, 1972.

Lerner, Gerda, ed. *Black Women in White America*. New York: Vintage Books, 1973.

Weinstein, Allen, and Gatell, Frank Otto. *American Negro Slavery*. New York: Oxford University Press, 1973.

MANAGEMENT

America, Richard F., and Anderson, Bernard E. *Moving Ahead: Black Managers in American Business*. New York: McGraw-Hill, 1978

Auger, B. Y. *How to Run Better Business Meetings*. St. Paul: Minnesota Mining & Manufacturing Co., 1979.

Benson, Carl A. "The Question of Mobility in Career Development for Black Professionals," *Personal Journal*, May 1975.

Bradford, Leland P. *Making Meetings Work*. La Jolla, Cal.: University Associates, 1976.

Broadwell, Martin M. *The Supervisor as an Instructor*. Reading, Mass.: Addison-Wesley, 1968

Clark, Chris, and Rush, Sheila. *How to Get Along with Black People*. New York: The Third Press, 1971.

Cohen, Peter. *The Gospel According to the Harvard Business School*. Garden City, N.Y.: Doubleday, 1973.

Cooper, Ken. *Nonverbal Communication for Business Success*. New York: AMACOM, 1979.

Drucker, Peter F. *The Effective Executive*. New York: Harper & Row, 1966.

———. *Technology, Management & Society*. New York: Harper & Row, 1970

———. *Managing in Turbulent Times*. New York: Harper & Row, 1980.

———. *Managing in Turbulent Times*. New York: Harper and Row, 1980.

Fernandez, John P. *Black Managers in White Corporations.* New York: John Wiley & Sons, 1975.

Fiedler, Fred E., and Chemers, Martin M. *Leadership and Effective Management.* Glenview, Ill.: Scott, Foresman, 1974.

Ford, David L., Jr., ed. *Readings in Minority Group Relations.* La Jolla, Cal.: University Associates, 1976.

Fordyce, Jack K., and Weil, Raymond. *Managing with People.* Reading, Mass.: Addison-Wesley, 1971.

Guest, Robert H., Hersey, Paul, and Blanchard, Kenneth H. *Organizational Change through Effective Leadership.* Englewood Cliffs, N.J.: Prentice-Hall, 1977

Hart, Lois Borland. *Moving Up! Women and Leadership.* New York: AMACOM, 1980.

Hersey, Paul, and Blanchard, Kenneth H. *Management of Organizational Behavior Utilizing Human Resources.* Englewood Cliffs, N.J.: Prentice-Hall, 1969.

Johnson, John H. "Failure Is a Word I Don't Accept," *Harvard Business Review,* March–April 1976.

Jones, Edward W., Jr. "What It's Like to Be a Black Manager," *Harvard Business Review,* July–August 1973.

Kanter, Rosabeth Moss. *Men and Women of the Corporation.* New York: Basic Books, 1977.

Kepner, Charles H., and Tregoe, Benjamin B. *The Rational Manager.* New York: McGraw-Hill, 1965.

Korda, Michael. *Power! How to Get It, How to Use It.* New York: Random House, 1975.

Lakein, Alan. *How to Get Control of Your Time and Your Life.* New York: Signet Books, 1973.

Likert, Rensis, and Likert, Jane Gibson. *New Ways of Managing Conflict.* New York: McGraw-Hill, 1976.

Lumsden, George J. *Impact Management: Personal Power Strategies for Success.* New York: AMACOM, 1979.

Maccoby, Michael. *The Gamesman: The New Corporate Leaders.* New York: Simon & Schuster, 1976.

MacKenzie, R. Alec. *The Time Trap.* New York: AMACOM, 1972.

Mager, R. F. *Preparing Instructional Objectives.* Belmont, Cal.: Fearon Publishers, 1962

Maier, Norman R. F., Solem, Allen R., and Maier, Ayesha A. *The Role-Play Technique.* La Jolla, Cal.: University Associates, 1975.

Mali, Paul. *Improving Total Productivity.* New York: John Wiley & Sons, 1978.

McFarland, Dalton E. *Managerial Achievement: Action Strategies.* Englewood Cliffs, N.J.: Prentice-Hall, 1979.

McGregor, Douglas. *The Human Side of Enterprise.* New York: McGraw-Hill, 1960.

Molloy, John T. *Dress for Success.* New York: Warner Books, 1975

———. *The Woman's Dress for Success Book.* New York: Warner Books, 1977.

Moskal, Brian S. "Ascent of the Black Manager," *Industry Week,* October 4, 1976.

Nierenberg, Gerard I., and Calero, Henry H. *How to Read a Person Like a Book.* New York: Cornerstone Library Publications, 1971.

Northrup, Herbert R., et al. *Negro Employment in Basic Industry.* Industrial Research Unit, Wharton School of Finance and Commerce, University of Pennsylvania, 1970.

Potter, Beverly A. *Turning Around: The Behavioral Approach to Managing People.* New York: AMACOM, 1980.

Roeber, Richard J. C. *The Organization in a Changing Environment.* Reading, Mass.: Addison-Wesley, 1973.

Saracheck, Bernard. "Career Concerns of Black Managers," *Management Review,* October 1974.

Schein, Edgar H. *Process Consultation: Its Role in Organization Development.* Reading, Mass.: Addison-Wesley, 1969.

———. *Career Dynamics: Matching Individual and Organizational Needs.* Reading, Mass.: Addison-Wesley, 1978.

Schleh, Edward C. *Management by Results.* New York: McGraw-Hill, 1961.

———. *The Management Tactician.* New York: McGraw-Hill, 1974.

Smith, Howard P., and Browner, Paul J. *Performance Appraisal and Human Development.* Reading, Mass.: Addison-Wesley, 1977.

Souerwine, Andrew H. *Career Strategies.* New York: AMACOM, 1978.

Vance, Charles C. *Manager Today, Executive Tomorrow.* New York: McGraw-Hill, 1974.

VanDersal, William R. *The Successful Manager in Government and Business.* New York: Harper & Row, 1974.

Walton, Richard E. *Interpersonal Peacemaking: Confrontations and Third-Party Consultation.* Reading, Mass.: Addison-Wesley, 1969.

Williams, Kenneth A. "The Black Executive as a Subject for Research," *Business Perspectives,* Fall 1972.

PSYCHOLOGICAL

Aronson, Elliot. *The Social Animal.* San Francisco: W. H. Freeman, 1972.

Berne, Eric. *Games People Play.* New York: Dell, 1964.

Bhagat, Rabi S. "Black-White Ethnic Differences in Identification with the Work Ethic: Some Implications for Organizational Integration," *Academy of Management Review,* July 1979.

Communications Research Machines, Inc. *Psychology Today: An*

Introduction. New York: Random House, 1979.

Fast, Julius. *Body Language.* New York: M. Evans and Company, 1970.

Grier, William H., and Cobbs, Price M. *Black Rage.* New York: Basic Books, 1968.

———. *The Jesus Bag.* New York: McGraw-Hill, 1971.

Harris, Thomas Anthony. *I'm OK, You're OK.* New York: Harper & Row, 1969.

Hill, Napoleon. *Think and Grow Rich.* New York: Fawcett Books, 1960.

Leavitt, Harold J. *Managerial Psychology.* Chicago: University of Chicago Press, 1972.

Schein, Edgar H. *Organizational Psychology.* Englewood Cliffs, N.J.: Prentice-Hall, 1970.

Sheehy, Gail. *Passages: Predictable Crises of Adult Life.* New York: Bantam Books, 1976.

Silverman, Robert E. *Psychology.* New York: Appleton-Century-Crofts, 1972.

Storr, Anthony. *Human Aggression.* New York: Atheneum, 1968.

SOCIOLOGICAL

Allport, Gordon W. *The Nature of Prejudice.* Garden City, N.Y.: Doubleday, 1958.

Billingsley, Andrew. *Black Families in White America.* Englewood Cliffs, N.J.: Prentice-Hall, 1968.

Pannell, William E. *My Friend, the Enemy.* Waco, Texas: Word Books, 1968.

Popenoe, David. *Sociology.* New York: Appleton-Century-Crofts, 1974.

U. S. Riot Commission Report. *Report of the National Advisory Commission on Civil Disorders.* New York: Bantam Books, 1968.

Young, Carlene, ed. *Black Experience Analysis and Synthesis.* San Rafael, Cal.: Leswing Press, 1972.

RESEARCH

Selltiz, Claire, Wrightsman, Lawrence S., and Cook, Stuart W. *Research Methods in Social Relations.* New York: Holt, Rinehart and Winston, 1959.

Statistical Abstract of the United States 1976, 97th Annual Edition. U.S. Department of Commerce, Bureau of the Census.

Turner, Roy, ed. *Ethnomethodology.* Baltimore: Penguin Books, 1974.

Index